About the Author

Sylvia Webber lives in Australia. She holds degrees in art history, and applied linguistics. She has worked as a teacher, and brought up two children.

Her Story in Four Centuries

S. M. Webber

Her Story in Four Centuries

Olympia Publishers

London

www.olympiapublishers.com
OLYMPIA PAPERBACK EDITION

Copyright © S. M. Webber 2019

The right of S. M. Webber to be identified as author of this work has been asserted in accordance with sections 77 and 78 of the Copyright, Designs and Patents Act 1988.

All Rights Reserved

No reproduction, copy or transmission of this publication may be made without written permission.
No paragraph of this publication may be reproduced, copied or transmitted save with the written permission of the publisher, or in accordance with the provisions of the Copyright Act 1956 (as amended).

Any person who commits any unauthorised act in relation to this publication may be liable to criminal prosecution and civil claims for damage.

A CIP catalogue record for this title is available from the British Library.

ISBN: 978-1-78830-356-9

First Published in 2019

Olympia Publishers
60 Cannon Street
London
EC4N 6NP

Printed in Great Britain

Dedication

This book is dedicated to Julia and Jason Passioura

Contents

PART ONE 23

MARGARET RUDSTON OF YORKSHIRE 25

    'To the Manor Born' 27

    The Civil War 43

    In the Aftermath of the Civil War 55

    Margaret Rudston and John Hall 67

    The Child's Portion of Katherine Leigh 84

    Margaret and Her Family 94

    Afterpiece: From Riches to Rags; A Story of the Cutler Family 100

    Appendix to Part One 105

PART TWO 113

MARIA BARSTOW OF DANZIG, AND THE STORY OF LITTLE ANN 115

    My Grandmother 119

    The Sieges of Danzig 135

    I Visit My Grandmother 145

    How Archibald Maclean Captured the Paris Mails for the Prussian Army In 1870 158

- Little Ann 163
- Appendix to Part Two 186

PART THREE 193
THE KELLY SISTERS OF IRELAND 195

- The Early Years 200
- Fanny Tries to Save Her Husband's Life 227
- Caroline's Work 244
- Bessy's Memoir Writing 254
- Fanny and Caroline Continue Life's Journey 264
- Appendix to Part Three 274

PART FOUR 275
MY MOTHER, JOAN WEBBER 277

- An Independent Woman 283
- The Escape from Malaya 308
- My Childhood With Joan, or Without Her 322
- Joan and William Settle in Tasmania 343
- Joan; Me 353
- Appendix to Part Four 374

Bibliography 385

Cover Illustrations 397

Lists of Art Works Held by Members of My Family, Not Shown Here: 398

Introduction

Motivation for Writing the Book

Her Story in Four Centuries is a narrative non-fiction book. Each part comprises a human interest story, mainly about the life of one woman. The women lived between the seventeenth and twentieth centuries, in Yorkshire, Danzig (Gdansk in Poland today), Ireland, Malaya (now Malaysia), and Australia. They lived in the British Empire as it spread. The book testifies to the strength of mind of women who were forced to cope with civil wars or wars abroad, while protecting and educating their children. The women and children encountered difficult situations, separation, illness, and death. Their stories show how family members worked together. They show how the human spirit survives.

I am grateful for the notes, letters, documents and memoirs that the women wrote. They are like a gift. Without them there would only be spaces and silences in the past in which women's lives took place. I felt inspired by what the women wrote, thought and did. I was the receiver of the love they felt for their descendants, love that was lacking in my immediate family. I was inspired by them to write about my mother and me. Being a woman, I could identify with the point of view expressed in women's stories. I felt elated in the way men usually feel when they are reading and writing about men. I felt able to communicate with the women across time.

In the past, women were often prohibited from doing many things, but writing family history seems to have been something they were allowed to do. I hope to encourage women to write about women in their family papers lying neglected in ancestral vaults, or to write about their own lives. They may think that the material isn't important because they have been educated to have a male point of view about what is important in the affairs of the world. Women writing about women creates a community and tradition that women can belong to and build on. Otherwise, each new generation of women may be overwhelmed by what men did, said, and wrote, before they can put themselves in the picture.

The women who wrote memoirs were conscious of writing in a genre. One aim of the genre was to provide genealogical information about their families. This could be widened into the history and meaning of their lives. They wrote about their relatives, friends, and the families who lived near them. Visitors, an important person, or refugees, may have stayed in their house. Sometimes they themselves journeyed and sojourned away from home. Another aspect of the genre was to account for heirlooms which were being passed down the generations. The family silver, or jewellery, was treasured. The women liked to include poems that were written by family members, quite often by women. They wrote death scenes.

Summary of the Parts

Part One of this book is about Margaret Rudston (née Dawnay), of East Yorkshire, who lived in the seventeenth century. She married Walter Rudston of Hayton, who was one of the landowning gentry, and they had six children. In 1642 they were caught up in the Civil War when Charles I, proceeding from York, dined at Hayton on the way to demand access to the arsenal at Hull from Sir John Hotham. Hotham denied the king entry to Hull on orders of Parliament. The king made Walter Rudston a baronet, and royalist soldiers were stationed at Hayton. In 1649, Walter was charged with 'delinquency' by the Commonwealth, and his estate was temporarily sequestered (seized). He died during his appeal, and Margaret had to continue with the court case on behalf of her son and the heir, Sir Thomas Rudston, who was twelve years old. She thought that the best outcome for her family would be to admit to the charge and to compound, or to 'go to a composition' for the estate, that is, to buy it back in the form of a fine. This result she achieved with assistance from her nephew John Dawnay, and Sir Robert Stapleton and lawyers. Margaret's sister-in-law Katherine Leigh had to go to court as well to get her child's portion paid.

Margaret managed the estate, brought up her children, and fought other court cases with the help of her family solicitor, John Hall. Mr Hall gave her *Satires 1* and *2* by the poet John

Donne, which he had copied in Donne's lifetime. After the restoration of Charles II, the Rudstons built a new house at Hayton. As she lived for so long (103 years), Margaret was to see her grandchildren grow up there.

The main story in Part Two is that of Maria Barstow (née Maclean) of Danzig, who lived in the eighteenth and nineteenth centuries. It was written by her granddaughter Elizabeth Barstow, of 'Garrow Hill', York. Maria married Michael Barstow, a merchant of York and Danzig, and they had six children. Michael died in the Napoleonic Wars when his timber business was severely compromised. Maria was married a second time, to Cornelius von Almonde of Danzig. He, as well as Michael Barstow's brother in England, and his business partner in Danzig, helped Maria and her children through twenty years of wars and sieges. Maria went blind. As Cornelius was the Dutch consul, the grand house Michael had bought for Maria in Danzig became the Dutch consulate. At different times, it provided quarters for the future queen of Holland (who gave Maria a ring), the French army, Napoleon, and the Russian army. Some of Maria's children were brought up and educated in England. Maria had both English and German grandchildren.

In a shorter, second story in Part Two, Elizabeth Barstow wrote about how her mother Ann Jones escaped from Ireland in 1798, as a baby, when the French landed at Killala to support an Irish rebellion. The Jones family lived near Killala, and Mrs Jones fled with her four daughters while her husband was engaged in suppressing the rebellion. It took three months for Mrs Jones and her children to reach their relatives in Yorkshire. The children had chickenpox on the way.

Part Three of this book tells of the lives of the four daughters of the Reverend Thomas Kelly of Ireland, in the nineteenth century. The Kellys were a Protestant missionary family who provided a progressive education for the girls, away from society life. The daughters' grandmother Mrs Tighe engaged an artist, Maria Spilsbury Taylor, to teach them to draw and paint. Elizabeth Wingfield (née Kelly) and Caroline Kelly wrote memoirs, and there are family letters and poems. Elizabeth wrote with emotional intensity of the Tighe, Kelly and Wingfield families: stories about illness and death, as well as education and achievements. Caroline Kelly worked in charities, and started a cottage industry (tatting) in the famine. She wrote about the Irish people who lived near their home, Kellyville. Fanny and Elizabeth married and had children, so they naturally had interests in bringing up and educating children. An unpublished poem by the daughters' aunt, the poet Mary Tighe, is included.

Part Four is about my mother, Joan Webber (née Wilkinson), and a little about my own life. Joan left Australia for Malaya in 1929 to teach English. She married William Webber, an English rubber planter, and they had three daughters. During World War Two in 1942, while William was fighting the Japanese, Joan managed to escape from Singapore with her one-week-old baby with only days to spare. The two older children had already been sent to relatives in Sydney. Joan wrote about her escape.

After the war, the family lived in Malaya again, through the Emergency. The children went to boarding schools in Malaya and Australia from the age of five. In 1950 the family settled in Tasmania and enjoyed a peaceful life, though not one without problems. I wrote about how my childhood was affected by war, separation, displacement, and boarding school.

History of the Documents

The book is drawn from a collection of family papers. The Rudstons of Hayton, East Yorkshire, kept their collection of papers together for seven centuries, passing it on with the property to the oldest son in each generation in accordance with the law of primogeniture. About half the documents were conveyancing documents, giving proof of ownership of property. Sometimes, because of marriage or other reasons, small collections from other families were included in it. Letters and notes were added, from which it was possible to make a family tree.

Trevor Rudston, the last 'lord of the manor of Hayton', inherited from an uncle the papers and what was left of Hayton. (As the Rudstons entered professions in the nineteenth century, they demolished the house and sold parts of the estate.) At his death in 1919, Trevor divided the Rudston papers into two parts. One half he stored in a bank in York, where it lay for seventy years. I believe this half was intended for his son, who had gone to America and who did not return to claim it. The other half he left with his daughter Evelyn and, when she died, she passed it on to her nephews, Evelyn and William Webber, the sons of her sister Annie, and the only grandchildren of Trevor Rudston. (Curiously, a note written by my mother's father was placed in the Rudston papers.)

In 1950 my father, William Webber, finally left Malaya, where he had lived and worked as a rubber planter for twenty-five years, and went on a trip to England to see his brother. They shared their collections of family papers, and William took all the Rudston papers they had to Tasmania. They did not know about the other half that was in a bank in York. William contacted Professor Stephen Roberts of Sydney University about the will and inventory of Sir John Rudston, an alderman of London, 1531. (We had met the Roberts family once in a holiday place at Burragorang Valley, New South Wales.) Professor Roberts made a copy of the will and inventory which I believe is now held by one of my sisters.

William slowly sorted and transcribed the Rudston papers as a weekend hobby. He did not particularly share his interest in it with academics, or even with members of his family. He put most of the papers into archival plastic containers, and listed and numbered them. He transcribed the oldest documents, which were written in Latin. As the words were often abbreviated, he put the missing letters in brackets, in the transcript.

While I was studying at Melbourne University, William contacted a historian again, this time Dr Lawrence Gardiner, about the will and inventory of Sir John Rudston. (In fact, my husband told his friend, the historian Barry Smith, about it, and he told Dr Gardiner!) As a result of this communication, the will and inventory of Sir John Rudston was discussed by W G Hoskins in his book *The Age of Plunder*, 1976. Dr Gardiner would probably have been interested in the civil war documents, I've been told, but William didn't tell anyone about the other documents, which he was still sorting and transcribing.

When William died in 1988, my sister Margaret brought all the Rudston material to her house on the mainland of Australia. She put it into the back of a cupboard for nine years while she was bringing up her daughter. Neither my sisters nor I knew much about what was in the collection.

The collection was passed to me to hold in 1997. I sorted through a pile of unsorted papers and letters in a tin trunk, and found a little booklet with copies of the poems *Satire 1* and *Satire 2* by John Donne. As the dates written in it were 1627 and 1632, I thought it was a significant discovery. I know my father hadn't particularly noticed it because he had made a point of getting valuations for a document signed by Cromwell, and a roll of engravings. My father didn't like poetry. If he had shown the Donne poems to my mother, who had an honours degree in English, she would have recognised them for what they were. But the Rudston papers were his hobby, and she didn't take an interest in them without being invited to.

I contacted, in 1997, Dr John Tillotson, a medieval historian at the Australian National University in Canberra, about the collection, and he came to my house to see it. He dated the earliest document he saw as 1353/4, but I believe there is one dated 1287. Dr Tillotson made a listing of medieval documents, and a brief summary of some of the others. He gave me some addresses to write to in Yorkshire. I found out, then, that there was another half of the Rudston collection. It had been found in the bank in York in 1989, and had been transferred to the East Riding of Yorkshire Archives at Beverley by the public trustee.

I contacted Barbara Ross, an archivist who had retired from the National Library of Australia, about the booklet of Donne poems, and she was keen to see it and kind enough to come to my house. These copies of the poems were not listed in the authoritative W Milgate ed. *Satires, Epigrams and Verse Letters,* 1967. Barbara referred me to Dr Graham Barwell of the University of Wollongong, who came to see the booklet also, and wrote a paper about it for the conference of the Bibliographical Society of Australia and New Zealand, 10-11 October, 1997. (The poems are now entered in the Donne Variorum.) When I phoned the National Library of Australia about our collection, its representative said that they would not be interested in having it.

Because my father was so secretive about the Rudston collection, it did not find its way into the listing by K V Sinclair, *Descriptive Catalogue of Medieval and Renaissance Western Manuscripts*, Sydney, 1969. The historians my father contacted didn't pass on information to other historians, or ask my father more about his collection.

I made a typed transcript of all the Rudston papers that we held. When my uncle Evelyn Webber died in England in 1999, he left to my sisters and me the family papers of the Webbers and the Kellys in Ireland, dating from 1768, including the memoirs of Elizabeth Barstow of 'Garrow Hill', York. Before this time, we did not know much about them. Evelyn did not look after the papers very well. He stored most of them in a couple of cardboard boxes in his boiler-room, where some of them became damp and mouldy. The letters written by the women, in particular, were extremely damaged.

The Rudston papers of the seventeenth century were originally written with abbreviations, variable spelling, and very little punctuation. I have represented these in the book in modern spelling, and with additional punctuation, but with the same words in the same order. This treatment reveals the beauty of the language being used. (In a couple of instances, I retained a spelling feature because I thought it was indicative of dialect.) I have slightly rewritten the memoirs of Elizabeth Barstow because she wrote in very long sentences, and she sometimes placed events in the wrong order. However, I have kept everything she wrote, and her way of expressing it, except for some archaisms and word repetitions. Part Three of the book is based almost entirely on the memoirs of Elizabeth Wingfield and Caroline Kelly. I have used a selection of what they wrote, and have either reported or quoted it.

Between 2001 and 2004, all the family papers I have mentioned were placed in public collections. Our Rudston collection was donated to the Beverley Archives, East Yorkshire, and was thereby united with its other half. A few items were sold, including the booklet with the Donne poems, which now resides in the Folger Shakespeare Library, Washington DC, USA. The letters and memoirs of the Webbers and Kellys were donated either as originals to the

National Archives of Ireland, or as copies or transcripts to the Genealogical Office, National Library of Ireland. The letters of Oswald Webber in the Boer War were placed in the National Army Museum, London. A copy of the memoir of Elizabeth Barstow was given to the Yorkshire Archaeological Society library at Leeds. The material referred to in Part Four of this book is held in Australia by descendants of the Webber and Wilkinson families.

I began to write the book in 2006, after completing the degree of Master of Applied Linguistics from Monash University, through Open Universities Australia. I had retired from teaching.

Acknowledgements

I would like to acknowledge the assistance given to me in England by the East Riding of Yorkshire Archives, Lincolnshire Archives, Staffordshire Record Office, Gloucestershire Archives, Burton Joyce Archives, Derbyshire Record Office, Borthwick Institute, and the British Library; and in Australia by the National Library of Australia, National Archives of Australia, Australian War Memorial, Australian National Maritime Museum, ACT Writers Centre, Embassy of the Republic of Poland, and Embassy of Germany. I would like to thank the Museum *Haus Hansestadt Danzig* in Lübeck, Germany, for photos, and the Gdansk Historical Museum in Poland, for information and a map. I would like to thank the Yorkshire genealogists Janet Roworth, Brenda Sharp, Derek Grocock, and Anita Lucas for their record searches. Thanks to my readers Patrick Brady, Jeanette Schultz, Julia Passioura and Katherine Tyson, for the help they have given. Thanks to Jason Passioura for maps and scanning, to Christopher Barstow for assistance; and to my relatives for answering questions, and for providing notes, which are acknowledged in the references.

PART ONE

MARGARET RUDSTON OF YORKSHIRE

Some characters, for reference:

Margaret Rudston and her husband Walter.
Their children: Faith, Barbara, Margaret, Thomas, Walter and Elizabeth.
John Hall, a solicitor.
Walter Rudston's brother William, and sister Katherine (Mrs William Leigh).
Margaret Rudston's nephew, John Dawnay.
Sir Robert Stapleton, a benefactor.

(A list of documents is in an appendix at the end of Part One.)

In this Rudston line, Elizabeth Rudston who married Sir Thomas Wotton in 1547 is an ancestor of Queen Elizabeth II. She was the daughter of Sir John Rudston, a cloth merchant who became Lord Mayor of London, and the richest man in England of his time (*The Age of Plunder*, W G Hoskins). I hope someone will write their story sometime.

Hayton Hall, from a Drawing by Samuel Buck c. 1720. The hall was built for the Rudstons probably in the 1660s, and was demolished in 1805. It was situated near St Martin's church and the former village school. (Reproduced by permission of the British Library.)

'To the Manor Born'

Margaret Rudston was a superwoman. She lived to 'a great age', as it says in a note, one hundred and three years. She was christened on 11 November 1595 at Snaith, and spent all her life in the rural countryside of East Yorkshire. She was buried on 14 March 1699 at Hayton.

The land in East Yorkshire that the Rudstons owned lay between the ports of York and Hull. It was flat or gently rolling farming country, suitable for a variety of crops, vegetables, and 'beasts'. There were rabbit warrens. Some of the land was wooded; some of it was bog.

Margaret married Walter Rudston of Hayton on 9 May, 1631. She gave birth to nine children when she was aged between thirty-five and forty-eight; six of them lived to adulthood. It's important to acknowledge the number of pregnancies women endured, and to respect them for their fortitude. In those times about half of all children died young or as newborns.

Margaret's husband, Walter Rudston, would die in 1650 in the middle of a court case. The Rudstons were caught up in the Civil War in England; Walter was an unwilling participant.

After the execution of the king, Walter was charged with 'delinquency' and he was threatened with the sequestration of his estate. This meant that the property could be seized by the state, and could be divided up, leased to other people, or sold. Margaret's task was to save the estate on behalf of her oldest son and the heir, Thomas, who was only a child; otherwise, the family would have nowhere to live, and no means of support.

Margaret's Family

Margaret was the daughter of Sir Thomas Dawnay and his wife Faith (née Legard), of Cowick Hall, near Snaith, which was situated about twenty miles west of the Rudstons' home at Hayton. Margaret's father was a landowner, and a wealthy and influential person in the county; he was the high sheriff of Yorkshire in 1610. Margaret was the youngest child in the family; she had one brother, John, born in 1593, and two sisters, Elizabeth and Frances, born earlier. The children of Margaret's brother and two sisters were much older than Margaret's children.

Margaret continued to live at home for many years after her brother and two sisters left. She sometimes sojourned in 'great houses', which was a typical experience for single women of her station in life, and became an educated and literate person. By the time she married, her brother had died, leaving three young sons behind. One of these sons, John Dawnay, would come to Margaret's aid after her husband died.

Their marriage may have been arranged, but Margaret and Walter truly loved each other. Margaret would write of Walter that he had always been 'so dear a loving husband'. Walter affirmed his love for Margaret in a letter at the time of his court case, in which he asked his solicitor to finish the case with all speed 'for that good woman's sake at Hayton whom my soul loveth, that we may not live longer at this distance, our hearts being truly united'.

Margaret's cousin, Sir John Hotham MP, became governor of Kingston-upon-Hull, or Hull, which lies about twenty miles to the east of Hayton. Sir John Hotham precipitated the armed conflict between the followers of the king, Charles I, and the followers of the Parliament, when he denied the king access to the arsenal at Hull in 1642. So it was that the Civil War began.

Walter's Family

The Rudstons were landowning gentry of moderate means, and resided at Rudston Manor, at Hayton, near the old church. Walter Rudston's father, also called Walter, had married Frances, a daughter of Sir Philip Constable, who lived nearby at Everingham. The Constables, like the Rudstons, were an old family of Yorkshire; they were related to everyone in the gentry in their part of Yorkshire. Differences of religion were not very important to these country people; they were like one family. The Constables were Catholic. Frances Constable was only fourteen when she married. She had ten children, the last two being twins born when she was thirty. She died a few months later. Many in her family died at a similar young age.

The Constables were a more powerful family than the Rudstons. The Rudstons went to court to defend their property and their enclosure of it, when small farmers claimed part of it as a common on which they had always grazed their sheep. The Constables arbitrated on the matter. The farmers said that John Rudston, the grandfather of Walter who married Margaret Dawnay, 'did slate and chase the sheep, and would in no way quit, and suffer them to depasture upon the ground called the ling as they have done in time out of mind of man'. The ling was heath land.

The Rudstons leased some of their land to tenants to farm. In order to ascertain what the boundaries of the land were, the court took statements from the tenants, especially old people, to see how long their leases had been operating. In one case a woman held a lease for so long that four men married her in succession; she outlived three of them before dying herself! They married her so that they had the right to farm the piece of land which was in her tenure.

It was important for landowners to keep all the documents from the past recording the ownership and acquisition of the land they claimed as theirs, as it was often contested. Collections of family papers were made for this reason, and were inherited by the oldest son and heir. It's these family papers I've been able to use for writing the story.

Walter, the oldest child of Walter and Frances Rudston, was born in 1597, and then followed Barbara, William, Charles, Mary, Samuel, Mathew, Marmaduke, and the twins, Philip and Katherine. A few years after his wife's death, Walter, the father of all these children, married Elizabeth, the widow of Samuel Saltonstall. She had six children of her own under the age of twenty, who were being provided for, and educated by, funds from Saltonstall properties in Hull. Walter and Elizabeth were both to live to a good age in retirement on the Rudston estate.

The Stage Is Set

Walter, the future consort of Margaret Dawnay, was groomed, as befitting the oldest son and the heir, to be lord of the manor of Hayton. He had to marry as well as possible because of the social connections and wealth it conferred, and his marriage was important to ensure that there were male heirs who would inherit the property. If his father died, he would be responsible for obligations, of both a formal and an informal nature, to his brothers and sisters.

Old Walter had to settle many matters before young Walter's marriage. To start them off in life, he made grants of money to each of his children, which were called child's portions. He found husbands for his daughters. The sons worked on the estate while they were growing up; now he placed the younger sons in apprenticeships, or found them employment in a trade or business. No Rudstons went to university. He made sure that he would receive an income from the estate, before handing it over to young Walter's management.

The Daughters

The daughters were found husbands, if possible. Young daughters might work at home, or their parents might arrange for them to work in a great house, very much like 'au pair' girls today. They would acquire some refinement, and would perhaps make a good match. Or they might meet prospective husbands in the closer family circle. The oldest Rudston girl, Barbara, married (twelve years before Walter) their step-brother Samuel Saltonstall, who owned a property, 'Rogerthorpe', and the couple soon had a young family. Mary Rudston married a cousin, John Rudston of Bessingby, and gave birth to a son, but she died at the birth. Women must have been daunted by the prospect of dying in childbirth.

Katherine, one of the twins, aged eighteen at the time of Walter's marriage, remained unmarried. She continued to live at the Rudston manor part of the time, and part of the time she was attached to the household of Lady Savile, her aunt. William Rudston, the next in line to Walter, had married Hester, the daughter of Sir George Savile of Thornhill (now deceased) and his second wife Elizabeth. The widow, Lady Savile, undertook to bring up Katherine Rudston for a few years as a gentlewoman. She was taken to London, sometimes, in the season.

The Sons and the Child's Portions

The sons William, Charles and Samuel Rudston were the trustees of an agreement in 1629 to pay the portions of the younger children, Mathew, Marmaduke, Philip and Katherine Rudston, by certain dates; therefore, William, Charles and Samuel must have already been paid their portions. It is not known what William or Charles Rudston did for a living. Samuel Rudston, described as a gentleman, worked in the courts of law at London, and was paid a portion of 200 pounds. Mathew and Marmaduke were employed as drapers in London, and likewise each received a child's portion of 200 pounds. It was common for younger sons in the Rudston family to seek their fortune in London, especially in the cloth trade.

Philip Rudston, one of the twins, was serving an apprenticeship with James Hopkinson, a merchant of York. Philip had full board in his master's house, was supplied with clothing, and was given a token stipend of sixpence a year. According to his contract, during the eight years of his apprenticeship he had to obey his master; he couldn't marry or leave; he couldn't frequent taverns to drink alcohol or play cards or other games; and he was not to hurt anyone or to commit fornication. Philip was to be paid a portion of 200 pounds, like the others, by 1634. Katherine, Philip's twin, was to receive the larger sum of 300 pounds by 1634, or at the time of her marriage if she married at an earlier date. Philip and Katherine would have reached the age of twenty-one in 1634.

As the trustees, William, Charles and Samuel Rudston were to hold and retain some of the Rudston estate to ensure the release of the portions by the oldest brother, Walter. If he failed to make the payments, the trustees could take the profits of the section of the estate assigned to them for that purpose, and having made the payments, they would then return the land to the oldest brother. In that way, some of the brothers would take part of the responsibility for seeing that the portions were paid. At the time of Walter and Margaret's marriage, Katherine Rudston's portion had not been discharged. This omission was to cause trouble in the future.

The House and Goods

Around the time of Walter and Margaret's marriage in 1631, old Walter Rudston transferred goods and chattels worth 2000 pounds to the ownership of his oldest son. There were no financial institutions like banks in the seventeenth century, so people kept their wealth locked up in house or castle. This wealth was more to be found in goods than coin. Very often business transactions were carried out in an exchange of goods and services, or barter.

Of greatest value on the Rudston estate were 1600 sheep worth 700 pounds. The wheat, rye, barley, oats and peas in the barns were worth 300 pounds. The hay was worth 150 pounds; some of it was lying on the ground in the ling. The cattle were valued at about 220 pounds altogether, in three equal holdings: draught oxen and four steers; twenty milking cows and two bulls; and young beasts, including thirty yearling calves.

The rooms of the house, and the furnishings, were described in the schedule. The silverware in the house was valued at 140 pounds. The damask and linen was worth seventy pounds. The remaining items, valued at 220 pounds altogether, were furniture in the dining parlour, a store room, and another nine rooms. These rooms were called the great chamber, the canopy chamber, the lodging chamber, the children's chamber, the closet chamber, the griddle chamber, the matter chamber, the gatehouse chamber, and the garret chamber. They contained seventeen beds in all, either standing beds or trundle beds. Other furnishings were tables, embroidered chairs and carvers (with arms), stools, embroidered cushions, carpets, cupboards, liveries, closets and chests. Liveries stored servants' uniforms and effects.

The document is incomplete, lacking the items of smaller value like farm equipment and tools, kitchenware, and stores of food and drink. These would have been worth about 200 pounds altogether. This would make the total value of the goods 2000 pounds. One third of the value of goods was held in sheep.

Some of the items were valued in pounds, and some in marks. The Teutonic mark was worth two thirds of a pound. Apparently the mark was a value that people were used to, just as today people often weigh in pounds or measure in feet and inches side by side with their use of a metric system.

The Rudston Estate

The Manor of Hayton, commonly called Rudston's Manor, comprised 'eight messuages, sixteen cottages, four and twenty gardens, six orchards, two hundred acres of land, one hundred acres of meadow, one hundred acres of furze and heath, one hundred acres of moor, common of turbary and common of pasture for all manner of cattle, with the appurtenances, in Hayton, North Cave, Bielby and Writeholme at Witham'. A messuage was a dwelling, with adjacent buildings, surrounded by land for growing produce for household use. The furze was gorse, and the turbary contained turf or peat. The Rudstons also owned thirty-five acres called Welwick Enholmes, at Ploughland in Holderness, the most eastern part of Yorkshire.

The description of the main dwelling at Rudston's Manor, and the fields around it, sounds like a poem. (I have written all the documents in modern spelling, but with the same words in the same order.)

The capital messuage or tenement called the old hall in Hayton, with all garths, gardens, orchards, barns, stables, dovecotes, edifices and buildings. Two closes or pastures called the feeding pastures lying westward from the said old hall. One close called Missick Close with a barn or sheepcote standing therein. Two closes called the setting closes, one close called the Far Ash Close, one close called the Little Beck Close, one other close called the New Intake adjoining upon the Ash Close, and two little ing closes adjoining upon the long close upon the south, and upon the tenants' field upon the north.

The garths were yards or courtyards. The ings were meadows which flooded.

The Marriage Agreement

In the marriage agreement of Margaret and Walter, Margaret's father, Sir Thomas Dawnay, was to pay 1000 pounds as a portion or dowry. In exchange, part of the Rudston property was to be limited to Margaret's use by placing it in a joint tenancy or jointure, with her husband. This part would be kept in trust to support Margaret for her life should her husband die before her, and it could not be sold, or encumbered in any way. It was common for one third of an estate to be held in a jointure. Walter could use the 1000-pound dowry but he was expected to pay 100 pounds a year for his wife's keep.

The main dwelling at Hayton, worth 200 marks or 133 pounds a year, was limited to Walter and Margaret in the jointure. Together with some fields around it ('the residue'), it was entailed, and was to be inherited by their male heirs. If they had no male heirs, it would be inherited by any male heirs of Walter (supposing Margaret died, and he remarried). If there were none of those, it would be inherited by Walter's brothers in order of age, and their male heirs.

Walter Rudston's father was to have 'one messuage or tenement with the appurtenances in North Cave, purchased from Robert Constable, with all garths, buildings and certain parcels of ground called Kiln Garth, Beck Close, Aunam Close, and five selions of land called Sayres with their appurtenances situated in North Cave, and two little closes in Bielby called Writeholme with the appurtenance'. (A selion was a small field for growing crops.) The residue of the premises in North Cave, known as Rudston's Walk, and the closes adjoining it and their appurtenances were for the use of Walter Rudston, the son, and his heirs.

Old Walter, in his retirement, was to be paid eighty pounds a year, in four payments, raised from all the lands in Hayton not limited to the use of Margaret. If he was not paid the money he could enter the property and take what he needed to cover the payment.

Daughters were provided for, in the marriage agreement. If Walter died without male issue but had a daughter with Margaret, then anything not limited to Margaret would be held by the trustees in order to raise 1000 pounds for the daughter when she reached the age of seventeen, or when she married if it was earlier. If there were two daughters, they would raise 1500 pounds to be shared between them. Once a daughter married she was the responsibility of her husband, and everything she owned belonged to him.

Margaret and Walter Marry

Margaret Dawnay and Walter Rudston were married in the old church at Snaith on 9 May, 1631. Margaret's father presented a moral tract to the couple in honour of the occasion. It was called 'A short treatise of the spiritual life leading unto perfection, wherein are declared nine impediments which occur to one desiring to go in the way of God'. The impediments which Margaret and Walter were to take heed of were self-love, the love of creatures, sensuality, pride, bitterness of spirit, propriety[sic], immoderate desire, neglect of the inward person, and lukewarmness.

The treatise said that human beings had to strive against desires and lusts, and mortify their senses. They should seek humility through thinking themselves vile and sinful. They should mourn how Christ suffered, and imitate him. They should train their desires to conform to God, and bear all adversity patiently; they should resign themselves to the will of God with contentment. The soul should be pure, clean, silent, quiet, and exclude imagination and remembrance. Humans should not only be led by custom and good works, but also by love of God, brotherly love towards all people, purity of intention, and denial of self. They should pray in this manner: 'Oh my God, Oh life of my soul, Oh my whole desire and joy, when shall I ardently love Thee and despise myself and all the world? Oh that I could be pulled out of myself and transformed into Thee by the burning of Thy vehement love.'

At this time, Margaret and Walter knew a lawyer, John Hall of London, who became a family friend. He was to play an important role in their lives. Just after the marriage, John Hall made copies of two poems, *Satire 1* and *Satire 2*, by John Donne, when he visited the houses of friends. He probably enjoyed the satirical poem about lawyers. He signed and dated the little booklet containing the poems and some of his legal notes. Later, he was to give these precious copies to Margaret.

Margaret and Walter enjoyed eight years of peaceful married life on the farm, and their family grew apace. One year after the marriage Margaret gave birth to their first child, a daughter, Faith. Their second daughter, Barbara, was born around 1635.

Wentworth

Walter underwent military training, and gained his commission as a captain who was authorized to lead a trained band of 120 foot soldiers in the East Riding of Yorkshire. He may have gone to Dublin in June 1634 to receive his certificate signed by Wentworth. A Yorkshireman, Viscount Wentworth was Lord Deputy of Ireland, Lord President of the northern parts of England, and Lord Lieutenant of the County of York. He was Walter's distant kinsman. Wentworth was raising an army in Ireland to support Charles I, as the English had no regular standing army.

Wentworth had a troop of English soldiers with him in Dublin, and Walter, or a friend of Walter's, may have served a term there and brought back to Yorkshire copies of 232 warrants of Dublin of 1634. A warrant was an official authorization or order to do something. The soldiers might have been amused by reading some of the warrants, such as:

Warrant for a falconer.

Whereas our servant and falconer H M hath complained unto us, himself and such as he employeth, all ready to kill hawks' meat, are oftentimes abused and threatened to have their penises taken from them, of which disrespective usage and carriage towards our servants we cannot but take special notice. And therefore we require all and every His Majesty's officers, ministers and loving subjects, not only to take due notice that the said M is our servant, but also to permit him to take and kill any kind of birds or fowls for hawks' meat, without any manner their lets or hindrances, whereof they are not to fail at their perils.

What peril might befall those who objected to their chickens being killed by the falconer for his falcon's dinner? Wentworth's regime was cruel and repressive; a person who was using a counterfeit licence for begging was pilloried and had one of his ears cut off. (In 1641, Wentworth would be impeached by the Parliament, and executed.)

Margaret Rudston's third daughter, also named Margaret, was born at Hayton in 1637. Margaret gave birth in 1639 to a son, Thomas, just before her mother died. Margaret had a son,

Walter, who died in 1640, and a second Walter born about 1642. Margaret's father, Sir Thomas Dawnay, died in the same year. In his will he bequeathed to his grandson and godson, Thomas Rudston, some lands at Goole in East Yorkshire.

The Bishops' Wars

In 1639 and 1640, Walter Rudston fought in Sir Thomas Metham's regiment in the Bishops' Wars, the wars of the Crown against the Scots. Sir Thomas Metham was a relative of Walter's through his mother's family, the Constables. Walter served as a captain in charge of his trained band of 120 foot soldiers. The war was fought over the attempt by Charles I to impose English bishops and the Anglican Book of Common Prayer on the Scots, who were largely Presbyterian. In 1639 there was a stalemate, and the two armies camped on either side of the border.

In 1640, the Scots captured the town of Newcastle in Northern England, and occupied the counties of Northumberland and Durham. Eventually Charles I paid them compensation so that they would leave England. There was, in all, very little fighting in the wars, and the English soldiers were poorly trained and armed. They endured cold conditions and lack of food and shelter, so there was a great deal of disease. Walter may have suffered illness in the wars, as later he was to write of being 'disabled by the relapse of my old disease'.

Walter must have thought himself lucky to return home to farm his land in peace, avoiding occupation by the Scots. He would see his old father before he died. Margaret had her hands full looking after the manor and the children while he was away. She lost one newborn baby during that time. In the year before the birth of Margaret's last child, Elizabeth, momentous events would shake the lives of the Rudstons of Hayton.

The Civil War

The English Civil War was a new kind of war. A war was usually fought against a foreign enemy. In this war, two sides representing the king, on one hand, and parliament, on the other hand, would fight each other for the right to hold the final authority in the country.

After the Bishops' Wars against the Scots, Charles I moved his court to York. He felt he had more supporters in the north than in London. At Hull, forty miles nearer the coast, there was the largest arsenal of weapons in England and an important port Charles wanted access to. His queen was expected to arrive at Hull with revenue borrowed overseas. Charles had very little money and he had to pawn the Crown jewels. He levied taxes, like ship money, without approval of parliament, to support the Crown. Even royalists like Sir Marmaduke Langdale, the Yorkshire commander, did not approve of the ship money tax.

The governor of Hull, Sir John Hotham, Margaret Rudston's cousin and formerly a royalist, held this town for the parliament. He could not allow the king access, by orders of parliament. While the king and his entourage were on their way from York to Hull in April 1642 to demand possession of the port, the king called in at the Rudstons' as he passed by, and dined with them. This would later be held against Walter when he was charged with delinquency, but a person could not refuse the king. When the king arrived at Hull he found the town gates barred by Sir John Hotham. He was not allowed to enter and was forced to return to York. The king was furious.

In July, the king set up court at Beverley, near Hull. He tried and failed a second time to gain entry to Hull, and engaged in the first military action of the Civil War. Sir Thomas Metham was active against the parliamentary forces, and a Captain Legard destroyed some royalist forces; people often had relatives fighting on the opposite side. The parliament brought in troops by sea, and these defeated the royalists, who withdrew to York.

The king conferred a baronetcy on Walter Rudston, because he had entertained him to dinner. Walter took oaths in support of the king. He sent horses to aid the Earl of Cumberland, who was almost a neighbour of Walter's, and lived in the grandest country house in East Yorkshire, Londesborough Hall. Charles I had put Cumberland in charge of the royalist forces in Yorkshire. But he was ineffective and the parliamentarians were easily able to raid royalist positions from Hull and other centres. By October, the Yorkshire royalists took their own action and gave control over their forces to the Earl of Newcastle.

Parliament's leading commanders in the north were the Yorkshiremen Lord Fairfax and his son Sir Thomas. The parliamentary leaders tried to reconcile the king and parliament, without success.

A New Kind of War

When the king declared war on the parliament, Walter, and many others who were like-minded, did not want there to be a war between the king and the parliament. They did not wish to take a side in it and fight the other side. They considered it necessary to have both a king and a parliament, and not an outright winner. Sir John Hotham wrote: 'No man that hath any reasonable share in the commonwealth can desire that either side should be conqueror. It is too great a temptation to counsels of violence.' Sir Walter Rudston said that he was not willing to meddle betwixt the bark and the tree.

But it was impossible to be neutral in the theatre of war. Many tried to persuade the Earl of Kingston-upon-Hull, Robert Pierrepont, to join the parliamentary party. He stated: 'When I take arms with the king against the parliament, or with the parliament against the king, let a cannonball divide me between them.' He prevaricated, and then took up arms for the king. He was captured by the parliamentarians. While he was being conveyed as a prisoner to Hull in the parliament's boat, royalist soldiers attacked from the river bank. The earl showed himself on the deck to prevent further shooting, but a cannonball from the king's army divided his head in two, and ended his life. Some say it was parliamentary soldiers who shot him. (So much for being in two minds.)

The earl had bought his title from the king for thousands of pounds, like many others had. Charles I was only too glad to sell titles because he was so impoverished. He inherited debts, and was denied funds by parliament. Sometimes the king lacked the wherewithal to pay for his own dinner.

The Agreement of the Yorkshire Gentlemen

The nobility and gentry of Yorkshire were called to a meeting in which they were required to support the king's cause. They were asked to sign the Agreement of the Yorkshire Gentlemen. It was a promise to offer subscriptions and raise funds, in proportion to each person's wealth, for the Earl of Newcastle's forces:

We, the nobility and gentry of the County of York, whose names are herewith subscribed, do mutually agree that all such moneys as were heretofore borrowed upon bond or shall hereafter be borrowed upon bond for the defence of this county, if the said money cannot be got by any act of parliament or any other loyal way, then the same shall be repaid by us portionably according to our estates, as the Lord Chancellor or Lord Keeper of the Great Seal of England shall appoint if we shall not agree in raising the said moneys amongst ourselves.

The gentlemen made oaths of loyalty and subscriptions at Stamford Bridge, a royalist garrison near York, and various people were appointed to collect money in different regions. Sir Walter Rudston was compelled by warrant from the Earl of Newcastle to get in 500 pounds in the division of Holme

Beacon, which was composed of a number of parishes surrounding his abode. This was ordered because Walter was a landowner who commanded a troop of foot soldiers. He did not subscribe to the agreement.

Trials and Tribulations

In February 1643, the queen arrived on the coast at Bridlington, just north of Hull, with arms and money she had raised on the Continent for the king. She was escorted to York early in March.

On 3 March, a contingent of the king's army commanded by Captain Mason tramped uninvited into the Rudstons' property at Hayton, and took control of it by force for the billeting of '1000 horse'. They were part of the Earl of Newcastle's cavalry under General Goring, and would remain quartered there for over a year. The soldiers occupied the house and made use of the amenities, including food, drink, firewood and coal. Margaret Rudston was trying to take care of five children, the youngest only a baby.

Walter was offered a place in Sir Thomas Metham's regiment by Captain Hildyard, either Sir Thomas's own position as a major, or as a lieutenant colonel under him. Walter refused the place, saying that he had resigned his commission in the army. He said he would not bear arms for the king against his parliament; he would not meddle or make any breach betwixt the bark and the tree.

Because of his refusal to lead his trained band in the service of the king, Walter's estate was plundered of men, arms, horses and 'plate' (silverware) in retribution. He was questioned about the 500 pounds he was to collect for Holme Beacon, and he said he had brought in IOUs. He would prefer to take responsibility for the payment himself rather than get it by order of warrant from the people of Holme Beacon.

Walter was made a prisoner in his home and was coerced under threat by Captain Cocks, the deputy treasurer of the army, to pay 100 pounds, so he gave him an IOU. Because he refused to subscribe to the Agreement of the Yorkshire Gentlemen, Captain Mason held a pistol to his breast and forced him away in a violent manner, not allowing him to speak to Margaret. He took Walter as a prisoner to the king's garrison at Stamford Bridge, where he was brought before the Council of War.

He was interrogated by the royalist general, Sir Marmaduke Langdale. Sir Marmaduke slated Walter and reckoned him not to be a cavalier. He said he must be an enemy because, when Hayton was under parliamentary control earlier on, Walter was not plundered. Therefore he must have sent money, horses and arms to representatives of the parliamentary party. Walter denied it, and said he had lent money to the king's party; he had just promised 100 pounds to Captain Cocks.

Walter refused to sign the Agreement of the Yorkshire Gentlemen and pay a fine, so he was sent to prison in York. They said he would be imprisoned until he subscribed to the agreement and paid 1000 pounds as a loan. He was detained at York prison for more than seven weeks. Twice he was brought before Sir William Widdrington, the President of the Council of War at York, and was asked why he would not subscribe to the agreement. He replied that he didn't know what the agreement was, and didn't desire to meddle in it. At one point his loan was reduced to 500 pounds, and at a later time to 300 pounds. But Walter remained in prison because he contended that he had no money.

Margaret Entreats Walter to Come Home

Margaret was still at Hayton trying to look after her five children amidst the '1000 horse' which had commandeered the house and property. She became ill. A yeoman called John Nelson was living with the Rudstons, and his being there was helpful to Margaret. In prison, Walter petitioned Sir William Widdrington for liberty upon bail to return to assist his wife 'in that great trouble', but he could not obtain it. Margaret wrote letters to Walter with arguments against his continuing to stay in prison. She pleaded with him to pay and come home. Eventually Widdrington agreed to Walter paying 100 pounds to procure his freedom, and this sum Walter managed to borrow. To gain his release he was also compelled to sign the Agreement of the Yorkshire Gentlemen.

After returning home at Whitsuntide, Walter sent eighty pounds' worth of silverware to the parliamentarian Sir John Hotham, in Hull. It was conveyed there by Lawrence Johnson, who fought with Walter in the Scottish wars, and John Nelson. They came back with a letter from Sir John Hotham:

Hull the 14th June 1643

This shall be to command all officers and soldiers whatsoever to forbear to meddle or plunder the house and goods of Sir

Walter Rudston, upon pain of severe punishment. Signed under my hand at Hull the day and year above written,
   John Hotham.
   To all officers and soldiers for the king and parliament.

Soon after this, Hotham was captured and imprisoned by the parliamentarians because they heard he planned to switch sides. He was charged with treason. Hotham was resentful that the parliament had promoted Lord Fairfax and his son Sir Thomas, above him and his son Captain Hotham, to be in command of the northern army. He would be beheaded eighteen months later.

The Fairfaxes had been appointed on their merit. Lord Fairfax became governor of Hull. He established a military base from which his parliamentary forces could attack the royalists who occupied towns and villages in the area. When the royalists under the Earl of Newcastle besieged Hull again in September and October 1643, the parliamentary forces were strong enough to drive them away, and most of their companies retreated to York. They plundered Hayton again on the way back.

The Rudstons still had royalist soldiers stationed at Hayton. They had no firewood or coal left at home; without them, they could not cook, or heat the house. Faced with the cold weather coming on, they decided that Margaret Rudston and the children were to go and live with Walter's sister Barbara Saltonstall, and her family, at 'Rogerthorpe', near Pontefract in West Yorkshire. Margaret and the children remained at 'Rogerthorpe' for nearly two years. Walter would visit them. As Pontefract was a royalist garrison, his visiting it would later be held against him in his delinquency case.

Walter went to see Margaret's nephew Sir Christopher Dawnay at his castle in Sessay, North Yorkshire, before Christopher left for the Continent. Many of the nobility locked up their castles, placed guards at them, and went overseas, so that they did not have to be involved in the vicissitudes of the Civil War. Christopher died a little later, and had no heirs.

Only one of Margaret's nephews, John, survived, and would play an important part in Margaret's life after Walter died.

The Solemn League and Covenant

In September 1643, the English Parliament passed a bill to accept the Solemn League and Covenant. It was a declaration to preserve the Church of Scotland and reform the religion of England and Ireland, and to protect the rights and liberties of parliaments. The Scots crossed the border again in 1644, this time to fight on the side of the English Parliament, against the king. The royalists were pushed back to York, which was besieged in April and June. They were defeated, and most of the north fell into the control of the parliamentary forces.

Sir Hugh Cholmley had held the castle of Scarborough near Whitby as a garrison for the parliament because he hoped it would bring peace. However, like his friend Hotham, he defected to the king. His royalist forces fought the parliament for a year. Sir Walter Rudston was seen in Scarborough a number of times, but he denied later, when he was before the court, that he was in the fight against the parliament at Sandsend, near Whitby, with Sir Hugh Cholmley. At that time

Walter had taken the oath to uphold the National Covenant according to the order of parliament. This proved that he was loyal to parliament.

Sequestration

A Committee of Sequestrations was set up in Yorkshire for the purpose of examining and charging those who had supported the king against the parliament. They examined Walter in November 1644. In 1645 they gave Walter a copy of his charge, for which he had to put in an answer. He did. They then could find no reason to charge him and the matter was laid aside for the time being, but the case was not dismissed.

The charges against Walter were: he sent horses, men and arms for the king's service. He fought at Sandsend near Whitby with Sir Hugh Cholmley. He consented to the drawing of the Earl of Newcastle's army into Yorkshire. He voluntarily lent 100 pounds to the king's army. He agreed, with other gentlemen, to charge the County of York for maintenance of the king's army. He agreed to collect the money for the division of Holme Beacon. He went frequently to Pontefract, York, Scarborough and Stamford Bridge, which were king's garrisons. He was accused of 'entertaining the king to dinner', not before the king went to Hull against Sir John Hotham, but afterwards, and the king had made him a baronet for his affection to him and his cause.

The committee sequestered, until further order, two parcels of the Rudstons' land about twenty miles from Hayton.

These had been set aside by Walter's father for the payment of portions, amounting to 500 pounds, to two younger children.

The Rudstons Are Reunited

Margaret Rudston and the children returned to Hayton from the Saltonstalls' house in Pontefract by the spring of 1645, or earlier. The royalist soldiers had departed. Margaret had given birth to her sixth child, Elizabeth. The Rudston family would be able to bring up their children, farm the land and live in peace again for a few years.

Walter's youngest sister, Katherine, married Lt. Col. William Leigh of Methley in 1644. The couple, finding themselves without any lodgings, went to Hayton for nine months. Margaret and Walter made them welcome. Walter paid for their food and other costs; they had one servant and four horses with them. Walter sold William Leigh thirteen oak trees for which he had to pay thirty pounds in the future, and suggested how he could sell the timber for profit. Walter had still not paid Katherine's portion of 300 pounds because he thought, in the past, that she would only spend it unwisely.

Katherine had lived at Hayton for three years after Walter's marriage at his expense. She then found a position in the household of Lady Savile, as a gentlewoman and companion, and was taken to London. But it was Walter who paid for her fine clothes. Now he gave William and Katherine seventy-eight pounds on one occasion, and forty-eight pounds on another, towards the 300 pounds still owed to them.

William and Katherine Leigh could have received the rents on the parcel of land sequestered by the government for the payment of their portion, and this procedure could have paid off the 300 pounds. But they did not apply for it legally and appropriately, so the money went to the government instead. The Leighs would cause Margaret trouble over this matter, in the future.

The Civil War raged on in other parts of England. In January 1649, Charles I was executed by the parliamentary government. Monarchy and the House of Lords were abolished, and the country was ruled by parliament for the next four years, as the Commonwealth, until Oliver Cromwell came to power. In Yorkshire, the Civil War ceased in March 1649 when Pontefract Castle was finally retaken by the parliamentarians.

In the Aftermath of the Civil War

Delinquency

Immediately after the war ended in Yorkshire in 1649, Sir Walter Rudston received news that the charges against him were about to be revived. Walter asked the MP, General and Yorkshireman, Sir Thomas Fairfax, to intercede in his case. Sir Thomas wrote to the Committee for Sequestrations in Yorkshire on Walter's behalf:

Gentlemen,

I understand by Sir Walter Rudston of Hayton in the County of York that you intend now to sequester him, he having, as I am informed, been charged by the Committee of the County (Mr Pierrepont being in the chair) in 1644 and never questioned since, they finding no case of sequestration; and that you intend to receive the profits of his estate, he having all this time enjoyed the same except for a small part thereof made over by deed for other uses. In case the Committee of Appeals had been settled he would have applied himself to them for a hearing concerning anything that could be said to his charge, but not sitting, he at present is remediless.

And therefore I make my request unto you, on his behalf, that he may, as he hath done all this while, enjoy his estate till he be heard upon his appeal if you intend to proceed against him, which I doubt not but he will ere long obtain, the Parliament intending shortly to settle a court for that purpose; and what favour and respect you show to him herein will be acknowledged by

Your very assured friend,

T Fairfax

Queen Street April 2 1649.

For my worthy friends the Committee of the County of York.

Walter wrote a petition to the Barons of the Exchequer in London saying that he was questioned in 1644 for a supposed delinquency, but they found nothing amounting to a sequestration. No land other than two parcels were sequestered, and no new matter was charged against him, but the sequestrators had lately threatened to sequester the rest. Walter said that he was imprisoned by the king's party and had had to present an IOU for his ransom. He would like the Chief Baron to ask the Committee for Sequestrations in Yorkshire to give him his charge in writing so that witnesses could be examined.

The Barons of the Exchequer granted an order to the committee in Yorkshire to send the charge in writing and examine the witnesses. Suddenly Walter found himself charged with delinquency. Because of the seriousness of the charge, some of the Rudston children may have been sent to live for about two years with aldermen and ministers of Beverley, and later with ministers in North Dalton, like the children of the disgraced general, Sir Marmaduke Langdale. The documents do not tell the complete story about them. The Rudstons knew the Langdales, who lived near them. The oldest Rudston child, Faith, was now seventeen and was working in a 'great house', Sizergh Castle, the home of Sir Thomas Strickland.

The Witnesses

On 12 June 1649, witnesses in Walter's case were to be examined at the house of Robert Bateson in Pocklington, near Hayton. Walter attended with John Lister and presented his witnesses, John Nelson and Ralph Shaw, and the answers to his charge. He was surprised to receive a further charge, and was given a month to answer it. When Walter returned, only the clerk was present, and nothing could be done. Hearing that the committee was to meet at Market Weighton nearby, and other places, Walter repeated his attempts to meet committee members but could never get two of them together to examine his witnesses.

At last, in November, Sir Richard Darley and a Mr Robinson agreed to meet him at the Sign of the Wild Man in York. Walter enlisted the services of the solicitor John Hall, whom he and his wife had known for nearly twenty years since their marriage. He went to the appointed place with his solicitor and the two witnesses and waited until four o'clock in the afternoon, but they would not examine his witnesses. He continued his endeavours to meet the committee, but they put him off with 'fair words', and would not examine his witnesses and let him present his appeal.

Walter wrote this general advice for his solicitor:

First to desire Sir Richard Darley well to observe my case as it lies, and he will find it apparent that I should be considered a friend to the parliament and not an enemy; these arguments being not bare pretences but full especially of the truth.

Secondly, I can make it appear under a thousand hands that since these evil times began I sent the county a thousand pounds, having not the least regard to myself in it, but only for the public good.

Lastly, for Sir Richard Darley he tells me to my face that I was the least delinquent in Yorkshire, therefore I wonder he should revive a new trouble against me, which shows more malice than matter to him that never deserved it at his hands.

During all Walter's efforts to have his witnesses examined, the Committee for Sequestrations in Yorkshire were taking statements from witnesses, both for and against Walter, including the witnesses he took to meet them. The witnesses reported what happened to Walter from the time that '1000 horse' from the king's army arrived at Hayton for billeting in 1643. One witness stated, to give credit where it was due, that because Walter refused to serve the king, he preserved the town of Hayton from plunder by parliamentary forces, and that he saved the money of the people of the county.

Walter's Appeal

In 1650, the Committee for Sequestrations in Yorkshire ordered the leasing out of Sir Walter Rudston's sequestered estate at Hayton, Cave and Pensthorpe, under the yearly rent of twenty-five pounds. In May, Walter presented a petition to the committee. He asked for haste in his case of appeal. On 29 May, he was summoned by the Commissioners for the Advance of Money to appear with his solicitor in the Painted Chamber at Westminster in June. They required him to explain the debts he incurred for the maintenance of the army raised against the parliament, according to the Agreement of the Yorkshire Gentlemen.

Walter wrote to his solicitor, 'Honest Jack Hall, I find by your truth you have been very careful of my business, for which I give you many thanks, desiring you would continue the same even to the end thereof, which I have no cause to doubt'. He thought it strange that the court would take no security but money, which was lent by Mr Hall's cousin, Dawson. Walter entreated Mr Hall to make the point, in pleading his case, that he was under the power of the king's garrison at Stamford Bridge. If he had been compelled by force to do anything, he could not be blamed under the ordinance.

Walter appeared in court on 28 June and confessed to having subscribed to the Agreement of the Yorkshire Gentlemen, but declared he was imprisoned until he subscribed and paid 100 pounds. He asked to be acquitted. However, the new order of the Painted Chamber made no allowance for excuses of this kind. It stated that any person who signed the agreement and received money or promises of money for the service of the king's army had to pay it to the Commissioners for the Advance of Money. If a person's appeal was overruled, the person would have to pay a quarter more. The commissioners had made a list of these debts, dated 16 June 1649.

Meanwhile, the Committee for Sequestrations in Yorkshire started to take new depositions concerning Walter's support of the king in the Civil War. It sent them to the Barons of the Exchequer in London in September, where Walter's case was still pending at Haberdashers' Hall. Among the depositions were those of prisoners at Scarborough who saw Walter in the street with soldiers. They said it was generally reported that Walter went in arms with Sir Hugh Cholmley to the fight at Sandsend near Whitby against the parliament. This information was sufficient to convict Walter of delinquency. The informants were paid.

By this time Margaret's brother-in-law, Sir Henry Vaughan of Sutton, was helping John Hall and Walter by attending court hearings, delivering letters and copying documents.

Walter Settles His Affairs

On 27 November, Walter wrote to John Hall from Hough End Hall near Manchester, the home of Sir Edward Mosley, where he was staying. Sir Edward was a relative of some Mosley women known to the Rudstons. One of them was the widow of Margaret Rudston's late nephew, Sir Christopher Dawnay. Another was the wife of Sir Thomas Strickland of Sizergh Castle, to whose household Faith Rudston was presently attached. Faith, who was now eighteen years old, was in some kind of trouble with Sir Thomas Strickland, and wanted to come home. Perhaps she had been mistreated. Sir Edward Mosley was trying to help in the matter. He was also in a position to give Walter advice about sequestration, as he had been sequestered earlier.

Walter was ill. He heard 'the damned devils' intended to sequester his family of their home before he was even judged a delinquent. Walter wrote a letter, as instructed by his solicitor, asking for help from Sir Robert Stapleton, his kinsman. Sir Robert Stapleton was a dramatist, poet and translator, and a royalist. He was the son of Richard and Elizabeth Stapleton of Carlton Hall near the Dawnays in Cowick; Elizabeth was the sister of the earl who was divided in two by a cannonball.

To get back his sequestered estate, Walter might have to compound for it, or go to a composition, which meant buying it back as a form of fine. But Walter wanted John Hall first to present his case privately to Baron Thorpe, a descendant of Walter's great aunt, who would be sympathetic. He made this impassioned request:

Debate the business with him as far as you may in my wife's behalf, and tell him her husband is so weak she humbly entreats his favour for a good and speedy end of these troubles. She will be wondrous thankful, being the absolute settlement of her and all her children for her husband's carriage in the cause, that it was fair and moderate. She can bring it under a thousand hands to testify in his behalf, and also you can show him what considerable things I have done for the parliament.

And if nothing will work but that I must be judged a delinquent, then labour the Baron by some powerful friend for his certificate or best assistance to finish my composition upon reasonable terms. For I would have no time elapse to settle a peace for my dear wife and me at Hayton. Or else you will hear that Sir Walter Rudston is for some new plantation where he may be quiet, for my spirit is not able to bear these suffrages which are acted by such instruments.

Therefore I prithee, honest Jack Hall, as thou lovest me and her whose happiness I esteem above all the world, negotiate for us to bring us to the harbour of rest at the truth, who have been tossed upon the wars and storms of these distempered times, full of years, greatly to the prejudice of our content and profits.

He added, 'The attendance of this suit has been more costly to me than the payment of the bills. I perceive my mare is dead, let her go, and all my ill luck with her, and then it would be a lucky loss to me. Still I will not despair, but there is a prudence will deliver honest men.' Walter sent many thanks to John Hall's friends Harry and Frank, who were trying to help him, and to Margaret's brother-in-law, Vaughan.

Walter was writing his will. He bequeathed his daughters to Hall's two friends, and to the landlord Bagford. He wrote, 'Tell Harry Linley and Frank Breake that I, being in a condition to make my will, have bequeathed two daughters to them upon a writ. If your landlord Bagford makes not haste he shall have the third, and then I am quit of them all.' He told John Hall, 'My whole trust is in you', and sent his love.

Margaret's Letter About Faith

Margaret Rudston wrote to John Hall from Hayton on 3 December. She had not heard from Walter and, not being able to find him at the house of his brother William, at Burton, she didn't know where he was. She knew that he was ill. She was disturbed about her daughter Faith, who was unhappy at the Stricklands' and wanted to come home, but Margaret didn't know what the matter was. She had her horse ready to ride, at a moment's notice, to wherever Walter was. Margaret wrote:

For Mr John Hall at the sign of the White Talbot in Fetter Lane in London, give this. The post is paid.

Mr Hall,

Your lines add much to my sorrows: first that Sir Rudston is not resolved yet what to do; secondly that I cannot hear from him nor of him. I charged Lory and John both to let me know by some means how he recovered, but I could hear nothing from them. So my desires were so much to hear from him that I sent George on purpose to see him, but he was gone from Burton, and they could give no further account of him but that he was gone to London. And you not writing of his being there, it troubles me exceedingly to think where he is.

Thirdly, his news of Faith seems very foreign to me. I am not willing at all that she should come home in regard of my present condition. I cannot give her the education that place affords. Therefore, I would entreat you to go and tell her, if it be a thing that may be discerned with all, let her waive it. She must know these are times of trials; she knows my sufferings are great. I hope she will not think much to be a sharer with me in adversity as well as in prosperity. I believe upon due examination it will prove but some small matter; women's failings are seldom grounded upon any great reason. I have lived in these great houses.

You are able to advise and give her good counsel, for which I shall think myself engaged to you. What's the matter I know not, but rather wish her to submit than lose such a place, though I must confess it is a place of no profit. Yet I hope she will get some breeding; that is all I look for. I fear the wench hath too great a spirit for these times, but she must humble herself.

I hope you will inform me fully of all things by your next post. I cannot so much as doubt of your care of all our businesses, they concern me so much. I long to see all my occasions at home.

Expect you daily, I being just now ready to take horse in great haste, I rest, your loving friend,
Dame Margaret Rudston.
Hayton 3rd of December 1650.
Bid Faith burn my letter when she hath read it.

Walter Agrees to Compound

Walter wrote to John Hall again from Hough End Hall, also on 3 December, after receiving a letter from him:

Seeing the late examples of so much necessity and so little sin against the parliament, I shall be judged delinquent. Therefore, I approve of your judgement in applying to composition. I shall desire you to take the transcribed copies to Sir Robert Stapleton, who is my noble friend, and entreat his good accommodation in my business, which so nearly concerns me and mine. Tell my cousin I think myself ever obliged to him that will step into a troublesome cause to deliver his friend in these dreadful times. It shows his real affection to us and our family. I pray present our kind respects to him with many thanks for his loan unto my daughter, whom I beseech the Lord to bless.

Good Mr Hall, let no opportunity slip for the facting and peace for that good woman's sake at Hayton whom my soul loveth, that we may not live longer at this distance, our hearts being truly united. All for expedition to compound, despairing now of deliverance, which makes us cry out, O tempora, O mores!

Walter anticipated that Mr Hall would be attending about three proceedings in London on his behalf. He said he would now go to his brother's place at Burton, and he sent 'love, love, love'.

Writing again to John Hall on 23 December, from Burton, Walter said he wanted to compound for his estate with all speed before worse happened, as rumour suggested that the property could be confiscated. He wanted to know how much time there was for payment of the money. He said he was assured that Sir Robert Stapleton was taking care of his wife and him. Walter passed on many thanks to Sir Robert. He enclosed the inventory of the estate that John Hall requested. He expected to be at Hayton to receive Mr Hall's next letter. He ended, 'With my love to all my friends with you resting, disabled by a relapse of my old disease which handles me so extremely that I long to see an end of my troubles, your affectionate loving friend, Walter Rudston'.

Walter had made an inventory of his estate, and had the court in York rate its value, based on the values of the particulars. It was ready to send to the Commissioners for Compounding with Delinquents, together with a petition. In the petition Walter said his appeal against the supposed delinquency was still pending, and outlined his attendance at the proceedings in London. He had paid 200 pounds to the commissioners in York since May. He had never acted against the government but, on the contrary, he contributed to it.

Walter Dies

Walter died the same day as the date on his petition, 29 December 1650, at his brother William's house at Burton. Margaret had word the same day to go to Burton as quickly as possible. She rode her horse for most of a cold, wet night to reach William's house, but she arrived too late to see Walter alive. He was buried in the church at Burton on 30 December. It isn't known at which Burton he died, as there were many. He was fifty-three years old. His youngest child was only six then. He died without a will, leaving debts of 1200 pounds. John Hall kept the letters for Margaret, which were, through him, the last communications of Walter, who had hoped soon to join her again at Hayton.

Margaret Rudston and John Hall

After Sir Walter Rudston's death, Mr Hall received a letter from one William Bernard, the lawyer of Walter Rudston's brother, William. He wrote these kind and tender words on behalf of Margaret Rudston and her children:

It is my Lady Rudston's desire, seeing that it hath pleased God to stop Sir Walter Rudston's course in this life by taking him out of this fearful vale, that your dealing with the committee at Goldsmiths' Hall may be delayed, and no proceedings in a compounding way be meddled with till you hear further from her Ladyship. Inform yourself, if you can, how any in the like case have been used, as she is informed that he being dead all matter of delinquency dies with him. Good lady, she is in a sad case much dejected, and it may be some mercy in her affliction that their thirst to his estate may waste with his life, though it were to her a far greater price than to him the estate.

Mr Hall, I beseech you, be faithful and careful in her business and her little children's, who have all received a great blow in the death of him who was so loving a husband, so tender a father, so upright a man, and to us all so kind and faithful a friend. You may counsel her Ladyship to Sir Robert Stapleton and ask his advice in her case, but be cautious in discovering the sad news to Mistress Faith Rudston too hastily, that too sudden and too violent a grief do her hurt. Enquire whether the Court of Wards be fully dissolved or no, and return a speedy answer unless any intervene betwixt my Lady and her son in compounding for the wardship.

The Lawyers Advise

William Bernard wrote twice more in January. He was very concerned that someone might compound for the wardship of the heir, Sir Thomas Rudston, who was eleven years old. The law about this matter was being revised. Sir Richard Darley of the Yorkshire committee for sequestrations promised a reasonable and speedy resolution of the business. Margaret's jointure and the deeds concerning the portions or annuities would have to be proved in a court. Margaret's nephew, Mr John Dawnay, promised money.

Mr Hall informed Mr Bernard, in reply, that he believed Margaret did not wish to stand upon Walter's appeal, but to confess his delinquency. Mr Bernard wrote back, with dignity: 'Sir, may you be faithful in her business, for assure yourself of this you have gathered from her discourse, she hath an especial esteem of your care and ability, and hath no mind of employing any in her business, whether at home or abroad, but yourself. I beseech you therefore to manage these her great affairs according to that prudence that is in you, and that trust reposed upon you.'

Mr Hall also received in January three letters from Marmaduke Prickett, the lawyer of Mr John Dawnay. Since Margaret's father died in 1642, and her husband was now dead, it fell to her nephew John Dawnay to act in their place as best he could. John was the only surviving son of Margaret's deceased brother; he was now aged twenty-six. Because of the delay, Margaret wrote a petition to the Commissioners for Sequestrations in Yorkshire to say that the case of Sir Walter Rudston was still pending, and could not yet be brought to judgement, but not because of her neglect of the matter. She prayed the commissioners to postpone proceedings with her son's estate.

Mr Prickett told Mr Hall that Margaret was prepared to take any action that was in her interest. The committee at York could only take witnesses for her jointure and deed. If the Barons in London did not clear the charge quickly, Margaret wished to apply to Goldsmiths' Hall at Westminster to compound for the estate. She hoped to finish this by Lady Day (25 March, and the beginning of the year) to save the rents then due, so that the price she had to pay would be two years of her rental income. After that date it would be three years' income. She wanted Mr Hall to stop the 200 pounds presently owed by Walter to Parliament, which was part of the money subscribed by the gentlemen of Yorkshire for the king's army.

Margaret wished Mr Hall to petition the parliament for maintenance of the children of Sir Marmaduke Langdale. Sir Marmaduke was the disgraced commander in the royalist army, who was forced to flee to the Continent. Most of his estate, which was near Hayton, was sold, and his children were now farming from the Commonwealth the land they lived on at North Dalton. The children's mother, a relative of the Constables, had died. Some of the Rudston children stayed in North Dalton during Walter's supposed delinquency and knew them well. Many of the committee for sequestrations at York pitied the Langdale children, and Sir Richard Darley helped them to write a petition. Margaret wanted Mr Hall to advise and assist with it.

Margaret Instructs Mr Hall

One month after Walter died, Margaret wrote to Mr Hall herself, on 27 January:

Mr Hall,

It hath pleased God to disenable me, if I have not been able to set pen to paper. God knows I have greater store of tears, than expressions, at this time. You will say I have great cause to sorrow that hath lost so dear a loving husband as he hath ever been to me. I am able to say no more but that my present necessity forces me to entreat you to make all haste you can to finish my great business. I am not able to take comfort in anything till the out of their fingers who seek to entail miseries upon his posterity.

I pray go as carefully to work as you can. If you do not take care to save Lady Day rents, I am quite undone. God knows this sad occasion hath brought me into a great deal of debt. I have letters from divers friends who think you move slowly for my advantage, it is true; but till you had orders I know not what you could have done. But now God hath enabled me so much as to let you know I commit my business solely to you. If you do not discharge the trust I put in you faithfully, my friends and I have instant cause to blame you; if found real and honest, you tie me with double cords of thankfulness unto you.

I conceive your first work is to clear my jointure; next, the deed of outlands for brother's and sister's portions. Then if forced to compound, all this, if taken out, will ease composition. But move the Barons strongly for clearing the estate. As for any entail, none can be found; careful search hath been made. He died without a will, and was buried in Burton church. His debts proved very great, twelve hundred pounds and more.

So you have an account from a distempered brain, and one who hath put all her endeavours to let you know this much. If anything may be done here, let me know and I shall get it effected. I am not able to give you any advice, but leave all to your discretion, and rest,

Your loving friend,
Margaret Rudston.

John Hall could make no progress with the Barons, so in February he applied to Goldsmiths' Hall for a composition. Margaret's brother-in-law Charles Rudston, together with the old retainer John Nelson, took the jointure, the inventory, and their affidavit as witnesses of Walter and Margaret's marriage agreement, to London. The affidavit was a written statement that they would swear on oath in court.

By the end of February, Margaret had written a petition to Sir Nathaniel Brent, Judge of the Prerogative Court, requesting that she be admitted as the guardian of Sir Thomas Rudston, a twelve-year-old child. She stated that she was his natural mother and that she had always been a Protestant of the Church of England, and in that religion educated all her children. (The Church of England was the religion of the state.) She wrote almost the same petition to the Lords Commissioners of the Great Seal of England, asking to be granted the tuition of her son. She attached an affidavit from John Hall in her support.

The Commissioners for Compounding

Through John Hall, Margaret petitioned the Commissioners for Compounding with Delinquents, on behalf of her son, Sir Thomas Rudston, baronet. Mr Hall stated, in long sentences:

Sir Walter Rudston, the petitioner's late husband, having estate sequestered for his supposed delinquency, did traverse the same by appeal before the Barons of the Exchequer and prosecuted it with all diligence, as by the certificate hereunto annexed appears, but could not bring it to a hearing during his lifetime and, on 29 December last, died and left his said case depending, his estate sequestered and above twelve hundred pounds indebted, and the petitioner with six small children destitute of competent subsistence.

Now for that the petitioner could not prove the said case to be heard the last term, and for that according to the ordinary proceedings before the Barons in Matters of Appeal it will be a long time before the same can be there heard, the petitioner confiding in the equitable favour of the board humbly submits her distressed condition, thereunto confessing that her deceased husband was assisting the late king's party in the first war, and humbly prays she may be admitted to compound for his estate according to a particular thereof hereunto annexed.

The particulars of the estate, with their yearly rental values:

An estate in tail, the Manor of Hayton:

The capital messuage rated at £133 6s. 8d. per annum.

The residue rated at £175 13s. 4d. per annum.

An estate in fee of sheep pasture and lands at North Cave and Drewton, at £13 13s. 4d. per annum.

A like estate of cottage and lands at Holme-in-Spalding Moor, at £8 3s. 4d. per annum.

A like estate of lands at Ploughland and Pensthorpe in Holderness, near Welwick, at £24 per annum.

A like estate of three tenements in Kingston-upon-Hull, at £8 per annum.

Personal estate in cattle, wheat, horse, swine, sheep, husbandry gear, household stuff, plate and apparel, corn and hay, of £116.

The capital messuage was the jointure in Margaret's marriage agreement. Together with the fields around it, it was entailed, or limited to a specified line of male heirs. She craved allowance for the jointure and for children's portions of 500 pounds in total for Katherine Leigh and Mathew Rudston. Sir Thomas Rudston confessed the delinquency of his father, through his mother and guardian.

Sir Robert Stapleton, through his lawyer, asked the commissioners in London to endear the case of his near kinsman, Sir Thomas Rudston, to Mr Moyer, that the composition might be favourable and the fine easy. 'Sir Robert knows you have power herein to befriend this young gentleman, which will be received as done to himself.'

A Mr Brereton was required to write a report on the petition to the courts at Haberdashers' Hall. His report stated that Sir Thomas Rudston desired to compound for the delinquency of Sir Walter Rudston, his father, sequestered about Lady Day last. Sir Walter's appeal was published in November 1650, but the cases were too far behind for it to be heard. Sir Walter's solicitor, John Hall, was authorized by Sir Walter in December to submit to a composition. Because Mr Hall was not thoroughly acquainted with the rules and Sir Walter lived at a great distance in Yorkshire, he could not effect the same in Sir Walter's lifetime. Dame Margaret Rudston, his widow, authorized John Hall in January to prosecute the composition on behalf of her son.

Mr Brereton based his findings on the marriage agreement of Walter Rudston and Margaret Dawnay of 1631, and on the particulars of the estate listed for the composition. He submitted them to judgement.

The court made its judgement. The Rudstons would be fined 878 pounds, 10 shillings. The total estate was valued at 381 pounds per annum, and this was doubled. The personal effects of 116 pounds were included once. No allowances were made.

All the proceedings were carried out with great speed so that they were completed before Lady Day. In this matter Margaret was helped by Sir Richard Darley and Sir Robert

Stapleton to prevent another year's rental value being added to the fine.

At the same time, a loan came through from her nephew John Dawnay for the sum of 1100 pounds, to be paid back over eight years without interest. So Margaret was able to pay the first half of the fine by 19 March 1651. Fast payment was required, in two parts. She paid the second half on 28 April. A receipt cites John Hall of Gray's Inn.

John Hall's Notes

John Hall kept some notebooks in which he listed his accounts and incidental expenses. In April, he attended Mr Dawnay at Cowick to present many thanks for his loan of 1100 pounds to Margaret. He asked him to make a choice of tenants for the Rudston estate, which was bound to him and his agents in return for the loan. He moved an order for Margaret to receive the Lady Day rents so that she could pay the second half of the fine.

Mr Hall saw Sir Robert Stapleton in London for advice about Margaret's debts. He spoke to him about the eighty pounds' worth of silver Walter had sent to Sir John Hotham, about the guardianship of Sir Thomas Rudston, and the case of Faith Rudston's debt from Sir Thomas Strickland. They were to choose a guardian for Faith, bring a writ against Sir Thomas Strickland, and start proceedings against him.

Mr Hall's life was going to alter a great deal because most of his work from now on would be in Yorkshire, and he would no longer need his rooms in London. He was a single man. He was not a particularly wealthy lawyer. In May, he outlaid funds for the making of clothes for himself, and saddlery for his horse. He bought two yards and a bit of black cloth for one pound, fifteen shillings, and paid almost as much for ten yards of fringe, and as much again on lace and silk for the making up of buttons, loops and sprigs. He bought stockings, two hoods, gilt paper and a seal. For his horse he purchased leather, buckram and silk, and paid for the making of a harness, saddle and saddle cloth, all for the cost of one pound, five shillings.

His costs for a trip to London of seventeen days were five pounds, fifteen shillings, of which more than one pound was for the horse, which needed 'blooding, drenching and shoeing', as well as its oats and hay. Mr Hall hired a Mr Fothergill to do administrative work for him in London, although Sir Henry Vaughan was still helping with it. Mr Hall was doing some legal work for Vaughan. Mr Hall sent money to his cousin Robert Dawson, an attorney in the Lake District, in part payment of his loan to Margaret Rudston; he was soon to engage him nearby for the suit of Faith Rudston against Sir Thomas Strickland and his wife Jane, of Sizergh Castle.

John Hall was in York at the end of May on the business of Sir Thomas Rudston's discharge. He bought there seven pairs of gloves for five shillings, put part payment on a bit and spurs, and hired a coat for the day. He spent some shillings on tenants at the court, and gave some pennies to poor men on the way.

The Commissioners for Compounding in London notified the Committee for Sequestrations in Yorkshire to stop all further proceedings upon the estate of Sir Thomas Rudston, unless further property was discovered that had not been listed, or if the rental values were higher than had been stated. The committee of Yorkshire sent a letter, dated 30 May 1651, discharging Sir Thomas Rudston's estate from sequestration. This would not be the last of the matter.

In June and July, Mr Hall was serving subpoenas and warrants on tenants at Hayton who were in arrears, signing leases with new tenants, and attending arbitrations in York. The guardianships of Faith and Sir Thomas were completed, and he was conducting suits on behalf of Sir Thomas. He travelled to places between York, Hull and North Dalton. He carried out work for Richard Wayneman and Robert Sotheby, and ate many meals at Richard Wayneman's house at less than a shilling each. He engrossed his bills, that is, they were to be paid for in corn (wheat) from the harvest.

On 8 August, Mr Hall wrote that 'all accounts were cleared betwixt my Lady Rudston and me'. There was a change now in the character of the entries in his notebook. Sometimes he stayed at Hayton, and paid for his meals there. He gave money to the mowers in the Missick and 'the music at the door'. He bought paper, four 'snips' and two glasses, and drank wine with Samuel Rudston and Mr Reed. Sometimes he went to Cowick and worked for Mr Dawnay. When he went on business to York, he sent oysters to 'my lady' and had her two little knives mended. Some of the tenants' arrears were being discharged, and Mr Hall's lady gave him two gold ducats.

Walter's Case Continues

The matter of Sir Walter Rudston's subscription to the Agreement of the Yorkshire Gentlemen would not go away.

The commissioners in York were still trying to charge Sir Thomas Rudston 200 pounds in respect of it; they tended to act independently of those in London. Margaret was again constrained to write petitions, on behalf of her son, both to the Commissioners for Sequestrations in Yorkshire, and to the Commissioners at Haberdashers' Hall in London. She wrote, in strong terms:

Sir Walter being dead, and an appeal of his still depending before the Barons upon a charge that was most maliciously prosecuted against him, which the petitioner, being a sad, disconsolate woman, and his son an infant, and at a great distance from London, knew not how to manage and therefore submitted to a composition, and hath his discharge, which she humbly conceives acquits him for the said subscription (if it were an offence) in these words, viz, that he shall be no further troubled, molested or proceeded against in the way of sequestration for any delinquency charged upon his said father for anything said or done against the parliament.

And the said Sir Walter's estate lying wholly under the power of the enemy, and he being imprisoned and forced to subscribe the engagement, and to pay 100 pounds as a fine for his refusal before he could be enlarged; all this notwithstanding, the commissioners are ordered to levy 200 pounds on the rents, estate or goods of this poor infant as due upon the said Agreement, without perusal of the said plea and proof, or hearing any on his behalf.

Margaret asked if she could produce more witnesses to prove her case. She requested the removal of the order to sequester the estate if the money was not paid. Her petition was accompanied by the affidavit of John Hall.

So depositions of witnesses had to be taken yet again, in September 1651, for the hearing in York of Walter's case. The matter was conducted on behalf of Sir Thomas Rudston, who was only twelve years old, by Lawrence Squibb, the lawyer of Sir Robert Stapleton. It took until November to complete. The lawyer said the case was similar to that of Dodsworth except that, because Margaret had acknowledged the delinquency in her composition, the commissioners would think Walter had subscribed to the Agreement of the Yorkshire Gentlemen willingly, and not by compulsion.

The whole matter was finally dealt with by April, 1652. The Commissioners for the Advance of Money at Haberdashers' Hall, London, had the last word:

...Upon reading the certificate of Mr Cary, our examiner, and hearing of counsel on behalf of the said lady, it is resolved that we do allow the plea of the said Lady Rudston in this case, and that the seizure upon the said Sir Walter Rudston's estate is hereby taken off and discharged, and hereof the Commissioners for Sequestrations in the County of York and all others are to take notice.

Mr Hall, the Manager

During this time, Mr Hall's notebooks recorded trips to York, Cowick, North Dalton, Hull and Holderness to find the witnesses. He had expenses for meals, lodgings and messengers, the shoeing of his horse, and for 'horse meat' or 'horse bread'. Many tenants were still paying off their arrears. They were placed under threat of having their corn seized if they didn't pay. Margaret gave Mr Hall a tree, which he sold to the co-op at Pocklington.

Margaret had a friend, Kathy Barnard, who sometimes stayed with her, and they helped each other with their affairs. Mr Hall bought a pint of sack (wine) to drink with his lady and Mr Rymer, and the next day he paid the waterman for a boat trip for Margaret and Kathy Barnard on the river 'to take the air'. In York he purchased groceries, lampreys, four teals and a mallard, and sent some sack to Philip Constable at Everingham.

It was Mr Hall who made the necessary payments to the school mistress and to Mistress Barbara Rudston's music master. He bought a book for Mistress Elizabeth Rudston. He recorded, 'I have bought of the Lady Rudston a cow for which I promise to pay three pounds, ten shillings'. As Christmas drew near, Mr Hall purchased a shag petticoat and 'à la mode' for his lady, a petticoat for Barbara Rudston, cloth for Sir Thomas, and stockings for a Mary Bishop. Margaret was able to afford a silver porringer and spoon for her grand nephew, John Acclome's child, at his christening at Moreby Hall.

In January, the young Master Walter Rudston went to school at Burnby for the fee of one shilling and sixpence the quarter, and handed his schoolmaster one shilling for an 'entering penny'. John Hall continued to make payments on behalf of Lady Rudston. His accounts were their joint accounts; he even offered eight pence 'for your Ladyship to give the poor women of the town', and two pence 'for two poor women in the minster when you went to visit my Lady Bethell', addressing her directly. He no longer paid for meals at Hayton, and surely lived there. He accounted for candles and his horse's shoeing and feed at Hayton.

His lady gave him eighteen shillings to buy a frieze coat for Sir Thomas, and fifteen shillings for a hat. There were expenses for the tailor and the shoemaker, for mending 'your Ladyship's' reading glass, for stationery, a watch chain, kid leather gloves, tobacco for Mr Sugden, a cheese, for French wine sent for late at night, and entertainments. Margaret sold some trees to people so that they could resell them and discharge their debts to her. There was always business with tenants, one of whom was a Mistress Langdale at North Dalton. The law suit of Faith Rudston against Sir Thomas Strickland still continued, and a sergeant was paid to arrest him.

After 1651, there was a period of good harvests. The price of wheat dropped in the abundance, but the wheat could be stored and sold at a higher price. Mr Hall engrossed his bills so that he was remunerated in wheat, and he helped to bring in the harvests too. There was much activity at Hayton: the felling and cutting of firewood, the planting of young ash trees, the 'bottling' of hay, and the bringing of oats from North Dalton.

The Thorpe Jetty and the Humber Banks

There was a project first set down, in 1614, by old Walter Rudston. It was an agreement with Edward Skeffling and John Newton of Patrington, William Wright of Ploughland, and John Sagg of Thorpe to remedy the 'great decay and insufficiency' of the sea dykes and the banks of the Humber River at the southern end of the area called Holderness, in the most eastern part of Yorkshire. The Rudstons, and the others, owned land there. The parties would contribute according to the proportion of land they owned. They would build up the ground with stones, make a fetter with timber boards, and repair the Thorpe jetty.

The work started as soon as Margaret Rudston finished paying her composition in 1651, and continued for three years. Edward Distance of Patrington, a yeoman and tenant, was bound to Margaret for the sum of forty pounds to oversee men to do the work, and record their time worked, and wages. He could deduct his expenses from his rental fees. John Hall kept the paperwork and wrote on it a couplet that he liked:

If breath were made for every man to buy,
The poor man could not live, rich would not die.

The labourers who worked on the project earned eight pence a day.

In 1652, it was decided to build a new jetty at a place called Sandriggs, at a cost of twenty-five pounds for materials and labour. In 1654, Edward Distance, the overseer, died, but his widow carried on the work for him. She wrote a note to William Widdall about some money he was owed:

William Widdall, my love to you. Mr Hall hath sent to me about the three pound which my husband did borrowed of you and doth think that I do forgit it, but neither he nor you need not think so, for I did send you word with my brother-in-law that I would pay it as soon as I can, and I pray you to be content and I will make all the haste I can to git it, and I will give you content for your money. For me lady is so hasty for money that I cannot git yours and hers both together, but would have you satisfy Mr Hall that I do not forgit you, but I

will pay you. For I must over to me lady the next week to carry her all the money I can, so with my love I rest,
   Your friend,
   Francis Distance, widow,
   from Patrington the 5th day of April 1654.

The Child's Portion of Katherine Leigh

Katherine's Bill of Complaint

Margaret's troubles were not over. No sooner was Walter's case completed in 1652 than Katherine Leigh, Walter's youngest sister, wrote a long Bill of Complaint to the Court of Chancery about her child's portion. Katherine, who had married William Leigh, was now aged almost forty. She alleged that the child's portion of 300 pounds had not been paid to her. She claimed that another 600 pounds was owed for the portions of three of her younger brothers. The events that followed revealed that, with the passage of time, the family members had forgotten which portions had been paid, and which had not. They did not know what the trustees were supposed to do, and did not hold copies of the documents.

Katherine Leigh knew about the deed of 1629 that stated the sums to be paid and named the three older brothers as trustees. She accused Margaret Rudston and her son Thomas, along with the trustees, William, Charles and Samuel Rudston, and unknown persons as well, of conspiring to defraud her of her portion. She said they had treated her like a servant in the past, and they had concealed the true value of their property. Her husband William and she often entreated in a gentle and friendly manner for the payment of the 300 pounds, without result, which was contrary to equity and good conscience. So they were compelled to bring the matter to the Court of Chancery for a proper remedy.

William and Katherine Leigh obtained an order at the assizes (a court) at York in August 1653, for Margaret Rudston to bring the deed to the court. John Hall held a discussion there with his legal counsel. The supposed validity of the deed raised difficult questions. Some of the lands set forth for the payment of portions had been sold. The remainder was compounded for and the sequestration discharged without claims for portions being made, so it seemed that the compounder should not be held responsible for payments. The trustees were at fault for not seeing that the lands had satisfied the portions, so perhaps they should compensate the compounder for any claims for payment made upon him. The Court of Chancery might hold all the lands liable. John Hall believed that the Leigh's case was false and insufficient in law, and he offered William Leigh twenty shillings to have the case tried legally.

Margaret Rudston's Reply

Through John Hall, Margaret Rudston and her agents put in their submission to the Lords Commissioners for the Custody of the Great Seal of England. They acknowledged the deed of 1629 and its attached schedule, and that William, Charles and Samuel Rudston were to hold certain lands belonging to

Walter in trust until the portions were paid. The lands were at Hull, Holme-in-Spalding Moor, South Cave, Ploughland and Pensthorpe, Drewton and the Manor of Hemingbrough. Margaret claimed that Walter paid the portions of Mathew, Marmaduke and Philip Rudston in his lifetime. William Rudston was now the only surviving trustee, as Charles and Samuel had died. William, with Walter's consent, had sold the land in South Cave for an unknown sum, and two messuages in Hull for eighty pounds, to satisfy the payment of portions. She believed that he kept some part of the price.

Margaret said that Walter and William thought, in the past, that Katherine would waste the money, and that they would hold back some of it till later. She described how Walter took care of Katherine's food, lodging and clothes for five years before she turned twenty-one, which cost him more than 100 pounds. He maintained her for the next ten years until she married, at the yearly cost of at least twenty-four pounds. In the three years she lived with Lady Savile, he paid for her clothes. Katherine admitted to it. This was why the trustees allowed Walter to receive, without interference, the profits of the lands held in trust. When Katherine married William Leigh, the couple stayed at Hayton free of charge, with a servant and four horses, for nine months. Walter gave them forty-eight pounds. He sold William Leigh thirteen oak trees worth thirty pounds, and William resold them to Charles Campleshon for a profit, but he did not reimburse Walter for them.

Margaret said that at present Katherine and William Leigh had combined with William Rudston to prosecute law suits in the upper bench for ejectment of her tenants in certain lands, and had obtained writs to take possession of them at the assizes in York. These were the lands in Holme-in-Spalding Moor, Drewton, Ploughland and Pensthorpe with a yearly value of fifty pounds. They had also taken possession of land in North Cave not covered by the deed. The Leighs had used William Rudston of Nottingham as the lessor, Thomas Thompson of Beeston as the lessee, and John Young of Methley as the ejector. They put in their own tenant, and collected the rent. William Leigh also threatened to sue for 800 pounds, including interest and damages, and to take the properties in Hull. But Margaret said she always made friendly motions to him concerning any remainder that might be owing to Katherine. Her relatives John Rudston and John Thorpe attempted to mediate the differences with William Leigh, but he rejected their efforts. Now she felt compelled to have the matter tried in a court.

Further, Margaret said, from 1644 to 1651 the land set aside for satisfying the portions was sequestered by the parliament, which received the rents. During all that time neither Katherine and William Leigh nor the trustees made any legal claim to the land for portions, which could have been paid for out of the rents. Margaret and Thomas compounded for the lands in 1652 and paid a great price for them. In Margaret's view they were not liable, but the trustees were. However, she thought that Katherine's portion was nearly discharged, and she was willing to offer a sum to complete it.

William Rudston, the Trustee

William Rudston, now living at Nottingham, replied to Margaret's submission. He recognised the existence of the deed and schedule, and that Katherine was to receive 300 pounds at the age of twenty-one years, or at marriage, if earlier. He confirmed that Walter paid Mathew, Marmaduke and Philip their portions in his lifetime. He believed Walter sold two messuages in Hull and land at South Cave, but denied that he, William, was involved or had any part of the purchase money. He denied that he was unwilling to give Katherine her money, or thought she would waste it. He understood that Katherine was brought up at Walter's house after the death of old Walter Rudston, until her marriage. He denied permitting Walter to keep rents for Katherine's support that were due for her portion. He knew nothing of the time Katherine and William Leigh stayed with Walter. He agreed with William Leigh on the ejectment, it was true, in order to force payment of the portion, but he denied combination or sequestration. He was unwilling any entry should be made on the lands, but found it to be just and a matter of conscience. Although he was the trustee, he did not hold the deed of trust, nor have knowledge of what was in it.

On 4 March 1654, the Lords Commissioners for the Great Seal of England stated that William Leigh informed them that Walter Rudston, the father of Katherine, and Walter Rudston, the son, did by deed of 1629 settle certain lands in trust on William Rudston (and Charles and Samuel Rudston, since deceased) for raising portions for younger children. All except Katherine received their portions. Lady Rudston brought the deed to the court. Copies would be given to William Rudston, to enable him to perform the trust, and to the Leighs. The scope of the bill was to have the trust performed and the portions paid.

At this time, William and Katherine Leigh were the plaintiffs in the case, and Margaret and Thomas Rudston, together with William Rudston, were the defendants. John Nelson tendered his affidavit of 27 March 1644, in which he witnessed that several sums of money were given to William and Katherine Leigh, who signed receipts for them. William Rudston said that if William and Katherine came to a just account of what was already paid, Lady Rudston would shortly donate the remainder. The bill would continue until the reply of William and Katherine Leigh was heard.

John Hall Attends Court

John Hall wrote to friends in London asking them to sign a warrant for witnesses, and giving his address as Hayton. In June, Mr Hall went to London on the legal business for Margaret. He travelled by coach, and was accompanied by Mistress Faith Rudston. For luggage, she took a trunk, and he a cloth bag. They carried a small pot of jam to eat on the way. Whilst in London, Mr Hall bought shoes and gloves, twelve plates, paper and parchment, and attended Mistress Rudston 'about her occasions'. Mr Fothergill still worked for him there as his law clerk. Back at Hayton they were ploughing the marshland and sowing and harrowing thirty-three acres of wheat. Ten pounds was paid off Mr Dawnay's loan for the month.

On 29 June 1654, the Court of Chancery gave notice that Margaret and Thomas Rudston exhibited their bill to be relieved of an action prosecuted at common law by William and Katherine Leigh and their agents. But only William Leigh answered the bill in court, so Katherine Leigh and her agents, Thomas Thompson and John Young, were in contempt of court. The court commanded them to cease their prosecution at common law until they cleared their contempt, and they could then proceed to trial at the next assizes. On 25 August, the sheriff of Yorkshire, Sir William Constable, having received a writ from London, asked his bailiffs to see that William and Katherine Leigh appeared before the Court of Chancery in three weeks' time to answer their charge of contempt.

Mediation Fails

In September, the Earl of Dumfries, by an order of the assizes at York, made an appointment for Leigh, Thompson, etc, on one hand, and Rudston, etc, on the other hand, and their solicitors, to meet on 11 October at John Rasin's house at the Sign of the Anvil, Doncaster, and endeavour to mediate their differences. The parties met. Margaret Rudston offered satisfaction for any money owed, after deductions were made for what had been given in the past. But William Leigh would only allow what had been paid in ready money, so they could not settle their differences. The Leighs gave their answers at the assizes in York to the Bill of Complaint of Margaret Rudston, and their contempt of court was discharged.

John Hall and Margaret received legal advice that they would not owe interest because of the non-payment of Katherine's portion. But they still took seriously the threats of William Leigh that he would sue for 800 pounds, or take their land from them. John Hall thought that the Muddiford case in early 1654, in which interest had been allowed, might provide a precedent. He and Margaret wrote down careful arguments about the payments that they contended were made to Katherine, and took depositions from witnesses. They detailed the interest they thought they might have to pay on what was owed. On balancing the account, they reckoned they might have to pay eighty or ninety pounds to Katherine. They had covered all William Leigh's court costs on top of their own costs of 120 pounds.

Margaret's Bill of Complaint, concerning the trespass on her lands and ejectment of her tenants by the defendants, was again brought before the Court of Chancery. William Rudston, the trustee, was now a defendant in the case, along with the Leighs. Margaret put her view that Walter had paid most of the 300 pounds. She wanted to account for any remainder and preserve the lands from sale by the trustee. William and Katherine Leigh answered that the portion had been due in 1634, and they only wanted the payment of the principal and any interest owing to them. They denied having received any part of the principal, but only forty pounds of the interest.

The court ruled that Margaret's bill would continue in order to allow her good time to bring in the principal money. If Margaret's husband had failed to release the money, it was the duty of the trustees to do so. The trustees took no action until 1652, but would and ought to have done so sooner if the portion was for long unpaid. Margaret was to pay any arrears as the court ordered at a future hearing, and the Leighs were to account for it. There was no interest allowed by the deed, nor any penalty for non-payment. There was only a power, in default of payment by the heir, for the trustees to enter and force the payment, and then restore the lands to the heir.

William Rudston had no option but to force the payment of the portion. In November, the upper bench at Westminster notified the Sheriff of York that William Rudston had leased lands in Drewton to Thomas Thompson on 1 March 1654 for a term, and that Margaret Rudston had by force and arms ejected Thompson on 1 May 1654. Margaret was to restore the lands to the possession of Thompson for his full term, and pay seven pounds in damages.

The Matter Is Resolved

Finally, after four years of trouble and expense, all the parties reached a solution in October, 1656. Margaret applied to her nephew John Dawnay for the loan and guarantee of the sum of 360 pounds to be paid in three instalments to William and Katherine Leigh. On receiving the payment, the Leighs and their agents agreed to 'remise, release, acquit and discharge' Margaret Rudston and her agents from 'all manner of actions, suits, recoveries, judgements, debts, demands, claims, rights, titles, estates and interests whatsoever'. John Hall's name appeared for the last time when he signed the document along with Dawnay's lawyer.

Farewell John Hall

After 1656 Margaret had another lawyer to deal with her affairs. John Hall was possibly a few years younger than Margaret but he may have died. At least he would have lived at Hayton for the remainder of his life. Margaret was the lady who looked after him, and he was her manager and companion. He had compassion for poor people. He kept all the Rudston family papers safe and in order; he read them, made copies of them, and wrote titles on them. He left with Margaret the poems *Satire 1* and *Satire 2* by John Donne, which he copied in Donne's lifetime in a little booklet with his student notes. He was her kind and trusty friend and solicitor. (The Donne poems now reside in the Folger Shakespeare Library, Washington DC.)

Margaret and Her Family

Margaret had to fight another suit on behalf of her teenage son, Sir Thomas Rudston, concerning the property at Goole which was given to him in 1642 by his grandfather Sir Thomas Dawnay. The property was to be held by Margaret until Thomas came of age. Some ash trees there were cut down and sold as a lot by Walter Rudston in 1646. The purchaser removed and paid for half of them, and left the other half to lie on the ground. In 1653, a tenant illicitly took and sold the remaining felled trees, and he claimed a right to do so. The purchaser threatened to sue Thomas, and then Margaret sued the tenant for damages. Thomas would later sell the property for 600 pounds.

Sir Thomas Rudston reached the age of twenty-one in 1660, the year of the restoration of Charles II. In the same year, the oldest Rudston child, Faith, now aged twenty-eight, married Cornelius Clarke of Culthorpe, Derbyshire. At this stage, Margaret and Thomas Rudston granted to Cornelius and William Clarke lands in Holme-in-Spalding Moor, North Cave, Drewton and Plowland for a term of 100 years, for the payment of 300 pounds. Cornelius and Faith had a son,

Stephen. Margaret's nephew and benefactor, John Dawnay, became an MP for Yorkshire, and would later be made Viscount Downe.

The New House

Sir Thomas Rudston, together with his mother, brother and three sisters, had a new house built in the 1660s, a sketch of which was drawn by Samuel Buck in about 1720. In their book *Lost Houses of East Yorkshire*, 1988, D Neave and E Waterson describe the new Hayton Hall as 'a pleasing small Dutch-style classical villa'. Presumably the house was small by comparison to country houses in East Yorkshire of the era. The house had a five window frontage, with four floors including the cellar and attic. It faced the canal garden and the corn mill on Hayton Beck. At the back of the house was the kitchen garden, and then St Martin's church, which is still standing today.

Details about the house are given in a list of repairs that were made between 1731 and 1733. 'Madam Cutler', Margaret Rudston's granddaughter, was living there at the time. In the cellar or ground floor, which had stone floors, were the kitchen, scullery, pantry, still room, wet and dry larders, beer, ale and wine cellars, and servants' room; and twelve doors, fourteen transom windows, and four chimneys and stoves. In the attic or garret floor, with plaster floors, the rooms were called blue garret, green garret, men's garret, yellow garret, housekeeper's garret, maid's garret. The two storeys between, with wooden floors, were described as comprising the common dining-room, dining-room, drawing room, sitting room, bedchamber, green room, red room, yellow room, lodging over hall, lodging over sitting room, Madam Cutler's lodging, hall, closets; these had eight chimneys, twelve dormer windows, and forty sash windows. The house must have been quite costly to build.

Margaret's Daughters

In 1675, Elizabeth Rudston, Margaret's youngest child and now aged thirty, married the Reverend Charles Remington, the vicar of Lockington, about twenty miles from Hayton. It is not known if they had children. A document shows that Margaret Rudston's daughter Barbara was still alive and single in 1679, as was also the third daughter, Margaret. The second son, Walter, died before 1685. Margaret Rudston the younger, in her will of 1693, listed her sister as 'Silburne'; Barbara must have married a Mr Silburne late in life.

Sir Thomas Rudston's Family

Sir Thomas Rudston married in 1679, when he was forty, Catherine, the younger daughter of George Mountaigne of Westow. (Catherine's older sister, Elizabeth, had married Francis Foljambe, and lived with her family in West Yorkshire.) Thomas and Catherine had a son, Thomas, in 1681, and a daughter, Elizabeth, in 1682. These two would grow to adulthood. A son, Walter, born in 1684, died when he was one year old. Three girls born between 1686 and 1690 died soon after birth. So the household was mainly one of older people: Margaret Rudston and one or two unmarried daughters, her son Thomas and his wife Catherine, and their two children. In spite of disappointment about the children who died, they must have lived there in contentment.

In those times only men of property had the vote, and there was no bureaucracy. In 1687, Sir Thomas Rudston was made a deputy lieutenant of the East Riding of Yorkshire. This position, which was for the keeping of law and order, he held by virtue of his status as a man of property.

Margaret, the Centenarian

When Margaret died in March 1699, aged 103 years, her daughter Margaret died four months later, at the age of sixty-two. Maybe they had the same illness, or her daughter simply had a shorter lifespan, and was affected by her mother's passing. Catherine, the wife of Sir Thomas Rudston, died a year or so after the two Margarets, at the age of only forty-six.

At the time that Margaret Rudston, the centenarian widow of Walter Rudston, died, her grandchildren Thomas and Elizabeth, aged eighteen and seventeen, were almost grown up. Their father Sir Thomas Rudston, the second baronet, would live for a further eight years. Both he and his mother would have had hopes for their line of descent to continue. They were spared the knowledge that Thomas, the third baronet, would die shortly after his father, perhaps in an accident, and that Elizabeth would marry but would be childless.

Margaret's Grandson Dies

A letter from Brian Thompson of York was received by Henry Cutler in 1710, not long after he had married Elizabeth

Rudston, and the young Sir Thomas Rudston had died. Henry Cutler had promised to pay any debts owed by the Rudstons. The writer of the letter spoke of such a debt. The old Sir Thomas Rudston, he said, was one of the best friends he had in the world, a worthy person and his good old friend to his dying day. Old Sir Thomas had a credit from Thompson's shop of twenty-eight pounds for some time, but paid twenty pounds when he heard Thompson needed money for house repairs, and promised the remainder soon. But after that Sir Thomas was often ill, and the matter wasn't settled. Then the young Sir Thomas ran up an account of forty pounds in a short time. When Mr Thompson accosted him about the debt in Pocklington Field, the young Sir Thomas told him to give the bill to Mr Stanfield, his steward, and he would be paid in a little while when the money came in. But nothing was done, and then Sir Thomas died.

Presumably Henry Cutler honoured this bill. The young Sir Thomas seems to have been something of a tearaway. But he was dead by the age of twenty-eight.

The Rudston Descent

Elizabeth Rudston inherited Hayton, and lived there with her husband Henry Cutler. However, the couple had no children. The estate would be inherited by Elizabeth's nearest relative. She had a cousin, William Rudston, but whose child or grandchild he was remains obscure. He died in 1721 without heirs. Before Elizabeth died in 1745, she willed the estate to a seven-year-old child called Rudston Calverley. He was descended from Walter Rudston's brother William, who married Hester Savile. Their only child, a daughter also called Hester, had married a Calverley. On inheriting, Rudston

Calverley added to his name the surname Rudston. At a later time the family was known as Rudston-Read to comply with the wishes of a benefactor. After a while, this name was changed to Calverley-Rudston by 'the lord of the manor'. My grandmother, Annie, was his daughter; her brother and sister had no children.

Afterpiece: From Riches to Rags; A Story of the Cutler Family

Elizabeth Rudston married Henry Cutler in 1708. Henry's aunt, Mary Cutler, had married Sir Edward Mosley, an acquaintance of Elizabeth's grandparents, Walter and Margaret Rudston. This was probably the avenue through which Elizabeth and Henry came to know each other.

Henry's grandfather, Sir Gervase Cutler, had Mary in his first marriage, and then his wife died. He married secondly Lady Magdalen Egerton, a daughter of John Egerton, Earl of Bridgewater. John Egerton's wife, born Lady Frances Stanley, was a descendant of Mary Tudor, the daughter of Henry VII. Magdalen was the seventh of the Egertons' eight daughters.

The verses written for Sir Gervase Cutler and Lady Magdalen Egerton's wedding in 1633 extol the virtues of the marriages which had been made so far in the illustrious Egerton family:

How limitless, how precious was your care
In getting matches for your daughters fair,
That, as their education did abound,

They might with husbands of like worth be crowned.
Lords given to riot or to wine, you knew
Would never make fit son-in-laws for you;
Therefore, your wisdom and your love did choose
Those that no sin nor error could accuse,
Husbands of temper and weighed virtues, who
Knew the best good was not to talk but do,
Who were not fairer in their outside seen
Than in the mirror of their worth within.

Such was the noble Sir John Hobart, he
With your fair Frances married worthily,
Such was the great and noble Bullingbrook,
To wife who Lady Arabella took,
Such is great Cecil, who (in spite of death)
Will make a Countess your Elizabeth,
Such our brave Herbert, in all noblesse rife,
Your noble Mary, who has ta'en to wife,
And such do all Sir Robert Napper see
In wedlock tied to your Penelope,
And such the matchless William Courten,
Wedded of late to your fair Katherine.

And such Sir Gervase Cutler is, whose hands
And heart is knit in matrimonial bands
Unto the happy Magdalen, the last
Married, though not in native worth the least.

Sir Gervase Cutler and his wife Lady Magdalen went to live at the Cutler family seat of Stainborough Hall at Silkstone, near Barnsley, South Yorkshire. The couple had nine children.

In 1642, the Civil War commenced. Sir Gervase was a royalist; he took his family silver worth 1000 pounds to Pontefract Castle to be coined into money for the king. He fought at that place and, when it was captured by the parliamentary side, he lay dying of a fever at the castle. The enemy's troops would not allow any provisions to be brought for him, but they relented, and let his lady visit him once and bring a cooked chicken and a joint of veal. When he died on 25 June 1645, they would not permit his wife to depart for three days. Then she was released to the first guard and was detained for a day more, without food or shelter, on suspicion of bearing secret intelligence. She was strip-searched, together with her maid, chaplain and a tenant who came to meet her.

So at the age of twenty-eight, the lady was left a widow with a large family. Sir Gervase was charged with delinquency posthumously, and his estate was sequestered. Lady Magdalen compounded for it, and was fined 792 pounds. But she appealed, and the fine was reduced to 492 pounds. She died in 1664.

Her oldest son, Sir Gervase Cutler, was a drunkard and a spendthrift. He married Dorothy Frankland. She gave birth to at least twenty-one children, most of them girls. Some of the girls were called Dorothy, Frances, Elizabeth, Grace, Penelope, Magdalen, Charlotte, Margaret, Helenor[sic] and Henrietta. Henry Cutler was the only son to reach adulthood. The daughters either married someone in a lowly station in life, or did not marry. Three of them married excisemen. Two of the unmarried daughters lived together on an annuity of twenty-seven pounds a year, which barely covered the basic necessities of life.

Soon after the death of the second Sir Gervase Cutler, in order to discharge his debts, his only son Henry sold Stainborough Hall to his neighbours, the Wentworths at Wentworth Castle. Henry was running a coal business known as the Galber Hill coal pits, near Skelbrook, South Yorkshire. All his life he helped to support his sisters. For this purpose he gradually sold the Cutler properties he inherited.

Henry Cutler wrote some verse, when he was still living at Stainborough Hall, to invite his newly-wed wife to dinner:

To Mrs Elizabeth Cutler at her seat at Hayton.

Dear Madam, I received your letter,
Though I was well, it made me better,
Not in body but in mind,
To find your inclination's so kind,
Tomorrow to my house to come,
Where shall be welcome all and some.

I hope you will not insist on
Meeting pretty Mr Pinninton,
For that's an honour I must not have,
The favour I will never crave,
And as for dapper Strickland,
I would not ask him for his hand;
But I will supply their places,
With Mr and Mrs Landale's faces,

And all that ever you will bring
Shall be as welcome as anything.

Your entertainment will be small,
And you must sup in the cold hall,
But your attendance will be all.
I fear you will hardly eat your fill,
A good fat ham of bacon,
A roast in the frying pan well scakon*[1]
Such kind of homely cheer,
Enough of it, never fear.
To attend only two besides a butler,
Who are at your service with Cutler.

If this letter you expose
I will pull you by the nose,
And from your face I will it wring,
Though it be thought a cruel thing,
Enough of it, you need not fear.

---

[1] *Shaken

Appendix to Part One

List of Rudston Documents

The Rudston documents are in the East Riding of Yorkshire archives at Beverley, East Yorkshire, unless otherwise stated. Those held by the Webber family were placed there in 2004. (When the documents are dated between 1 January and 25/27 March in the reign of Charles I, I have dated them with two years' dates, because the New Year was sometimes regarded as 1 January and sometimes as 25/27 March. The same applies to dates between 1 January and 30 January in the reign of Charles II, which started immediately after Charles I died in 1649.) The list of documents that were used for the story of Margaret Rudston, approximately in chronological order, are:

Booklet: *Satire 1* and *Satire 2* by John Donne, copied and signed by John Hall, dated 1627 and 1632, with other notes, now in the Folger Shakespeare Library, Washington DC.

The wedding verses of Sir Gervase Cutler and Lady Magdalen Egerton 1633, with family trees and coats of arms (sold).

'Old' volume:

The will and inventory of Sir John Rudston, died 1531.

'The Ling'. Undated, late sixteenth century.

Walter Rudston and the Saltonstall family, 1615, 1618, 1628.

'A perfect schedule of all goods and chattels movable and immovable which by these present indentures whereunto this schedule is fixed or annexed and bargained and sold by the said Walter Rudston the father to the said Walter Rudston his son.' Undated.

'A schedule declaring the trust and intent for which these present indentures were made.' This is referred to, in later documents, as the schedule of 1 May 1629, appointing trustees to oversee the payment of portions to Rudston children.

Indenture 10 December 1631 between James Hopkinson of York and Philip Rudston of Hayton.

Samuel Rudston's release for his child's portion 1633.

Mathew Rudston's release for his child's portion 1633.

Marmaduke Rudston's release for his child's portion 1633.

The marriage agreement of Margaret Dawnay and Walter Rudston 21 April 1631.

The commission of Walter Rudston from Wentworth 7 June 1634. (In volume of 232 warrants of Dublin 1634.)

Volume of 232 warrants of Dublin of 1634 (copies).

Booklet: 'A short treatise of the spiritual life leading unto perfection wherein are declared nine impediments which occur to one desiring to go in the way of God.' Undated, signed TD or JD.

'Delinquency and Sequestration' volume:

Copy of the Agreement of the Yorkshire Gentlemen, 13 February 1642/1643.

Sir John Hotham's letter to Sir Walter Rudston, 14 June 1643.

Mr Leigh's acknowledgement of no payment of his wife's portion 15 March 1646/1647.

Sir Thomas Fairfax's letter concerning Sir Walter Rudston's sequestration case in 1644, 2 April 1649.

Copy of Sir Walter Rudston's petition to the Barons of the Exchequer.

Rudston interrogatories for witnesses, after the death of Charles I (copies).

Charges of delinquency against Sir Walter Rudston 11 June 1649 (copies).

Sir Walter Rudston's answers to the charges (copies).

Depositions of witnesses 11 June 1649 (copies).

Examinations of Raph Shaw and Lawrence Johnson concerning Sir Walter Rudston's delinquency 1649 (copies).

Affidavits concerning Sir Walter Rudston's appeal made by John Nelson, Raph Shaw, and Sir Walter Rudston before W Belt 17 November 1649 (copies).

Sir Walter Rudston's advice to his solicitor John Hall.

Sir Walter Rudston's draft of affidavit.

John Hall's brief notes.

Solicitors' advice (W Ward, John Henry).

Copy of the Committee for Sequestrations in Yorkshire's demise of Sir Walter Rudston's estate 4 April 1650.

Copy of Sir Walter Rudston's petition at York May 1650.

Summons from the Commissioners for the Advance of Money 29 May 1650 for Sir Walter Rudston to appear in the Painted Chamber Westminster on 28 June.

Sir Walter Rudston's letter to John Hall 4 June 1650.

Depositions of witnesses June 1650 (copies).

Sir Walter Rudston's answers to the charges (copy).

William Oglethorpe's letter to John Hall 24 June 1650.

Copy of Sir Walter Rudston's answer and petition 3 July 1650.

Order in Painted Chamber 3 July 1650 concerning Yorkshire Agreement (copy).

John Nelson's examination concerning Sir Walter Rudston's imprisonment at York 10 July 1650 (copy).

Deposition of Andrew Grant August 1650 (copy).

Covering letter for depositions concerning Sir Walter Rudston 10 September 1650 (copy).

Sir Walter Rudston's letters to John Hall 27 November, 3 and 23 December 1650.

Margaret Rudston's letter to John Hall 3 December 1650.

The petition of Sir Walter Rudston 29 December 1650 to the Commissioners for Compounding with Delinquents, and particulars of the estate (copy).

William Rudston's letter to John Hall through William Bernard 31 December 1650.

William and Katherine Leigh's petition to free the estate from sequestration (copy).

Depositions of witnesses 21 January 1650/1651 (copies).

The Committee for Sequestrations in Yorkshire's demise of Sir Walter Rudston's estate 1 January 1650/1651.

William Bernard's letters to John Hall 2 and 7 January 1650/1651.

Marmaduke Prickett's letters to John Hall 4, 12 and 25 January 1650/1651.

Margaret Rudston's letter to John Hall 27 January 1650/1651.

Charles Rudston and John Nelson's affidavit referring to the marriage agreement of 1631.

John Hall's legal queries about compounding 4 February 1651.

Marmaduke Prickett's letters to John Hall 11, 18 and 28 February 1651.

Sir William Belt's opinion concerning Lady Rudston.

Margaret Rudston's petition to Sir Nathaniel Brent of the Prerogative Court for guardianship of Sir Thomas Rudston (copy).

Margaret Rudston's petition to the Committee for Sequestrations in Yorkshire for stay of proceedings.

Margaret Rudston's petition for grant of tuition.

John Hall's affidavit.

Margaret Rudston's petition to compound and particulars of the estate (copy).

Margaret Rudston's petition confessing delinquency (copy).

Particulars of the estate (copy).

Sir Thomas Rudston's petition confessing delinquency, and particulars of the estate (copies).

Reference to Mr Brereton 26 February 1651 (copy).

Mr Brereton's report to the courts at Haberdashers' Hall (copy).

Copy of Sir Robert Stapleton's letter to Mr Osbaldeston.

Receipt for 439 pounds 5 shillings paid for fine 19 March 1650/1651.

Com. for Compounding to Com. for Sequestrations in Yorkshire, notice of termination 19 March 1650/1651.

Particulars of the estate.

Receipt for 439 pounds 5 shillings paid for fine 28 April 1651.

Final notice of termination 28 April 1651.

Margaret Rudston's petition for discharge to the Committee for Sequestrations in Yorkshire (copy).

Copy of Sir Thomas Rudston's petition to the Commissioners at Haberdashers' Hall concerning the Yorkshire Agreement.

Discharge of Sir Thomas Rudston's estate from sequestration by the County of Yorkshire 30 May 1651.

John Hall's affidavit concerning Sir Walter Rudston subscribing the Yorkshire Agreement 23 August 1651.

Henry Davison's additional interrogatories.

Lady Rudston's petition to the Commissioners for Advance of Money, and legal opinion on it (Lawrence Squibb).

Lawrence Squibb's letter to Lady Rudston 20 September 1651.

Com for Sequestrations in Yorkshire order for examining witnesses for Sir Thomas Rudston 3 October 1651.

Covering letter for depositions 14 October 1651 (copy).

Depositions of witnesses 10 October 1651 (copies).

Depositions of witnesses 30 November 1651 (copies).

Lawrence Squibb's letter to Lady Rudston 8 November 1651.

Commissioner for Advance of Money to Margaret Rudston, final release from sequestration 9 April 1652.

John Hall's accounts.

John Hall's notes and accounts 1651-3.

'New' volume:

The agreement to pay costs by Dawnay 1651.

The Thorpe jetty and the Humber banks: copy of 1614, and 1651-4.

The case of Katherine Leigh concerning her child's portion 1652-6.

Concerning Gibson's bond for wood of Lady Rudston 31 March 1653.

Thomas Rudston v Richard Empson about the ash trees.

Letter of John Hall 3 April 1654.

Notes and accounts of John Hall 1654.

The case of the fine clerks 1654.

A suit of Margaret Rudston 1656.

Grant of land to Cornelius and William Clarke 1660.

Indenture of sale of property at Goole to John Tripp 1 June 1669.

Half document naming Sir Thomas Rudston and Barbara Rudston 1679.

Two bits of a document naming George Mountaigne, father-in-law of Sir Thomas Rudston.

Sir Thomas Rudston and Stephen Clarke 1691.

Funeral of Sir Thomas Rudston 3rd baronet 1709.

Brian Thompson's letter to Henry Cutler 1710.

Henry Cutler's poem to his wife.

Henry Cutler's coal business 1711.

An estimate of bricklayers' and carpenters' work for a house for Cutler at Hayton 1731-3.

A bundle of documents: List of births, marriages and deaths in the Rudston family, seventeenth century. Tombstones in the church at Bessingby concerning John Rudston and Mary Rudston. Booklet: The Penal Laws and Test Act 1687-8 naming Sir Thomas Rudston as DL in the East Riding. Three newspaper cuttings about the Cutler family from the Barnsley Chronicle, 19 and 26 February, 5 March 1881.

Copy of document with dates of deaths.

Henry Cutler's note about Sir Thomas Rudston 2nd baronet died 1707.

Plan of Hayton estate 1763.

Rudston family tree with coats of arms.

(The references at the end of the book list primary and secondary source material used in writing all parts of the book.)

PART TWO

MARIA BARSTOW OF DANZIG, AND THE STORY OF LITTLE ANN

Based on a memoir by Elizabeth Barstow, of 'Garrow Hill', York.

Characters, for reference:

Michael Barstow of York married Maria Maclean of Danzig (Gdansk today, in northern Poland).

They had six children: Marie, Everilda, Thomas, Frances, Emily and Matilda.

Maria Barstow married secondly Cornelius von Almonde, and had Marianne.

Maria's son Thomas Barstow ('Tom') married Ann Jones, the daughter of Mr Robert Jones and his wife Elizabeth (née Irwin), of Ireland.

The author of the story, Elizabeth Barstow, was their daughter.

(Genealogical notes are in an appendix at the end of Part Two.)

The story of Maria Barstow was written by her granddaughter Elizabeth Barstow, of 'Garrow Hill', York, in 1898. Elizabeth was born in 1827. She visited her grandmother at Danzig (Gdansk today, in Poland) in 1840. She called her account 'My Grandmother'. Her grandmother was known both as Maria, and Mary. The story follows.

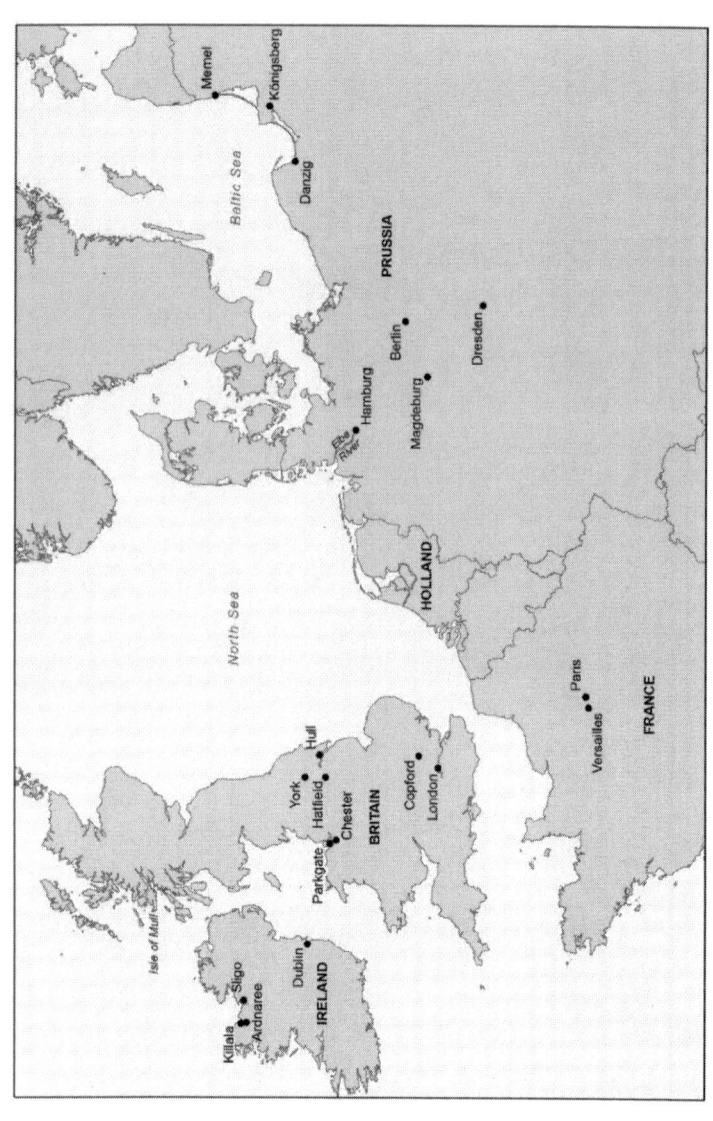

A Map for the Barstow and Jones Families.

Government House, 88 Langarten, Danzig. The building was demolished in 1905. The Barstows' house, which was opposite it, was similar, except that its courtyard aspect faced the back garden. (Photo kindly provided by the Museum 'Haus Hansestadt Danzig', Lübeck, Germany.)

Maria von Almonde (nee Maclean) when old and blind. She was also Maria Barstow (private collection).

My Grandmother

The Queen of Holland's Ring

My sister-in-law often asked me to jot down my reminiscences of my grandparents, and some of the stories I had heard of the troubled times in which they lived. She was particularly anxious to know the history of a beautiful diamond ring which was left to her, as the wife of the eldest son, by my mother. My mother and I were visiting my grandmother in Danzig in the year 1840 when my grandmother gave her the ring.

'Here, Ann,' she said, as she slipped the ring on mother's finger, 'here, Ann, this ring ought to belong to Tom's wife. It was given to me by the Queen of Holland when she thanked me so prettily for my great kindness to her and hers.'

The future Queen of Holland and her daughter found refuge in my grandmother's house in the *Langgarten* in 1806. They fled their country when Napoleon made his brother Louis King of Holland. The future queen came to Danzig because she was a member of the Prussian royal family; her husband and sons escaped also. I will return to these events later in the narrative.

My grandfather, Michael Barstow, went to Germany to seek his fortune after his father, old Thomas Barstow of Fulford, near York, married for a third time in 1777 (note 1). Michael, the oldest son, was born in 1740. He was brought up by the second wife, his natural mother having died when he was only four years old. He had no fancy to be still living at home while there was a buxom new mistress of the house. He was already in his late thirties; his younger brother, Thomas, had entered holy orders, and his sister had married.

Michael, as his portrait shows, had a nice, refined face and well-proportioned features; the line from forehead to tip of nose is quite straight, and the forehead rather receding. He wears a dark blue coat with stand-up collar, and his hair is *en queue*. The portrait was painted in Danzig.

I do not know what fate led him to Danzig, on the Baltic coast, unless it was his connection with the Barnards of Cave in East Yorkshire; however, he became a Baltic merchant, and went into partnership with one Adam Elliot. They traded in timber on a very large scale, chiefly with France and Holland. At that time Danzig was part of the Polish-Lithuanian Commonwealth, but it was predominantly a German society.

Courtship and Marriage

The story of how Michael met the love of his life was passed on in my family. *'Honi soit qui mal y pense'* (Shame upon him who thinks evil of it). One day, walking in the streets of Danzig, Michael saw a lovely young woman, and was immensely taken with her. Desiring to find out who she was and where she lived, he followed her. Suddenly, without noticing it, she dropped her garter. Michael quickly transferred it to his pocket, vowing to himself that, if she were free, he would make her his wife. The Fates befriended him. That very evening, he was introduced to Mary Maclean at a ball. This history tells how he kept his vow.

Mary, or Maria, was the daughter of Archibald Maclean, the British consul in Danzig, and her mother, Mary, was the daughter of a John Simpson of York and Memel. The Macleans' family home was at Memel, farther east on the Baltic coast, where lived their son Lachlan. There was a younger son, Archibald, still a child. The father had come from Scotland (note 2). Memel exported timber for the Royal Navy's ships.

Michael fell desperately in love the first time he set eyes on the beautiful Mary Maclean. For two years he besieged her heart with the most fervent expressions of devotion. He became desirous of increasing his means, and of offering her a home that was more luxurious than the one she presently occupied. He was more than double her age, only four years younger than her father.

The first letter I have, dated 1783, was addressed to his 'loveliest angel'. He told her, 'My heart, being full of you, grew too large for my bosom, and stopped for a time all utterance'. Again, he told her, 'This night I saw you lovely and more charming than Venus when first she sprang from the waves'. In another, he wrote, 'Oh that thy angel form could descend into the midst of our circle, and I could hail thee, my Marichen, and thou be once more restored to us to bless us with thy smiles, thou rosy-featured maid. Âme de mon âme, for thee I well could die, for thee alone I wish to live.' Written across the cover was 'I hope you liked the herrings I sent you, and that they were good'. This practical remark probably carried as much weight as all the high-flown nonsense.

The love letters are full of poetry in various languages which I cannot decipher, but one dated 10 February 1783, I will render more fully:

Dearest Mary,

If you could possibly conceive the dread anxiety of my situation, I think you would drop me some small line of comfort; it certainly cannot be indifferent to you or I am wretched indeed. Is it possible that I have not as yet made any impression on your heart, or is that so cold as to yield up implicitly its feelings without as much as daring to acknowledge them? You cannot possibly think the man whom you allowed to ask your hand, base enough to take advantage of the graceful weakness of your heart. Should you refuse me, I would derive such comfort from your kindness that it might keep me from a deed of desperation.

The letter I have just received from your father is not a refusal, but it is so very civil and polite that I tremble at the thought of what may follow. All my hopes are in your grandfather, Mr John Simpson, who, I believe, wishes me well. Oncle Henry will doubtless tell you more; if all depended on him I should then indeed be happy.

Oncle Henry and his capelmeister are not long gone; they came at 8.30 and supped with me, and your health was drunk in a bumper, as it always is when we meet. Our Marichen is our first and our last toast – and do you sometimes think of us, loveliest angel? You have now letters I wrote to you under cover to your father, under cover to your Oncle Henry, and under cover to your best of mothers, and still I have not a syllable from you. You might have told me how my demand was taken, what your hopes and fears were. Indeed, sweetest Mary, I think you are too hard on me.

Oh, it strikes twelve o'clock, too soon as yet to wish you good morrow, for you are now, I fancy, buried in sleep. Could I but hope your best dreams were of me, then must I sleep too that our spirits might hold pleasing converse. I will search for you through boundless space and should I meet with you, I will tell you tomorrow. 'Good-night, good-night! parting is such sweet sorrow that I shall say good-night till it be tomorrow', loveliest angel, dearest Mary, good night then.

I have seen my sweetest Mary. I met with her at Conradshammer. It was spring, and in the garden, green as lovely May, your bower had been repaired and was covered with woodbine and jessamine. The parterre in front was replete with roses and other fragrant flowers. Under the weeping willow grew beautiful forget-me-not. The pond was beset with gloomy cypress, but there the sun shot its dazzling rays on the sporting of gold and silver fishes. It was an enchanting scene.

But the figure that gave the most charm to the scene was thine, dearest nymph, for like one of Diana's fairest thou seemed to me, clothed in a loose morning gown, beautifully white, at the waist closed by a sky blue silk girdle. Your hair hung carelessly upon your shoulders, for you were just come from bathing.

There, seated in the bower, your head reclining on my breast, you confessed your passion and vowed eternal love. You swore by the little symbol of fidelity that hung in your Garter on my breast, that you would ever be faithful to your word to me and to yourself, which you confirmed with so tender a kiss as penetrated my very soul and awoke me in the most perfect scene of imaginary happiness.

Oh Mary, what can this vision mean? Is it a true one, and shall I indeed be happy? Best and truest of girls, say yes. Give me your hand upon it. Thanks dearest, loveliest Mary, thanks from your trembling Barstow.

The affair still hung in hand, and there were other suitors in the field. (I find a tender letter from one Jameson. Why has it been preserved?) Michael Barstow wrote again on 8 July, 1783:

Sing angels, sing the raptured lay,
Send every blessing from above,
'Tis dearest Mary's natal day,
Oh, win her heart to tenderest love;
Teach her my passion to requite,
For oh, for her my soul doth burn,
Oh that she soon may bless my sight,
My love with equal love return;
Then who so blessed on earth as I?
No one, indeed, loveliest Mary.
No healing joys relieve my constant smart,
No line of love rewards the loss of heart.

Now, my dearest Mary, you are twenty-one, entirely of age and your own mistress. Let the first kind thing you do be entirely in my favour. Present me this day with your heart, and promise to be mine forever. It is now time to throw off the mask and confess that I am deserving of every return of love you can make. Say that you will share your happiness with mine and then I shall be blessed indeed. At this distance you can do so without a blush.

In August 1784, he wrote to her in a more sensible strain, as now at last his 'loveliest angel' had yielded to his entreaties. After he promised to make her a loving, tender husband, they were engaged. He told her, 'We must begin by loving within bounds, as it is an easy matter to enlarge as our fortune increases, then we shall ever be roomy, well and happy. This situation makes the mind to be at ease; then the heart will be light, the spirits good, and the whole man well and contented.'

He tried next to persuade her to marry him at once without the usual *verlobung* (betrothal). 'I should be more happy to be presented to your friends as your husband than as your bridegroom, and a number of foolish ceremonies will be saved. The good people can keep their money in their pockets and we stay free from obligations. Believe me, my Mary, nothing is more conducive to being on favourable terms with the world than having nothing to thank it for. According to my way of thinking, the person who confers the obligation is the person most obliged, but this is logic which few people understand and which fewer still feel. It is, however, just. I hope before you die to make you sensible of it, as well as of a number of other things which appear at first sight equally odd, but of which the firm possession adds a hundred little charms to many actions, trifling in themselves, yet giving a vast zest to life; it adds everything to the happiness of dearest, loveliest Mary, and of your faithful and most affectionate M. Barstow.'

However, in spite of Michael Barstow's urgings that they should forego the usual matrimonial programme, Maria's family delayed the marriage. In the meantime, Maria's grandfather, John Simpson of York, became ill. Michael made a trip to York, and reported on her grandfather's return to health. The doctor said his disorder might return. Michael saw his father again, and dined with his old friends. Michael and Maria were then married in Danzig in the summer of 1785. A Dresden china tea and coffee service, ornamented with the initials *MB* in flowers, was made especially for the bride. (It remains in our family.)

The Barstows' first child, Marie, was born the following year. About the same time, Michael's father Thomas died of dropsy. Michael returned to visit his old home at Fulford, near York, and brought his family with him. The second daughter, Everilda, named after Michael's long-dead mother, was born there. She did no credit to her birth-place, as in her earliest days she contracted jaundice from her mother, who was suffering it at the time of the birth, and her complexion never recovered.

Maria Barstow had the choice as to which country she would make her home. She elected to return to the German society of Danzig, as her friends and relations were all there, and English manners and customs were not to her taste. So the good farms in Fulford, which Michael had inherited as the oldest son, were sold. The proceeds were invested in the timber trade, in the partnership with Adam Elliot and others, at Danzig. Some property in Yorkshire remained for Thomas Barstow's widow. Michael's only brother, the Reverend Thomas Barstow, had married by this time; he had been a Fellow of Clare Hall at Cambridge University.

Michael and Maria returned to Danzig with their two daughters. A son, Thomas, was born to them in 1788. They lived in a very large house that Michael bought at 47 Langgarten Street; it was situated more or less opposite the Government House at number 88, and the house which was built by Catherine the Great of Russia for her minister, at number 74. The Barstows' house had nine windows frontage, and was built around three sides of a court. It had three floors, including the attic. The Barstows had more daughters: Frances, Emily, and Matilda. In 1793, the Prussians annexed Danzig, and would soon take Poland too. They purchased the Government House opposite the Barstows'.

During these years, the French Revolution drastically changed the conditions of trade for Michael Barstow. The European countries and Britain were forced to fight the French for twenty years, until they finally defeated Napoleon.

In March 1793, Michael was writing a letter to his brother Thomas, now living at Marks Tey, near Colchester. Michael said that his health had suffered considerably. He was full of anxiety about money matters. The breaking out of the French Revolution had crushed all commercial speculation, and had ruined the timber trade with France and Holland. His company had timber worth £24,000 stranded on the docks, and numerous outstanding debts. Meisner, a banker at Warsaw, owed them large sums.

As if he saw the end, he was worrying about making provision for his daughters. Then he wrote, in the middle of all the financial chaos he was relating, that an old lady residing in Danzig, Miss Anna Bendlowes, had promised to leave her property to him. He and Maria had at an earlier period performed for her a deed of no small kindness, so after inheriting some property in Yorkshire she was anxious to show in this way her appreciation of their goodness to her. Michael wrote, 'Her heir at law is one Mr Concett, who lives near Thirsk in North Yorkshire, and who will probably dispute the will'. He appointed his brother to be the executor, as well as his wife's brother, Lachlan Maclean of Memel. He went on to say, 'Possession is nine points of the law; however, you will take the best advice and throw not good money after bad'.

Michael Barstow did not finish writing the letter to his brother. After four days he became so ill that he died. He was fifty-three years old, and had not long enjoyed his married bliss. (Was his anticipation of happiness too great to be realized?) He left his family, a widow only thirty-one years of age, and six children aged between one and seven, the grand house in the *Langgarten*, and some funds from the timber business. But Maria Barstow was a young and beautiful woman, and her fortunes would change again.

Maria Marries Cornelius

Maria Barstow did not long remain a widow. The 'loveliest of angels', with her lustrous grey eyes and rosy complexion, was still good to look upon. She was very musical, and had a splendid singing voice. Cornelius von Almonde was first enraptured by hearing her sing in church. Cornelius, a merchant, was the Dutch consul in Danzig. He was the same age as Maria.

About a year and a half after Michael Barstow's death, Cornelius and Maria were married (note 3). Adam Elliot, Barstow's business partner, who was still managing to run the company, wrote to the Barstow relatives to tell them of the marriage. He spoke highly of Almonde, and said that he thought Mrs Barstow would now have a greater chance of happiness than ever. This was a sad remark considering all the fervent expressions of devotion Michael had made.

The Almondes went to live in the house that Michael Barstow had bought, which now became the Dutch consulate. Cornelius turned out to be a most devoted husband, writing Maria lover-like sonnets on her birthdays, and sweetening her life by every possible kindness and attention. He certainly deserved all the encomiums of Adam Elliot.

The Almondes' first child was born in 1796. Adam Elliot wrote to the Reverend Thomas Barstow about the young family springing up around them. He said that one son died of smallpox on the day of another's birth, and that the shock had nearly cost the young mother her life. (Only one child, Marianne, out of seven children that the Almondes had, would survive to adulthood.)

Adam Elliot was a true friend of the family, and did all he could to realize funds. Two years after Maria's second marriage he wrote again to the Reverend Thomas Barstow, recommending that he send for little Tom Barstow, to bring him up in England. He wrote of the child as being 'sound in head and heart, and likely to make a useful member of society'.

Then he went off to speculate as to General Napoleon's next move, whether on Russia or Egypt, which seems so strange now in 1898. (General 'Nap', he called him.) So when my father, Tom, was nine years old, he was dispatched to his uncle and aunt, who had just moved to Copford in Essex. They had no children of their own. Tom was sent to school at Felsted as a boarder, and spent his vacations with them.

Four years after Michael Barstow's demise, his children's would-be benefactor, Miss Bendlowes of Danzig, died. As it turned out, the property she left them in her will had been previously disposed of by her brother Philip, from whom she had inherited it for her lifetime only. These were the estates of Littlethorpe, Howgrave, Sutton, Thornborough, and Upton Hill, in Yorkshire, and Bolam in Durham; therefore the Barstow children might have been rich. The case was settled by an amicable law suit, so that the Barstows were to inherit eventually. W Concett, and his representative, D'Arcy Preston, who took the name of Concett, were to enjoy the estates in their lifetimes.

Meanwhile, Cornelius von Almonde made some dreadful journeys into Poland, endeavouring to recover the money owed to Michael Barstow's firm, particularly by the banker Meisner at Warsaw. I remember hearing how he once had a very narrow escape, being pursued by wolves.

Another time, when darkness overtook him, Cornelius passed the night in a primitive den. Though half famished, he could only look in dismay at his hostess and her surroundings. Then he remembered the proverb 'An egg and a nut you may eat after a slut', and he begged for an egg. To his horror the good woman broke the eggs into the corner of her leathern dress of sheep skins. This covering was often the sole garment of the Polish peasant, with the wool worn inside. She quickly beat up the eggs with her filthy fingers, and in a few minutes offered him this most savoury omelette, which hunger compelled him to eat.

The woman's husband returned, and all retired to bed. In the night Cornelius was awakened by a poisonous stench. He looked up and saw that his host had just killed a goat, which he had hung up at the foot of the bed. He was proceeding to disembowel it, the blood dropping down upon him. Cornelius rose and fled as quickly as possible, though in all probability the goat was killed in his honour.

A few years passed, and Adam Elliot again advised the Reverend Thomas Barstow that his wife and he should make a home for Michael Barstow's children, this time the younger daughters. However, for ten years now Napoleon had either been at war either with Great Britain or another country, and commercial shipping was often threatened by the warfare. In 1802, after the Treaty of Amiens, there was a short period of peace. The Almondes took advantage of the truce to send Frances, Emily and Matilda over to the Essex parsonage of their kind uncle. The girls were then aged thirteen, twelve and ten.

They had a terrifying voyage; such a storm in the North Sea that they were driven up nearly to the North Cape. The crew, reduced to starvation, were fed on soup made of tallow candles melted in hot sea water. They were very thankful when they sighted Spurn Head in East Yorkshire. The captain went off by boat to Hull to report himself and lay in a stock of provisions for his passengers. He rather disappointed them when he brought back only a leg of mutton. They had been subsisting on a small allowance of biscuits for several days and had hardly any left. The ship made its way down the coast and at last it reached the river Thames.

My father, Tom, was staying in London, where he had gone on purpose to meet his sisters; the relatives had become greatly anxious on their account. One day, to divert him, his friends proposed that they should go out for a row on the Thames. Somewhere near Woolwich their attention was drawn to a very shattered barque, with ragged sails, vainly striving to beat upstream. As they approached they saw the Prussian colours flying. They hailed it and learnt it had come from Danzig. In another moment the young men were on board and, to their great joy, they found the long-lost girls. The sisters were quickly rescued from their wretched prison and taken to London in a chaise, grateful indeed to be on dry land. After a short stay in town, they proceeded to their uncle's house.

So my father and his younger sisters escaped the horrors of the sieges of Danzig in 1807 and 1813. They were to be brought up and educated in England by their childless uncle and aunt, as if they were their own children. Tom would be sent to university.

Now, when Maria von Almonde was about forty, close to the time of the Treaty of Amiens, she was afflicted with cataract, and went to Berlin to be operated on. She was successfully couched, but, being of an impatient and energetic nature, she became tired of the necessary restraint, and declared she was dying of *langeweile* (boredom) and would return to Danzig. The weather was very hot, and she got dust in her eyes during the long journey, which was followed by inflammation. She became totally blind before half her life had passed.

The two older daughters of Michael and Maria, Marie and Everilda, were still living in Danzig, together with their half-sister, Marianne. The oldest daughter, Marie, who was very beautiful, had married. But she was already a widow at the age of twenty, and returned to her home. Marie and Everilda shared many of their mother's troubles and anxieties.

For the last three months of 1806, the Prussian royal family moved to Danzig. Queen Louise, with her sons Frederick (who became King of Prussia) and William (who became the first German Emperor), occupied the Government House in the *Langgarten*, opposite the Dutch Consulate established by the Almondes. It was a great relief to them, because they had been living in a state of misery and discomfort.

Sir George Jackson writes of their life at Ortelsburg where the king, Frederick William III, and his queen, had but one room on the ground floor of the wretched barn they called a house. They could not leave it without getting wet up to the ankles, the village being one of the dirtiest, and 'the king taking a morning walk while the room, which serves for sitting-room and bedroom, is arranged for their Majesties' breakfast'. He also mentions that the royal family were fearfully devoured by bugs. Poor, beautiful Queen, she bore all her misfortunes with a dignified resignation and nobleness of character which endeared her to people, and won for her the admiration of the world.

So it happened that when Napoleon overran Holland and made his brother Louis king, the reigning family fled, and the future Queen of Holland and her daughter took refuge in Danzig at the same time that the Prussian royal family was staying there. Naturally, they came to the Dutch Consulate. The queen, Wilhelmina, was the sister of the Prussian king.

They were my grandmother's guests for about six weeks and, of course, she did everything she could for the comfort of the refugees. Princess Paulina was able to play with her cousins residing just across the road. The queen was most considerate and thoughtful, and even begged my grandmother to roll up the carpet in the dining-room as, she said, people were so careless and made crumbs. Carpets were an uncommon luxury in Prussia in those days. It was a handsome Axminster carpet with a rich gold ground, and was still in a very good state of preservation when I was in Danzig in 1840. The queen gave Maria von Almonde a ring in return for the great kindness that was shown to her.

The royal families did not stay long in Danzig, however, because the French army was swarming on all sides. Shortly before Christmas they withdrew to their castle at Königsberg, about a hundred miles to the east. The little princess died, but another princess would be born in the future.

The Sieges of Danzig

Danzig was garrisoned by 16,000 men in preparation for the coming siege against the French, which was now inevitable. The English, Russian and Prussian forces were in an alliance against the French.

Marshals Ney, Lannes and Lefèvre commanded the French forces. The Russians tried in vain to halt the siege. An English brig of twenty-two guns attempted to run the blockade. She had 150 barrels of gunpowder on board. After a cannon shot had struck her rudder and the sails had been cut to pieces, she surrendered to the French. (The flag of this ship now adorns Les Invalides in Paris.) Later in the two-month siege a Russian naval force landed fresh troops, but the French also brought in new troops.

The French Occupy Danzig

A tremendous cannonade which continued for a week set the town on fire in many places. At last, the ammunition of the besieged was exhausted. The Prussian commander, General Kalkreuth, capitulated on 24 May 1807. The garrison had been reduced to less than half its complement. When I was visiting Danzig in 1840, I was shown many cannon balls that had been built into the roofs of the churches through which they had broken their way; the shells which set fire to the buildings had red flames painted on them. I was taken to the Hagelsberg, an outwork which bore the brunt of the cannonade. I was told how every night it was freshly garrisoned, but half of the men never returned to give an account of themselves. At last none returned. When the French took possession of this key point of the town there was not a whole man left, nothing but a few shattered remains of humanity amongst the dead and the dying.

My grandmother and her family were in Danzig during this siege. They lived on half rations, and suffered a good deal from hunger, and alarms. First Marshal Ney and his staff were quartered on them. I have heard many stories of the reckless conduct of the invaders. My aunt Everilda told me how a French officer rode up the half dozen steps of the *beischlag*, an elevated terrace joining the front of the house to the street; he raised his whip and threatened to strike her with it. She said, 'I called my mother and she did give him it. She was better than any man.'

Napoleon himself occupied the house in the *Langgarten*, and attended a meeting there with the burghers of Danzig, who were concerned about trade, on 2 June 1807. He slept in the room my aunts commonly used as their dining-room, and he had a bolt put on the door. It remained black and unpainted. Perhaps Napoleon also stayed there in June 1812 on his way to Moscow. I think I never went through that room without shooting the historic bolt.

Marshal Rapp, as the French commandant of Danzig, appropriated my grandmother's house during the chief part of the French occupation, until 1813. My grandmother and her family turned out of the house to make way for the intruders, and resided principally at a country house they had at Pietzkendorff, between two and three miles out of Danzig. Almonde went continually back and forth to look after his property and the affairs of the consulate. At the same time, Marshal Rapp sent to France for fruit trees, with which he replanted the garden. They flourished and did remarkably well; when I was visiting Danzig the garden was reputed to be the best in town and, indeed, the currants and greengages were not to be surpassed.

Shortly after my father Tom Barstow graduated from Trinity College, Cambridge, in 1809, he decided to set up house-keeping. He wrote to his mother to beg her to send him his father's valuables, which for security's sake she had walled up in the cellar of the house in the *Langgarten*. My grandmother had given her other valuables to the government, like all good Prussians, to help raise fresh armies to fight the French, and had received in exchange the small iron cross on which was engraved 'They gave gold for iron'. But as her son's silver was not hers to give, she had it walled up. Tom did not properly appreciate the difficulty and danger of complying with his demand during the French occupation of Danzig. All trade with England was prohibited. The valuables had to be taken from their place of concealment in their home, which was occupied by the French. It could not be effected without a mason, who had to work in the dead of night.

At last Almonde, hearing of a ship in the offing which he knew was bound for England, succeeded in conveying the property safely on board. This was done at great personal risk as the expedition had to be made at night, and he was fired at by the French battery both in going and returning. However, the valuables were fated never to reach their destination. It was said that the vessel foundered and that the silver went to the bottom. But years later, the old family Bible with silver clasps was brought to my great uncle, Archibald Maclean, who found his sister's name inscribed in the register. I saw it when I was first in Danzig, and certainly it showed no signs of being submerged, so doubtless the silver was all stolen. Amongst it was a cup presented to old Thomas Barstow, as master of the York Harriers.

The Russian Army

During the dreadful winter of 1812 and 1813 Danzig was destined to undergo another siege, but this time the Russians were the assailants and the French the defendants. Though most of the inhabitants of the countryside fled into the town at the approach of the wild Cossacks, my grandmother's horror of the siege was so great that she decided to remain where she was, in Pietzkendorff. The country was in a dreadful state, between fleeing remnants of the Grand Army escaping from Moscow, and their ruthless pursuers.

One day my grandmother sent her servant out on a shopping excursion. He asked for final orders. 'Oh,' she said, 'should you find any of those poor, half frozen Frenchmen in the snow, you can bring them in to me'. But she was really rather aghast at the too literal way in which her servant obeyed this injunction, after he returned with two French soldiers in his sleigh. He had picked them up nearly dead from cold and hunger. My grandmother set to work at once on her task of mercy. Their frost-bitten limbs were rubbed with snow. They were but scarcely fed when a party of Cossacks arrived, clamouring to know if any French had taken refuge in the house. The wretched invalids were hastily stowed away, one in a chimney, and the other in a boiler in the out-house.

Meanwhile the Cossacks swarmed over the premises, plunged their swords through and through the bedding, and searched all round. My grandmother hastily produced her store of good things, in the hope of turning their thoughts in a different direction, and they left the house well satisfied. It was a long time before the two Frenchmen dared to stir or show their faces. Later, when it was proposed that they should go back to France, they fell on their knees before my grandmother, and implored her to keep them. They 'would bear anything and do anything', they said, rather than return to France and have to serve again in the French army, after the miseries they had undergone.

They were clever, intelligent men. My grandmother succeeded in finding them occupations. One, who had been a silk weaver at Lyon, became foreman to a large linen factory in Silesia. He married my aunt's maid, and was still living when I was at Danzig in 1840. He sent a letter yearly to my grandmother with accounts of his family and prosperity, full of gratitude to her who, under Providence, was the cause of it. The other soldier did not recover his health after the hardships he endured, and died in a short time of typhus fever.

About 35,000 men of Napoleon's Grand Army took refuge in Danzig, but they were so worn out by suffering that they were not a very effective force, and were soon decimated by disease. Marshal Rapp defended the town with heroic bravery, and the garrison made constant sorties. They often repulsed the Russians with great loss. They scoured the adjacent countryside for grain and cattle, till all the land was devastated, and the wretchedness of the inhabitants was quite indescribable.

After the Battle of Leipsig, the Duke of Württemberg arrived to help the besiegers, with a considerable force under his command. A furious bombardment recommenced, and the town was set on fire in twenty-eight different places. When provisions had become very scarce and all hopes of being relieved had vanished, Marshal Rapp surrendered in November 1813. He stipulated that the garrison should be allowed to return to France on condition of their not serving again. The Emperor of Russia refused to sanction that condition, and Rapp and his French soldiers were marched into Russia as prisoners of war. The rest of the garrison joined the allied ranks.

Holland, about the same time, received back with enthusiasm the representatives of the House of Orange. Danzig was now garrisoned by the Russians.

Near Pietzkendorff where my grandparents lived, there was a rising ground, from which there was a very good view of Danzig. From this point of vantage Almonde often walked to assure himself that their house in the Langgarten was still standing. One evening, he saw volumes of smoke issuing from what he judged to be their house. He hurried into the town and, only too true, it was their house that was on fire. He met all the Cossacks leaving it, just as, they say, rats leave the sinking ship. They had not the least endeavoured to extinguish the flames. The fire was caused by over-heating the stoves while burning the banisters in them. Almonde enlisted some aid and the fire was soon put out, the roof alone having been much damaged. He would not have it repaired until after the Russians vacated the premises and had them returned as unfit for habitation. In this manner, Cornelius got rid of the destructive guests.

The Almondes' house had a double hall, and from the second one there was a double staircase that met under a central window which had been handsomely carved, as was the fashion with the Danzig houses. It was broken up and burned by the Russians, and completely destroyed. They incinerated the chairs and furniture and, in fact, everything they could lay their hands on. 'Oh, save me from my friends!' was the universal cry. The Russians were real pigs, and did more mischief in the few months in which they occupied Danzig than the French did in as many years.

Maria and Cornelius continued to help poor refugees who came their way. One day a most lamentable object presented himself at the door and begged to speak to the Dutch consul.

His language was very superior to his appearance. He was a Dutchman, and said he had served in the Grande Armée and was taken prisoner after the retreat from Moscow. Most of his companions in misery died. He decided to attempt an escape. He was about nine months effecting this purpose, not daring to use the beaten track. He journeyed mostly by night, and hid by day, for long supporting his existence on berries and roots. He was in the last stage of exhaustion, and covered with vermin, when he reached Danzig.

The first thing to do was to give the poor fellow soup and a good shake-down in the stables. He slept twenty-four hours without moving, so they woke him up to give him more soup, fearing he might die of hunger. After another twelve hours he woke up seemingly refreshed, and was tubbed by the old garden woman. He was dressed in new garments, and his rags were burnt in the courtyard. He wished to stay with his newly found friends, but that was impossible. The Almondes paid his passage to Holland, and gave the captain of the ship something substantial to hand over to him when he landed.

Maria's Children Marry

Frances Barstow, who went to live with her uncle and aunt in England in 1802, was the first of the girls to marry (after Marie had been left a widow, as I mentioned earlier). She married William Farmer of Nonsuch Park, Surrey, in 1809. She was very clever and bright, and had inherited her mother's kindness and generosity, but was rather unconventional, the effect of her early education in Danzig. She would have a large family of seven sons and four daughters, and her daughters were to marry Germans (note 4). In Prussia, Marie married August Adolphe Guenther. They had three sons and two daughters (note 5). Everilda Barstow married first Heinrich Richter, and second Johann Neumann of Danzig, and had several sons and daughters, and I make mention of two of them, Thomas Richter and Mary Ann Neumann, later in the story.

Tom Barstow married Ann Jones in 1817 at Skreen, County Sligo, Ireland, near Ann's birth-place. Her family fled from Ireland to Yorkshire in 1798, when Ann was a baby. At that time the French landed at Killala, on the west coast of Ireland, and threatened to lead a rebellion of the Irish people against the English. (I have written the story of Ann's escape.) Tom and Ann, my parents, lived first at Skipton-on-Swale in North Yorkshire. In 1835 they bought a house 'Garrow Hill', near York. They had a very large family of eight sons and five daughters, born between 1818 and 1845, a span of twenty-seven years (note 6).

My father, Tom, sustained four great losses during his life. First, when he was a minor, a tenant occupying his house in Fulford died intestate and in debt, and his creditors seized upon my father's property, furniture and pictures. Second, all his silver was sunk with a ship, or stolen, as I have related. Third, the house we lived in at Blossom Street, York, was burnt down because our next-door neighbours, by over-heating, accidentally set it on fire. Fourth, a heavy bond which stood first in a schedule of debts was maliciously placed at the end by false friends, so that my father was defrauded of a very large sum. These misfortunes he bore in an exemplary manner.

In 1820, the Reverend Thomas Barstow died (note 7). Up to this time he and his wife had provided a home in England for their unmarried youngest nieces, Emily and Matilda Barstow. They were now aged thirty and twenty-eight. Emily suffered from asthma all her life. They returned to their mother in Danzig after an absence of eighteen years, and would now live with Maria and Cornelius.

Marianne von Almonde, the only child of Maria's second marriage to survive to adulthood, married Carl Heinrichsdorff of Danzig, proprietor of the Salmon Restaurant. She had a beautiful singing voice. Like her mother, out of a family of seven, she had only one surviving daughter, Marie, born in 1828. After her husband died, Marianne married her cousin, Archibald Maclean of Czerbienczin, near Dirschau. They had two sons and three daughters (note 8).

So it was that in the long peace after the sieges of Danzig, five of Maria von Almonde's children were busy bringing up their young families, either in England or in the German states, while Emily and Matilda remained at home, unmarried. Matilda looked after her asthmatic sister, and they were companions to each other. They were both a help to their blind mother, just as the daughters Marie and Everilda had been at an earlier time.

I Visit My Grandmother

At intervals of about ten years my father made pilgrimages to Germany to see his mother and other relatives. Sometimes he met them on the Rhine River, and sometimes he journeyed all the way to Danzig to see them. In 1840, when he proposed to pay his mother another visit, she most kindly made it a special request that I should accompany my parents, who had only intended to take my older sister with them. She suggested, as there were four places available, and as they had to drive from Hamburg, my presence would make little difference in the expense. So it was happily decided that I was to go. I was thirteen years old.

How well I remember it! We saw on the road to Hull the debris of some railway carriages in which seven people had lost their lives the previous day, in what was then the worst railway accident that had occurred in England. We drove about Hull, as my father was intent on seeing 'the land of green ginger'. The name had amused him, but it was an unremarkable suburb.

Then came a sea voyage in which I distinguished myself as being the worst sailor that was ever launched on the deep.

We were to weigh anchor on a Saturday, but the vessel was too heavily laden, and it was not until the Sunday afternoon that the tide rose high enough to bear us away. Just as we reached the bar of the Humber River, the captain most unkindly proposed having prayers. The first line of the confession was too much for me, and few stayed to the end of it. None of us crawled out of our dens of misery till we reached the Elbe River, in Germany, excepting my sister. She flitted about the ship and often came with cheering words to comfort us poor sufferers. As soon as we reached smooth water, she dressed me and put me on my feet.

Meanwhile my sister had picked up an ardent admirer amongst the passengers. He, to do justice to the occasion, put on a clean collar before every meal, never removing the inner one; he had a fringe of dog-eared linen around his neck, looking altogether comical and repulsive. At Hamburg was my first *table d'hôte*; there a beautiful American pushed her plate into the middle of the table and, alternately with knife and fork, dexterously pitch-forked her food into her mouth.

My father bought a carriage at Hamburg, into which we and all our luggage were packed. We travelled *vetturino* fashion to Berlin, a long, dreary drive. We halted there three days, staying with the Guenthers at their charming apartments *unter den linden*. I spent most of the time in bed with a bad sore throat. My cousin Carl, then a very young doctor, entertained me by showing me his cases of needles and surgical instruments.

We continued our journey, travelling fast. Our drivers were beautiful objects in yellow breeches, top boots, plumed hats, and horns slung over their shoulders with red and green ropes and tassels. Oh, the monotony of those endless miles of stubble; nothing as far as the eye could see but the undulating waste, just occasionally edged by black lines of Scotch fir. It was quite a pleasant excitement when, our driver having fallen asleep, the horses took us over the stone edging. We were within an ace of being overturned into a deep ditch which bordered the road. The driver, poor fellow, fell on his knees in abject terror, lest my father should complain of him and he should lose his situation. He kissed the hem of my mother's dress, pleading, 'Beat me if you like, give me no *trinkgeld*, only don't report me!'

We travelled in the wake of the king's kitchen, which was on its way to Königsberg; here, the new king, Frederick William IV, was going to hold high court in honour of his *Huldigung* (the swearing of fealty). These heavily weighted carriages were like flocks of locusts in the land, devouring everything before them. What a capacity for food these Germans had, for they fed at every station, and we did not. For several stages we could not procure any food, and only wretched, tired horses. But to our great joy we passed the convoy at last.

About noon on the third day, after driving all night, we reached Danzig. I was quite ill. I never recovered from my sea-sickness, and had a very bad cold as well. I was put to bed with a big poultice, and kept there several days. It was the same bed the Princess of Orange had slept in, and this pleased my young imagination. I was in the *belle étage*, in which my aunts lived;

it had a large, square *saal*, and rooms of equal length opening right and left out of it, and these were again divided in width.

The Almondes occupied the ground floor, and we always dined downstairs with them. Our grandmother, though seventy-eight at the time of our visit, was even then very energetic. In spite of her blindness, she had much of the vigour of a young woman. She still had a reputation for her singing. Once when the young singer Clara Novello was on her way to St Petersburg, she came from Dirschau to Danzig on purpose to listen to the blind musician of whose fame she had heard. She spent a day of happiness with my grandmother in singing, and being sung to.

On fine mornings my grandmother breakfasted in a summer house in her garden, nominally at seven. My father thought he would breakfast with her, and appeared on the scene punctually at seven, but the breakfast was all over and the old lady was seated at her knitting. On another morning he tried 6.30, but again he was late for the fare, so he gave it up as hopeless. Maria did not sleep well, and was always tormenting her companions to get up at the most unearthly hours.

After her breakfast, the orphans she had in the house came to read to her, and to say their lessons before going to school. She generally had three or four of them. When they had undergone this examination, any grandchildren whom she might have staying with her appeared with book in hand. They too had to say their lessons, and woe betide them if they had not been learnt. She held the book as if she could see, and corrected the mistakes with wonderful precision. She never failed in administering justice should the lessons not have been duly learnt: the outside of the book always made acquaintance with the culprit's head. Mary Ann Neumann, Everilda's daughter, stood in great awe of her grandmother; she often felt the weight of these blows and could not believe that Maria really was blind.

On completing the morning duties, Cornelius usually came and read to Maria till dinner time, which, of course, was at midday. In the afternoon friends called to tell her the news, and have coffee with her, a refreshment that went by the name of 'vespers'. It was quite as important a meal as five o'clock tea has since become in England.

We were a very large party, for, besides my two aunt Barstows and my aunt Marie Guenther, three cousins were invited to be our playfellows. Numerous relatives were always coming and going, to say nothing of the young orphans that were being brought up. The footman, the cook, indeed I think the whole of the household had been orphans whom the Almondes took compassion on and educated. They became so renowned for their kindness that, at times, they were quite besieged by people entreating them to take in stray children.

Of course we were made much of, and driven to see all the pretty and interesting places in the neighbourhood of Danzig. One drive I remember was to Neufäler to see a house that was literally cut in two by the great flood the previous year. The Vistula River flooded as a regular occurrence, and had torn for itself a new mouth, the Durchbruch, as it was called. It was hoped that this new outlet and shorter cut to the sea would prevent such dreadful catastrophes in future. During the flood my grandmother and aunts took in about fifty homeless people, clothed many of them, housed them in their stables as well as they could, and fed them for many days. My Aunt Matilda told me her first purchase for them was fifty combs, for there was nothing they so much needed.

The Huldigung

The great event of that first memorable visit to Danzig was the return of Frederick William IV, the King of Prussia, from the *Huldigung*, or homage, at Königsberg. The belles of Danzig, clothed in white, presented bouquets of vast magnitude. Then came the *Bourgemeister* (a tailor) with yards of parchment, at which the king looked askance. He begged him to cut short the thread of his discourse, as he was hungry.

At Government House there was a grand reception, and all the notables of Danzig were present, Cornelius von Almonde amongst the rest. The king caught sight of him at once. Though thirty-three years had elapsed since he had met him, the king called out when he saw *'den alte Almonde'*, and asked him to come forward. He supplemented the formal presentation with a hearty squeeze of the hand, and reminded Almonde of how he, the king, used to go to Almonde's house to play with his cousin, the young Princess of Orange, and he asked after his wife. The dear old gentleman, Almonde, came back radiant with pleasure from the royal interview.

In the evening the whole town was illuminated; every pane of glass had its burning candle. The fantastic pointed gables and the beautiful architectural lines of the old houses were bordered by lights of various shades and colours. The ships moored on either side of the many bridges were all dressed, their rigging hung with coloured lamps, which enhanced the fairy-like scene.

While we were gazing in admiration, a party of rowdy young fellows came charging down upon us, elbows well in position. My father gave the foremost of the party a box on the ear, which sent him reeling on his comrades, and redirected the current of the charge. At this, Marie Heinrichsdorff delighted us by crying out, 'Oh, my Uncle, that was a heavenly box!'

We returned home shortly after the royal visit. Before we left, my grandmother gave my mother the ring she had once received from the Queen of Holland.

We lodged for a week at Dresden, and my father sold his carriage for exactly what he had paid for it. We picked up a travelling companion, a General von Yochmus, who had just been fighting in Spain. He entertained us with many stories. He could not quite make out my name, and called me 'Fraulein Lizard'.

At Magdeburg the landlord of the hotel shocked us by his insistence on giving us only one sleeping apartment. He said the room was large and he could bring in plenty of beds, and he thought us ridiculous people for objecting to such an arrangement. I should say that in those days German provisions for the toilets were very meagre.

From Magdeburg to Hamburg we went by boat, a most tedious navigation, as we were always running aground. On one occasion my father sent back some raw ham which they had brought us for supper. The girl who was waiting on us turned upon us with a look of scorn, exclaiming, 'They are

Jews, they are Jews!' Of course, my father returned the meat because it was raw, not because it was pork.

My grandmother and Cornelius von Almonde both died in 1844, within a few months of each other. They were both aged eighty-one.

The following summer my two unmarried aunts, Emily and Matilda Barstow, came to live in England. Before they left they had a church built at Osche, a desolate place on the Vistula River, in memory of their parents. They dedicated it to St Michael, with pious reference to their father Michael Barstow. By now they had lived for twenty-five years in Danzig, their birth-place, after they were largely brought up in England. They were passed back and forth between Danzig and England according to who could accommodate them.

In 1851, Emily, who had long been a great sufferer of asthma, was called away. One day, when she was more ill than usual, the family assembled around her bed thinking every breath would be her last. She quietly said, 'Don't trouble yourselves about me now; I have seen St Michael beckoning to me, so I shall not leave you till Michaelmas Day', and on the morning of September 29th, she died. What perhaps was still more remarkable was that I, her favourite niece, had a like vision. It so impressed me that, on the strength of it, I went up from Brighton to Reading, and was with the aunts when the end came. Aunt Matilda mourned her sister like a widow.

My Second Visit to Danzig

Between 1853 and 1854, I went to Danzig a second time and stayed with my uncle and aunt Maclean. I had fallen into very bad health, so my good aunt Matilda proposed, for a little change, taking me to Kissengen, and then on to Danzig. My uncle and aunt, Archy and Marianne, mainly lived at Czerbienczin; I rested with them there for a while, and did some sketching. My cousin Thomas Richter and his wife visited us. The Macleans usually went into Danzig with their daughters for lessons during the winter, and nothing could exceed their kindness but that they asked me to stay longer and spend the winter with them there. (Their two sons were away at school, and were both to serve in the Franco-Prussian War. There is a story about one of them which I have placed at the end.)

I occupied the upper storey or attic of the house in the *Langgarten*, as my uncle and aunt were on the ground floor, and President Blumenthal had taken the floor in between. The upper floor had only three rooms, and two large attics for the storage of fuel and stores, and for the drying of clothes and linen. It was a weird-looking place, full of beams, ropes and cordage, enough to induce anyone to commit suicide who was so disposed. At the farther end of the gable there was an iron door, which my aunts had placed there as an escape in case of fire, but from it there was a most perilous drop onto the roof below. I had two locked doors on the staircase dividing me from my relatives. One morning I was nearly suffocated by the valve of the stove closing; I had just enough sense left to jump out of bed and fling open the window and hang my head out of it, in spite of the keen and bitter frost. It was several days before I recovered from the effects of the fumes.

Afterwards, I had another adventure. A young lady, who was not quite right in her mind, came to stay with my aunt. She had one of the spare rooms in the attic, which communicated with mine. One night she shook me out of my sleep, and was very perturbed; she thought she was dying. So there was nothing for it but to go downstairs and wake up my aunt, and call up the servants, as the carriage had to be sent for the doctor. I crossed the courtyard three times that night, ankle deep in snow, in my dressing-gown and slippers. I think the excitement of the whole affair prevented me from catching cold. These houses en suite were very inconvenient; the servants locked up the inner communications so that there was no way of getting to their quarters at night except by crossing the courtyard.

The Vistula Floods

There came a rumour that the banks of the Vistula had again given way, and consternation was depicted on every face. One bright Saturday in March we walked along the Chaussée, which was a raised embankment, and watched the water gradually rising in the ditches. The inhabitants of the houses were hard at work making rafts and getting their things together. All night long we heard the tramp of cattle being driven into the town, and the roll of heavy waggons laden with children, pigs, and sheep. Early in the morning we heard the rattle of artillery. We really felt as if we were on the eve of another siege and, indeed, the town was beleaguered, but this time by the waters. The cannon were used to weigh down the bridges and prevent their being washed away by the rushing flood.

On Sunday morning we again walked along the Chaussée, and there beheld such piteous sights. Groups of women who had escaped from the flood were trying to make fires with anything at hand, in order to heat some coffee for their poor little ones. Their husbands, in boats or on rafts, were still endeavouring to save what belongings they could. Some of the people were two or three days on the roofs of their houses, and were half dead from hunger and cold before they could be rescued. There were about twelve square miles submerged in this flood; it was more than two months before the waters abated and the people could return to their homes. They then suffered terribly from typhus, which followed in the wake of so much exhaustion.

Soon after this disaster, I returned to England.

My aunt Matilda died about ten years after her sister Emily. She was the kindest and dearest of old ladies. She left me the furniture she had imported with her from Danzig. It included the bed occupied by the Princess of Orange in 1806, in which I had slept in 1840. It is, strange to say, my resting place again in my old age. As for the Queen of Holland's ring, my mother passed it on to Mary, the wife of her oldest son, Thomas.

The house in the *Langgarten* was left conjointly to my father and his half-sister Marianne, by Matilda, who had inherited it from her older sister, Everilda Neumann. It had been rented out for some years. It was sold in 1863 to the Prussian government, for the use of the military authorities. The proceeds of the sale were only small as the woodwork was in a bad condition and needed renewing. Danzig became part of Germany in 1871. The house is now, in 1898, the residence of the President and government officers.

Towards the end of March 1890, I was one day surprised to receive a box from Germany. On opening it I was still more surprised to find it contained the portrait I described earlier of Michael Barstow, the hero of all the love letters. The picture is not a work of art of the highest order. Michael's expression recalls to my mind those lines of Milton:

And looks commercing with the skies,

Thy rapt soul sitting in thine eyes.

Was he thinking of his loveliest angel? Probably the picture was painted for her.

This is an extract from the letter that accompanied the picture:

Liebwalde, 20th March, 1890.

You remember perhaps having seen in the year 1853 your cousin Thomas Richter and his wife, then visiting Czerbienczin. I preserve still a fine sketch of the home from your hand, a very dear remembrance of you, and of all the dear, beloved persons of this place who are no more in this charming world.

A year and nine months ago a sudden death tore away my dear husband after a long and happy marriage of forty-three years.

Under the heritage of my husband, we found the portrait of your grandfather Barstow, which I had seen in former times at my mother-in-law's. Mary Ann Neumann, who was months last summer at Liebwalde, adjoins the letter of promise of Mr Barstow. She is of the same opinion as me that this portrait and letter have only value with your family, so I think you will be glad to receive them.

Johanne Richter geb Baum.

The letter she enclosed was written to Mary Maclean by Michael Barstow, and is much the same as some that have already been transcribed.

How Archibald Maclean Captured the Paris Mails for the Prussian Army In 1870

I first read of this episode in the life of my cousin Archibald Maclean, the older of two brothers, in *The Times* newspaper in 1870. Archibald was attached to a regiment of Uhlans in the Franco-Prussian War. He was directed to make a reconnaissance sixteen miles ahead of the column, as it was reported a French force was in the neighbourhood. He picked out five well mounted men, and they rode off. Not finding the expected army, they rode on and on, and at last descried a large town with spacious buildings and gardens.

'Why,' he exclaimed, 'that must be Versailles! Let us go and look at it.' They approached, and found the gate unguarded. Archibald left two of his men in charge, and rode up to the guard house. He commanded the guards, in the name of the King of Prussia, to lay down their arms. They demurred, and then one man unwittingly remarked that it did not signify as their guns were unloaded. Archibald's were loaded. They obeyed.

Charging his men to shoot anyone who moved, Archibald Maclean asked his way to the *Maré*. That functionary was filled with horror on seeing the dreaded foe. Maclean commanded that billets should be in immediate readiness for 60,000 men. The mayor offered *Monsieur, le colonel*, as he called him, the keys of the town. These Maclean refused, saying that the king would soon send the proper officials for them. He asked his way to the post office. At the post office he took possession of the Paris mails, which he handed to his attendant, and they rode off.

He had been greeted with cries of dismay, *'Ah, les Prussiens!' 'Les Uhlans!'*. But, as the following of 60,000 men failed to appear, there was a change in the note to *'À bas les Prussiens!'* ('Down with the Prussians!'). The surprised deputies were just coming out of the Chamber, and the crowd was thickening and growing dangerous. So Maclean rode to the guard house, called off his men, picked up those at the gate, and they all galloped away for dear life. Many parting shots were fired, but happily none found their mark.

They reached headquarters safely. Maclean reported himself to his general, and presented the Paris mails. The general desired him to make his report to the Crown Prince, who lay about twenty miles away. Maclean replied, 'My General, neither my horse nor myself can do anything more, we are quite exhausted. We have been full seventy miles.' So fresh men were dispatched in haste to the Crown Prince, who lost not a moment of availing himself of the information as to the defenceless state of Versailles. He marched all night and, within twenty-four hours, really took possession of the place.

A few days later Maclean was decorated by William, the first German Emperor, on the Grande Place before all the army. He was presented with a commission in the regulars, but he did not accept it, being, he thought, too old. King William was proclaimed German Emperor at Versailles. He had once lived opposite the Almondes in Danzig.

The hero of the adventure, Archibald Maclean, remarked to me that it was a marvel to him that he was still alive, and that the French had not shot him. He supposed they were so unprepared for such a sudden apparition that, like the guards, none of their weapons was loaded.

Arranged by E Barstow. Mimeographed by F A Jones.

***

Interlude

In March 1945, the Barstows' old house in the *Langgarten*, and the important buildings opposite it were bombed out of existence. What the bombs did not obliterate, was finished off by bulldozers. But in a Baedeker guide to Northern Germany of 1904, the buildings are clearly indicated in a map of Danzig, as *Kommandantur* on one side of the road, and *Kas* and *Russ Konsulat* on the other. The floor plans of the buildings are drawn, and I can easily identify the Barstows' old home, the commandant's house, built around three sides of a court. At one time, a great grand-daughter of Maria Barstow, Helene Guenther, married the commandant, and they may have lived there (note 5). Later, Maria's house was purchased by the Bergholdom bankers.

Elizabeth Barstow, the author, wrote for the purpose of informing her relations about the history of women in their family. 'How I wish I could remember more of the stories I heard of those days', Elizabeth said. Elizabeth did not marry, and she lived until she was ninety-nine years old. What did she do all that time? Even though she was privileged, I feel sad about a certain lack of opportunity in her life; for work, for study, for marriage. Elizabeth and her unmarried sisters, as Elizabeth's diary records, tended a smallholding at 'Garrow Hill', York. They kept cows, pigs, and bees, made hay for the horse, and grew fruit trees, vegetables, and flowers. They held garden fetes in support of charities, and sewing afternoons. Probably Elizabeth often stayed with her numerous brothers and sisters, and the like, including Matilda and Thomas Webber and their family, in Ireland, who recounted stories of the past. Matilda was the only one of the five Barstow girls to marry.

Matilda and Thomas sometimes made trips to Germany, and visited their relatives there. They left their children with their Barstow aunts at 'Garrow Hill', in the care of a German nanny. Their son Oswald wrote to his parents in 1880: 'I hope you are enjoying yourselves travelling from one place to another. Thank you for the paper you sent me from Stuttgart. I got a cricket bat, ball and wickets for a birthday present from my aunts, and Fraulein plays with me when the grass is not too damp. It is now thundering hard and we are frightened.' Other nephews and nieces, and occasionally German relatives were guests at 'Garrow Hill'.

Elizabeth Barstow, as 'Aunt Lise', sent letters and chocolates to her nephew Oswald Webber, while he was fighting in the Boer War in 1900. After Oswald returned, he was invited to a ball at 'Garrow Hill', at which he met his future bride, Annie Rudston. When Elizabeth died in 1926, Oswald wrote about it to his son William, who was in Malaya. Another grand-nephew, George Gibbs, remained in contact with German descendants of those in Elizabeth's story over two world wars, in which they were on the opposite side, until about 1960.

Elizabeth Barstow also wrote a story about how her mother Ann Jones escaped from Ireland as a baby, at the time the French landed at Killala in 1798 to support an Irish rebellion. She called it 'Little Ann'. It represents the point of view of the English, not the Irish. She put the two stories in a booklet with a leather cover, and a title page inscribed 'Memoirs of Elizabeth Barstow of Garrow Hill, York'. The title is written in pencil in the hand-writing of her brother-in-law, Thomas W Webber. Thomas contributed some notes towards the story about her mother, dated 1882, which I have included. But the main sources of information were notes and letters collected by Elizabeth Barstow's cousin, Elizabeth Agar, who died in 1881. These no longer remain. Elizabeth's aunt Frances Jones mimeographed the memoirs in 1898. She was aged in her nineties.

I have slightly rearranged and rewritten both of Elizabeth's stories for this book. Her second story follows.

Little Ann

As I have given an account of my grandmother, once Mrs Michael Barstow, it is in the due order of things that I should say something about the Mrs Barstow of the next generation, my mother, for she too passed through many perils and adventures in her earliest days, though, infant as she was, she was hardly conscious of them. No one who saw the beautiful girl, the delight of all eyes, or the goodly matron, conspicuous for every grace and virtue, or the lovable and beloved old lady of riper years, could have imagined the hardship and dangers which beset little Ann on her first appearance in the world.

Know then that she was born in the north-west of Ireland, in the year 1798, when the whole world was distracted with wars and rumours of wars. The preachers of sedition and discord were no more wanting in Ireland then, than they are at this present time of 1898. They coquetted with the French, and invited them over to help them drive out the English, and murder their landlords. The whole country was honey-combed with secret societies, and your deadliest foes might be those of your own household.

A Traitor

When Ann first saw daylight, her father, Mr Robert Jones, was living at Ardnaree. An old tenant of his came to him in great distress, saying that the tenant's son was in danger of being arrested. He entreated Mr Jones if by any means he could save him. The son had joined the United Irishmen, a rebel group.

Mr Jones was very much impressed by the old man's earnest manner, but he little imagined that the anxiety was more on Mr Jones's behalf, than on the son's. Mr Jones promised to do all he could for him. Mr Jones met with the son and assured him of his pardon if he would divulge the names of his associates. The young man then confessed that their names would be found in the ledger of a certain shopkeeper.

Mr Jones went off immediately as directed, taking a constable with him, and insisted on seeing the ledger. He found the names of the traitors written on alternate pages of the book. But his surprise was very great on discovering the name of his own steward, Dwyer, at the head of the list with a donation of fifty pounds, an entry which occurred several times. The money had been purloined from Mr Jones.

The young man then disclosed a plot in which Mr Jones and his family were to be murdered that night. Dwyer had secured his firearms. On further examination it was found that the bullets were drawn from the pistols, and the guns were spiked. But all of this was a great shock to Mr Jones, who had had a very high opinion of Dwyer, and had thoroughly confided in him. Only a few days previously they had gone together to the bogs to arrest a prisoner.

Dwyer himself was immediately arrested and sent to Castlebar jail, tried, and condemned. The French arrived before his execution and opened the jail, and he escaped punishment. But he died despised, wretched, and in poverty, always fearing lest he should be re-arrested and his just sentence carried out.

The French Arrive

Because the French made several attempts to land in Ireland, the coast was kept constantly guarded by English vessels. Consequently, it was a subject of interest rather than alarm when three frigates, with English colours flying, anchored in Killala Bay on Wednesday, 22 August, 1798. Some of the young men of the place, from motives of curiosity, went out in boats to the fleet. It is easier to imagine than to describe their astonishment at finding themselves prisoners on board French ships. However, they were soon released after they took an oath of secrecy and promised not to serve against the French.

Harlow Irwin, one of the party, was Mrs Jones's cousin. He was so terrified that he hid himself with his wife and family at the foot of Mount Knocknaree during the subsequent struggle.

The French, expecting the whole country to rise, brought with them arms for 100,000 men, and nine guns. They landed about 1000 troops under General Humbert. The small garrison of Killala made an ineffectual resistance. Humbert occupied the bishop's house, making it his headquarters. He treated the family with the greatest civility, a striking contrast to the behaviour of the Irish rebels.

Humbert marched with the principal part of his force, augmented by Irish rebels, to Castlebar, and a detachment was sent to take possession of Ballina. A fruitless attempt would be made to defend that place by a few volunteers, on the curiously formed bridge across the Moy, the stream which separates Ballina from Ardnaree. Mr and Mrs Jones, and their four little girls, aged six, four, two, and eight months, were living at Ardnaree.

The Journey Begins

On 23 August, while Mr Jones and some of the neighbouring gentlemen were dining with Colonel King, Mrs Jones and her sister Mrs Duke went to drink tea with their Aunt Letty. Aunt Letty was an old lady of seventy years, who lived in a cottage called 'Palmyra', prettily situated close to the banks of the river near to Ardnaree. The tea tray had just been brought when a messenger rushed in with the dreadful news that the French had landed at Killala. The ladies were in the greatest consternation, debating what they should do. Robert Jones's brother, Charles, appeared on the scene with the further news that the French were marching on Ballina. He bade them instantly flee.

Charles Jones kissed Mrs Jones and said, 'Goodbye, Bess, God bless you'.

'What,' she said, 'will you not speak to Nancy at such a time as this?'. He had quarrelled with his sister, Nancy Duke, and had not spoken to her for a long time. He turned, then, and took an affectionate leave of Nancy. They wished to take their Aunt Letty with them, but the good old lady refused to depart her house, saying that she was too old and too poor to be molested. (So it proved, and she peacefully breathed her last some years later in her little cottage of 'Palmyra' – note 1).

After this hasty leave-taking, the two ladies soon met Mr Jones. He was busy collecting his yeomen, still dressed in his evening clothes of red coat, knee breeches, and silk stockings, in which attire he did much service. He marshalled his men in the old church yard. But as soon as the French appeared they would all run away. Meanwhile Mrs Jones hurried off to look after her children, and prepare for flight.

Half an hour had completely changed the aspect of affairs at Ardnaree. The gentlemen had dispersed. They were attending to their military duties, and were trying to kindle a spark of loyalty amongst the people.

The servants were in rebellion. Mrs Duke's coachman had decamped on one of her horses. Mr Jones's horses were out in a distant field, and it was a while before anyone could be persuaded to go and fetch them. At last Fleming, the gardener, brought one of them up, but then came another difficulty: who could and would drive? Not one of their own servants would drive the coach. Then John Moyle, an old, superannuated coachman who had been pensioned and who could hardly sit on horseback, offered to do his best for them.

The children were hurriedly taken out of bed. There was no time to dress the youngest, Ann, who was only eight months old. She was wrapped in a blanket and stowed away in the carriage. So Mrs Jones fled from her home with her four little daughters, accompanied by her sister Mrs Duke, and her faithful nurse Austin. She concealed about her person a packet of important papers and a miniature of her father, set with diamonds.

A short distance from the house the carriage stopped close to the Redgate, where Mr Jones had drawn up his band of yeomen that he might take leave of his wife and children. No sooner had they settled in their seats than a ball came whistling through the carriage window. Mrs Jones saw the flash, and pulled her eldest daughter, Catherine, towards her, or she would have been killed. The shot was deliberately fired by one of their own men. But Mr Jones, not daring to excite any opposition or increase the excitement of the moment, was obliged to accept the excuse that the gun had gone off by accident. Some of the men were highly incensed at such villainy, and he had difficulty in appeasing their wrath.

Charles Jones's family were even more to be pitied as, living at Ballina, they were in more immediate danger. In the confusion, two of his children disappeared, and he feared they were lost forever. But unknown to the parents an old nurse had taken them to the mountains, and had passed them off as her own. Eventually they would all be united. Charles's two boys, Vaughan and Robert, clung to Mrs Jones's carriage.

As the unhappy party reached Enniscrone, a particularly wild part of the country, darkness closed over them. The old coachman declared that it was impossible to proceed farther without danger of overturning the carriage. There was no help for it but to make the best of a bad business. Feeling thankful they were in comparative safety, they opened the carriage doors and let down the steps for the two boys, who sat on them, resting their heads against the knees of those within. In this manner they passed the night.

At dawn of day they proceeded on their way to 'Fortland', the home of Mrs Jones's uncle, Robert Browne (note 2). On arrival, Mrs Jones found her uncle and his daughter on the point of starting for Sligo. Mr Browne threw his keys to his niece, and told her to help herself to what she wanted, and to remain as long as she liked. So the party rested and refreshed themselves, and Mrs Jones made a dress of some towels for little Ann, the baby. However, as 'Fortland' was only nine miles from Ballina, she was afraid of prolonging her stay. They started early the next day for 'Tanrago', the residence of her brother, Colonel John Irwin.

The road ran along the sea coast then, and was much longer than the present one, hilly, and in a very bad state of repair. The cabins by the side of the road were all closed up; the inhabitants had fled either from fear, or to join the rebels. Mrs Jones's children were crying from hunger, but at Chapelfield, beyond Skreen, they managed to obtain some mouldy bread and half-boiled potatoes. Margaret, the second girl, being delicate and fastidious, refused to eat this unpalatable food, and was whipped for her refusal.

At 'Tanrago'

When the family arrived at 'Tanrago', the first sight that greeted their eyes was three men hanging on an oak tree before the dining-room windows. Margaret always remembered it. Colonel Irwin was absent with his regiment, the Sligo Militia, at Wexford, where shortly afterwards he engaged in the Battle of Vinegar Hill. But many were the friends Mrs Jones found at 'Tanrago', the house being filled to overflowing. Perhaps, for once, company in distress did not make the evil less, as it was so difficult to cater for such a multitude.

After the children were put to bed, Mrs Jones washed their clothes to be ready for the morning, though she had no soap. She made a point of having a few clean shirts in readiness for any gentleman who called on his way to Ballina, who would leave his own, in exchange, to be washed for the next comer. Clean linen was often a luxury in those troublesome times, though it seems but a trifle to those who never felt the want of a clean shirt.

Whilst at 'Tanrago', Mrs Jones had the pleasure of seeing her husband again, as he managed to get over twice during her stay. Tom Fleming, the gardener, succeeded in carrying off a bundle of wet linen for them from the wash house at Ardnaree, which was a great joy. Fleming was an honest, good fellow and was the means of preserving his master's liberty, and probably his life, more than once, being always on hand with his horse in any emergency.

Mrs Jones and her children drove away from their home at Ardnaree only a few hours before it was occupied by the French. A handsome silver inkstand, which was a wedding present from Mrs Jones's relations, Lady Rich and the Countess of Harrington, was left on the drawing room table in the bustle and confusion of flight. Nurse Austin's son secured it by jumping out of the window with it in his arms as the French entered the door. They fired after him, but luckily he escaped, and returned the inkstand to his master. The rest of the silver had been buried, but a traitor who helped bury it told the French where it was hidden. They, of course, took possession of it.

Another relic long preserved in the family was the mahogany dinner table. Not having candlesticks at hand when required, the French quickly improvised by firing bullets through the table, and candles were stuck into the holes. As preparations for a great entertainment had just been made at Ardnaree, the French discovered an unexpected treasure in some excellent sweetmeats. They enjoyed the good cheer very much and said Mrs Jones must be a capital house-keeper. They next attacked the medicine closet, but the contents were not so palatable, and they threw them out on the floor.

Mr Jones had a large apiary of which he was very proud, and hoped to have gained a premium for his honey. But the Frenchmen fancied it, and decided to take the hives by storm. They wrapped their cloaks over their heads and ran backwards against the hives, upsetting them, and then made a hasty retreat. They left them until the bees had deserted their topsy-turvy habitations, and then they returned and carried off the honey in triumph.

The French slaughtered the farm animals for food and discarded the skins and refuse about on all sides, creating disgusting sights and smells. Some valuable folios were flung upon the manure heap after the bindings had been torn off for saddles. A new mistress was soon installed at Ardnaree, who flaunted about in Mrs Jones's smartest dresses. This annoyed the neighbours, who recognized the profanation.

Many were the promises of safety and honourable treatment made to Mrs Jones, if she would but return to her home. These were all rejected through Tom Fleming, the gardener. It was thought that a man who had taken a lease of Ardnaree from the French wished to get Mrs Jones into his power, in the hopes of having his insecure lease confirmed by Mr Jones. So fearful was Mrs Jones of having the place of her retreat discovered that she would not even send to Sligo for bread, but contented herself with the mutton and potatoes she could get at 'Tanrago'.

Her fears were probably increased by the remembrance of the adventures which befell her great grandmother just a hundred years before, in the rebellion of 1689. The Mrs Irwin of that time started from 'Tanrago', intending to join her husband and father at Enniskillen, a stronghold of the Irwins. She escorted her children and carried a few household utensils in creels. Her eldest son John, nine years old, was mounted on horseback and brandished a spit (note 3).

They were encountered by Sir Teague O'Regan. He was struck by the martial bearing of the boy and inquired who they were. On being told, he exclaimed, 'Though the Fox has escaped, I have got the cubs!'. (Mr Irwin was known as 'the Fox'.) O'Regan carried the fugitives off and kept them prisoners in a fort at Strand Hill, where Mrs Irwin was in such distress and want that she was obliged to pawn her wedding ring for bread.

The Bay of Ballysodare

I must return to the story of Mrs Jones. Hearing that the French were in Sligo, Mrs Jones feared that they might raid her present quarters at 'Tanrago', so she decided to leave. With her nurse and children, she crossed the Bay of Ballysodare in a small boat. Mrs Duke and the sons of Charles Jones were no longer in the party. Mrs Jones took with her two feather beds, a shoulder of mutton, and the small box of papers. At the farther shore they started to trudge on with some troops who also escaped by boat.

Mrs Jones's cousin, Harlow Irwin, met them on the road dressed in a French uniform, which at first gave them all a fright. They accompanied him to the cottage on Mount Knocknaree where he and his family were hiding. The sight of the shoulder of mutton caused great joy amongst them, for they had not tasted meat since the landing of the French. Harlow gave up his parlour to Mrs Jones, and there she spread her feather bed and watched over her children's slumbers.

Their next march was to Sligo, for they now learnt that the French had not occupied it. Mrs Jones carried little Ann, and led Margaret by the hand, and the nurse Austin carried Elizabeth and led Catherine. Catherine cried bitterly; her shoes were worn out and full of holes, and the stones cut her feet. On 15 October Mrs Jones wrote from Sligo to her brother, Colonel Irwin, recounting the details of their journey after leaving 'Tanrago':

As Bob wrote to you, my dear John, from Tanrago, I need not tell you in what manner we contrived to get there, and sorry indeed am I that we were obliged to leave it. When the army was ordered for that part of the country, and we were told that our forces were breaking down the Bridge of Balladread, it would have been imprudent for us to have remained there. After that our only way of escape was by water, as Ballysodare was in the possession of the rebels. George Beaty was exceedingly civil, and as soon as I expressed a wish that his boat should be mended, had it done, and fortunately it was finished, all but the pitching.

We were glad to get into it, and after tacking and retacking, the water dashing over us, we were at last landed at the sand bank. We waited there till we got horse and baskets to put our very few things in: a small box of papers of yours, which I intend to protect as long as I can, and a couple of your beds, which I fortunately brought with me, or we should have lain on the ground. I took my little Ann in my arms, and my cowl over me, as it was raining, and on we trudged with Mr Wood's corps and the remnant of Bob's, who were also obliged to take to the sea.

Harlow Irwin met us, and he insisted on the children and me going to his house, which saved us from the hurry bustle of the flight from Sligo. But we had our fears, thinking that Sligo was in the possession of the French and the rebels, and we did not know in what manner we could make our escape from them. I had neither horse, car, nor man, and very little money, so I was obliged to remain quietly till Bob returned with the army from Ballyshannon. He brought us to Cavanaugh, which is noisy and disagreeable, last Sunday. The town is so full that there are no lodgings to be had. Mr Phillips has kindly offered us part of his house, and we intend to go there today.

We had not been long gone from Tanrago when a large party of armed rebels went there and took away all the saddles and bridles, drank some wine, asked where the horses were, and said they would return for them, which they did. They took your milch cows and a chestnut mare of Bob's, drank more wine, and went away again. Mrs Queen packed up everything she could, including the pipe of wine, and brought them to this town.

Mr Tyler was on picket last Thursday, and he went to Tanrago and found everything to be still safe. Nancy Carrol, with the assistance of a good stick, and fighting two or three battles with the women who were left to herd the cattle, has recovered two of your cows; one she got near Ballina, and the other at Ballinary. She set off again to try and get the rest, so I hope you will not be a great loser.

The people at Tanrago were very attentive. John Chamberlain was kind and affectionate; indeed, he has given me linen of his own to make four shirts for Bob. I agree with you that the best thing I can do is to go to England. I wish to wait till Ballina is retaken, as I might perhaps get a few things for me and the children. If we could sell the chaise, which I am told is still safe, the money would help to bear our expenses.

I am puzzled to know what to do with Austin and the two girls. I shall only take one with me. Austin doesn't like to leave her son, but if she would consent we must bind him to a trade.

God bless and preserve my dear John to his affectionate sister, E Jones.

PS Old Hay has just sent me two geese and two turkeys, and some butter. Tanrago is still safe. Mr O'Hara's troop is gone to Tubbercurry, Mr Wood is at Leekfield, and General Trench and 3,000 men are on their way to Ballina. The rebels have put every Protestant they could find into Colonel King's house, God help them. Bob has at last got lodgings at Mr Black's; they pay a guinea and a half a week.

Eventually Mrs Jones found shelter at 'Hermitage', the residence of her cousin Mrs Tyler. During her stay in Sligo, Mrs Jones witnessed the flight of many of her female friends to Manor Hamilton, County Leitrim, mounted on the gun carriages. They wished her very much to accompany them, but she refused their entreaties. Shortly they all returned, for the French, after the Battle of Collooney, instead of marching to Sligo as was expected, pushed on by Drumahaire to Manor Hamilton. (The French then headed for Longford.)

Whilst at Sligo, Margaret had a narrow escape from being drowned. A young nursery maid, not being able to resist a sailor's attentions and her own foolish curiosity, was going on board his vessel when the little girl slipped off the plank. The sailor caught her just as she was disappearing into the water. The children's regular nurse, Austin, had returned to her own family.

On leaving Sligo, Mrs Jones took charge of the Perceval children of Temple House, and went with them in their old coach to Athlone. She stopped on the way at Armaghmore, where her friend Mrs O'Hara supplemented little Ann's scant wardrobe. (Immediately after Mrs Jones and her family departed, Mrs O'Hara and her daughters were obliged to seek refuge at the Bishop of Elphin's.) At Athlone Mrs Jones met up with her brother Crinus Irwin; he had set out for Enniskillen in the hope of finding her. They travelled by canal to Dublin, which they reached safely, and took shelter in Crinus's lodgings.

Here one would have thought that all their difficulties and dangers would have ended. But, indeed, it was far otherwise, and there were still great troubles in store for them. Little Ann became very ill. A medical man, who had been called in, pronounced her to be suffering from itch, and rubbed her with sulphur.

Crossing to Wales

It was Mrs Jones's intention to join her mother Mrs Irwin, then living at Hatfield near Doncaster, in Yorkshire. Mrs Jones and the children left Dublin by a packet (a ferry) which, owing to the disturbed state of the country, was crowded to excess. It was so old and leaky that, in spite of all hands being employed at the pumps, the water could not be kept out of the cabins. The mother sat up to her knees in water, with little Ann on her lap. She took what care she could of her other children, expecting every moment to go down. The scene of confusion around her was dreadful; some were praying, while others were drinking and cursing. Amongst the sea stores some bottles of brandy had been broken and had saturated her dress, and this probably saved her from cold. The dress was a black muslin one, the only one she had; it was the same dress in which she had escaped from her home on 23 August. They reached land at Parkgate, in Wales.

The miseries of the voyage nearly proved fatal to little Ann. The effect of cold, after the treatment with sulphur, almost cost her her life, especially as her illness proved to be chicken-pox. The group made their way to Chester, partly by the Bridgewater canal, and were detained there several weeks because of Ann's illness. I will quote some of a letter which Mrs Jones wrote to her husband from Chester, dated 10 November:

My dearest Bob,

You will be astonished you did not hear from me before this, and you will wonder at my not having got farther than Chester. I was not able, and had not spirit to write. As I could not give you a satisfactory account of us, I thought it better to be silent. Our dear little Ann has been very ill. I hope in God she is now out of danger.

Crinus left us on board the Dartmouth at six o'clock on Monday, and all went well till we got to the Bar. I undressed the three older children and put them to bed, but sat up and nursed little Ann. The wind and tide were high, and the vessel was in such a bad state that, when the waves washed over her, the water poured into the cabins, and everyone was ill and wet to the skin. But for Murry, my sister's maid, the three girls would have been lost.

The rigging was so rotten that it could hardly bear pulling, and we lost one of the sails, and were nearly gone, but the only thing that saved us was the fair wind. What a night I passed. All our clothes were wet, and our trunks full of water. Captain Edwards, who was a very civil man, when he knew we were all safe, said that if he had known the situation of the vessel he would not have ventured his life in her. (He is captain of the Prince of Wales. The owner of the vessel was sick.)

We landed at Pargate at three o'clock, and I found myself and the children so ill I could not proceed. Ann continued very ill, her skin perfectly crimson and very hot. We had a restless, bad night at Pargate, and we got here the next day. Ann was all swelled, and her head so much so that she could only partly open one eye. I had a letter from Mrs O'Hara to a Mrs Venables, so I sent my compliments and begged she would send a physician; and she did so, a Mr Ogle, who seems a clever man.

He immediately put Ann into a hot bath and, as that succeeded, he blistered her back to rouse her and relieve the oppression. At night she had another hot bath, and the redness on her skin continued and spots came out, some of them as big as a sixpence. On Friday there was an alteration in the colour of her back, it being purple, and he feared mortification. This morning he said he hoped she would do. We cannot give her more than a teaspoonful of liquid at a time, her stomach is so weak, and her support is principally wine. I take bark in a glass of mulled wine three times a day, but I have not had my clothes off since I came here. Please God we shall be able to leave in a few days.

I am at the hotel, and Mrs Jackson is very civil, and has given me old linen, but I am afraid my pocket will pay. Ann was too ill even to move into lodgings. I don't want money, as

I have forty pounds, and thirty pound notes on Manchester. Mr Ogle says she had the chicken-pox, and that the cold, wet, and fatigue drove it in and caused it to turn purple. I am astonished I did not kill the other children, for I am now certain that they had the chicken-pox in Dublin, and I had them rubbed with sulphur.

I shall write again in a few days. I hope to find a packet of letters at Hatfield. Don't be uneasy about me, I am as strong as a horse. God bless you, my dearest Bob, and preserve our dear little one to her sorrowing mother, E Jones.

This letter was addressed to Robert Jones, Esq, Ardnaree, Ballina. Postage one shilling and sixpence. Chester post mark, 13 November, 1798.

Mrs Jones was detained a long time at Chester, but she had the pleasure of meeting some old friends there. One such was Mrs Bruin, who had been a Miss Knox of Nappa. They all sympathised with her in her trouble; even the landlady of the hotel, whose name happened to be Jones, showed kindness to her.

At last Mrs Jones was obliged to communicate her distress to her anxious mother, as the long delay had almost exhausted her finances. Mrs Irwin immediately sent her confidential servant, Richard Farrel, to her assistance. With her delicate children Mrs Jones could only travel slowly, so another fortnight elapsed before they arrived at Doncaster.

As they drove up to the inn at Doncaster, Farrel recognized Mr Agar's coachman standing at the door. Mr Agar was Mrs Jones's brother-in-law. Farrel learnt from the coachman that his master was in town on business, and was just sitting down with some gentlemen to dinner. As soon as he received a message about the arrival of the forlorn travellers, Mr Agar rushed out to welcome them. He helped them out of their carriage and took Ann in his arms, opining as he did so, 'What a blessing it would be, my dear Bess, if it would please God to take the poor little thing'.

Mrs Jones's relief at this providential meeting with her brother-in-law can be better felt than described. She had spent her last sixpence. Mr Agar returned to his friends, and told them of the sad plight of the poor fugitives. The gentlemen immediately sent them a couple of chickens from the table, together with other substantial comforts. After they were rested and refreshed, Mr Agar forwarded them in his carriage to Hatfield, where they happily reached their journey's end, to the unbounded joy of their relations. Their journey had taken over three months. Their joy was crowned by the complete recovery of little Ann.

Amy Chamberlain's Story

There were many other members of the family, beside Mrs Jones, who had strange and sad experiences in these troubled times. The following one was related by Amy Chamberlain. (She married Crinus Irwin, who was afterwards Archdeacon of Ossory.)

Amy accompanied her mother, and her father Judge Chamberlain, and Judge Downes, who were going to hold a special commission in the south of Ireland, and were to be guests of Colonel Pennyfather. They slept at Naas. While walking in the garden the next morning, they saw a great crowd. On enquiring the cause of it, they were told 'watering cucumbers'. However, after they observed that the men were digging pike heads out of a hole, they lost no time in setting off for Kilcullen. From Kilcullen they were proceeding up a steep hill when Mrs Chamberlain put her head out of the window and saw the pikes glittering on the top of the hill. They held a consultation and decided that, as holding His Majesty's commission, they ought to proceed. But shortly an immense body of armed men became visible and it seemed folly to go on.

Judge Chamberlain ordered the postillions to return. They refused to do so until the judges pointed pistols out of the carriage windows, and vowed that they would blow their brains out unless they did. The post boys said they would break the pole in turning, and they did break it, but they managed to gallop back to Kilcullen. The rebels came after them, and even piked the carriage. Luckily, the military came to their assistance, and helped them to obtain entrance into a castle, in which they found shelter with a friend, Major Ferkell.

They were escorted back to Dublin, but were stopped on the road by a party of soldiers who were drawn across it, and were on the point of shooting some rebels. They requested permission to pass before the executions took place. As the request was not granted, they were obliged to witness the executions. On their arrival in Dublin the military escort was lodged in their house in Harcourt Street. A week later, after being well fed, these men of the escort all joined the rebels.

One more word about the French whose inroad into Ireland raised the spirit of rebellion and caused so many sorrows. General Humbert with his army left Castlebar on 3 September 1798, marching by Swineford to Tubbercurry, and then on to Collooney, missing the coast road, and Tanrago. At Collooney, Colonel Vereker and a small body of militia made a gallant stand against the French, but were defeated, after an hour's fight, by superior numbers. Colonel Vereker (later Lord Gort) returned to Sligo. Billy O'Beirne helped him over the high wall around Markree, but, not being able to climb through lameness, Billy was taken prisoner (note 4).

The French pushed on to Longford where Dean Burke, the Bishop of Waterford, entertained the French general. On arriving at the village of Ballinamuck, they were surrounded by an overwhelming force collected from all parts by Lord Cornwallis. Humbert then surrendered at discretion, leaving his Irish auxiliaries to the tender mercies of the enemy. The French were treated well, but these others received no quarter.

This French army returned to their country, but another attempt was made afterwards to land in Lough Swilly, which an English fleet under Admiral Warren intercepted. On board were some expatriated Irish, amongst them Wolfe Tone, the leader of the rebellion. He was sent to prison in Dublin, and committed suicide anticipating the sentence of a court martial.

Mr Jones

Ireland continued in a disturbed state after the fighting was over. Little heed was paid to law and order, and Mr Jones's family could not return. However, it was a considerable time before Mr Jones could arrange his affairs to follow them to England. Indeed, it was a while before he heard anything of them, nor could Mrs Jones obtain information of her husband. He took cold sleeping in a sod fort at Sligo, which brought on deafness from which he never recovered. He was overturned in a coach near Belturbet, was much hurt, and for a spell was laid up at Enniskillen, being attended by a doctor.

Another time when the spark of rebellion was again kindling, there was a combination to stop and plunder all the mails. It was well known that the magistrates received information they were sending to the government. A meditated attack came to the attention of certain Sligo people, and Mr Jones, who was obliged to go to Dublin, was the only passenger. The guard said, 'Have you pistols? Shall I fire, or give up the bags?'

'No use firing on forty or fifty men', replied Mr Jones. 'Put out the lamps, and get into the coach with me, mischance of being overturned.' The rebels let it pass, not thinking that, without guards or lights, it was the mail. The Sligo was the only mail that reached Dublin that night.

Besides rebels, the country was infested with bands of robbers. Mr Jones had been to a fair and sold some cattle, and was returning with his herdsman, who carried the money on horseback in a portmanteau. Mr Jones followed with his pistols ready cocked. They saw in the mist a troop of men coming through Barnes Gap and they prepared for an attack of robbers, but they were surprised and comforted by finding that it was a group of police who were in search of the plunderers.

After the union of Ireland with Great Britain in 1801, when all the family were together again and living in York, the Joneses had five more children (note 5). Mr Jones did not live long after this time, but his wife did.

These notes were chiefly collected by Elizabeth Agar, Mrs Jones's niece, who was born in 1796 and died in 1881, aged eighty-five years.

(There is another story about women and children in a time of war in Part Four of this book.)

Appendix to Part Two

Notes for Maria Barstow, My Grandmother

1. Thomas Barstow of Fulford, 1712-1786, married first in 1738, Everilda, daughter of R Hewan or Newman of Meldrake Hall; second in 1752, Judith, daughter of W Stainforth, rector of Simonburne; and third in 1777, Grace (née Dickons), widow of Alderman Blanchard of Beverley. Thomas was elected sheriff of York in 1762, and lord mayor in 1778. The Gazette records that 'Thomas Barstow, the lord mayor, after attending the Minster service in state, not only entertained all the corporation, but also his own friends with great elegance'. It mentions that he received the thanks of the prisoners confined in York Castle for gifts of potatoes he made between 1774 and 1777.

The Barstows were merchants of York. A Michael Barstow acquired Holme House in 1663, and married Alice, who founded Barstow's Hospital in 1702. Their son, Nathan, married Ellen Favour. And their son Benjamin, was the father of Thomas Barstow, as above. Thomas imported timber.

2. Archibald Maclean, 1736-1810, was a descendant of the Macleans of Duart on the Isle of Mull, Scotland. He went to Danzig in 1753 as a trader. He died at Königsberg (Kaliningrad, in Russia, today). His wife's father, John Simpson of York, was Mayor of Memel (Klaipeda, in Lithuania, today). John Maclean, and Anna Maclean who married Andreas Brahl, appear to be of the same family. For descendants of the son Archibald, see Kogge, D and Spencer, A, *Zur Geschichte der Familie Mathis, Tagebucher und Erinnerungen*, Norderstedt, 2000. Some of the Macleans left Scotland after the defeat of the Stewart cause in the 1745 uprising. They went to France, Poland, USA, Canada; later, Australia.

3. Cornelius von Almonde was the son of Cornelius von Almonde of Hohen Tor, Danzig, and his wife, Anna (née Eggerath). Their children were Anna, Magdalena, Cornelius, Maria, Hermann. The ancestral home of this Mennonite family was Holland.

4. Elizabeth, 1810-1893, married in 1840 (at Munich, Bavaria), Charles Wiltshire of the Frythe, Welwyn, Hertfordshire.

Emily, born 1814, married Hippolyte von Klenze, Bavarian Guards.

Everilda married Gustav von Ascheberg, Prussian Guards.

Mary married Maximilian von Gumppenberg, Bavarian Guards.

5. William, born 1815, was for long a member of the Prussian Cabinet, and became His Excellency, the Ober President of Posen. He died in 1892, full of years and honours. (He had five sons; and a daughter, Helene, who married General Alexander von Seydlitz-Kurzbach, commandant of Danzig.)

Carl, born 1817, was a doctor. He died in Danzig.

Frantz of Marksdorff, born 1820, was a member of the Reichstag.

Mary married Dr Wilhelm Baum, and had a family.

Augusta Emily married her cousin, His Excellency Lachlan Maclean, a member of the Prussian Cabinet, and had a son and two daughters.

6. Thomas, 1818-1889, MA Trinity College, Cambridge, stipendiary magistrate, married Mary Leader, and did not have children.

Robert, born 1820, Jesus College, Cambridge, stipendiary magistrate, died in New Zealand 1890, married Jane Hulme, and had children.

Mary Anne, 1822-1882, died unmarried.

Michael, 1824-1866, M A Christ Church, Oxford, perpetual curate, married Louisa Ingram, and had children; one of them, Montague, married Baroness Orczy, author of *The Scarlet Pimpernel*.

George, 1826-1868, a colonel in the army, married Annie Strahan, and did not have children.

Elizabeth, 1827-1926, died unmarried.

Lewis, 1829-1900, a captain in the navy, married Mary Ann Agar, and did not have children.

Frances Amy, 1831-1922, died unmarried.

Charles, 1834-1890, died unmarried.

John, 1836-1899, a major in the army, died unmarried.

Henry, 1838-1922, in the Indian civil service, married Cecilia Baillie, and had children; one of them was Sir George Lewis Barstow. (Four of these children were sent to England for six years, without their parents, when they were seven, five, four, and three years old.)

Matilda, 1842-1918, married Thomas W Webber, and had children.

Flora, 1845-1910, died unmarried.

Fuller details are available in the Barstow family tree.

7. Thomas Barstow, born 1745, second son of Thomas Barstow of Fulford, married Mary Ann Pickard of Colchester in 1778, and did not have children. He was Fellow of Clare Hall, Cambridge. In a pocket book he wrote: 'I wish to be buried about the middle of the north side of Aldham Church yard.' Written in another hand is: 'Thomas Barstow MA, 49 years rector of this parish ob. May 6th 1820, aged 75.' Some lines of verse are included. His wife survived him nine years.

8. The Maclean children were Archibald, Lachlan, Anne, Emily and Flora. Archibald married Erna von Tiesenhausen. Archibald or his son (Archibald) of Czerbienczin Castle attended a gathering of the Maclean clan at Duart Castle, Isle of Mull, Scotland, in 1912. Lachlan (of Roschau) married von

Tiedeman. Anne married von Mellentine. Emily married Glüer.

Marie Heinrichsdorff married in 1847, Adalbert von der Marwitz of Wundichow, Pomerania, and had four sons and five daughters:

Adalbert, 1850-70, a lieutenant in the guards, killed at St Privat. He went into battle carrying the colours and was shot in command of his regiment, after the retreat was sounded.

Carl, 1854-72.

George, a major in the Second Grand Regiment, married Helena von Kameke. (He was a General in World War 1.)

Fritz married Margaretha, daughter of Count Flemming.

Celestine married von Brockhusen.

Marie married von Zitzewitz.

Herta married Major von Waldow.

Anna married von Eisenhart-Rothe.

Katie married von der Osten.

Notes for 'Little Ann'

1. Aunt Letty was Mrs Webber, the widow of Capt Thomas Webber who died fighting for Frederick the Great of Prussia. She was the mother of Daniel Webb Webber QC, and MP for Armagh. She was born Letitia Irwin.

2. Robert Browne was familiarly known as Bob Browne, and he married the beautiful Peggy Irwin (sister of Letitia), who, as wits said, 'had been so often the toast of the country', that she was at last 'toasted Browne'. Browne was the heir of the Monteagle title; however, being advanced in years before he

could have inherited, and having only one daughter, he declined to take it up. His sister Catherine (the second wife of Vaughan Jones) was the mother of Mr Bob Jones in the story 'Little Ann'. The Jones family were descendants of Sir Theophilus Jones, a Cromwellian general.

3. Col John Irwin was born in 1680, served under Marlborough, and was ADC to the Prince of Hesse. He married first Lady Mary Dilkes (née O'Brien), the daughter of the first Earl of Inchiquin, who had married twice before. They had a son, (also John), who died fighting at Cartagena, Colombia in 1741, at the age of twenty-one years, according to Thomas W Webber. (As Lady Mary's first son, Henry Boyle, was born in 1682, this seems unlikely. Irwin had probably married her to advance his career.) Col John Irwin married secondly Susannah Cadden, and had Lewis, Letitia, and Margaret (Peggy). Lewis, who married Elizabeth Harrison, was the father of Mrs Elizabeth Jones in the story 'Little Ann'.

4. Billy O'Beirne married Charlotte, the sister of Daniel Webb Webber.

5. The Joneses had two sons and seven daughters altogether: Robert Jones of 'Fortland', County Sligo, Lewis, Catherine, Margaret, Elizabeth, Ann, Beatrice, Frances and Amy. Of the children that married, Robert married Margaret Sapte; Catherine married in 1821, the Revd George Trulock, sometime archdeacon of Killala; Ann married in 1817, Thomas Barstow of York; Amy married J Ormsby of Sligo; and Lewis married Catherine Dixon in Canada in 1845.

PART THREE

THE KELLY SISTERS OF IRELAND

Based on the memoirs of Elizabeth Wingfield and Caroline Kelly.

Characters, for reference:

Mrs Tighe, mother of Mrs Kelly.

Mr and Mrs Kelly: They were the Revd Thomas Kelly and his wife Elizabeth, née Tighe.

They had four daughters: Sarah ('Sally'), Frances ('Fanny'), Elizabeth ('Bessy'), and Caroline ('Cassy'); and three sons (Tom, Edmund, and William).

Fanny Kelly married the Revd Thomas Webber, and had William ('Willy'), Thomas ('Tommy'), Charles ('Charley'), and another son.

(They lived at Avoca, County Wicklow.)

Elizabeth Kelly ('Bessy') married the Revd Hon. William Wingfield, and had Elizabeth ('Bena'), Richard ('Dicky'), and other children.

Mr Kelly's married sisters had the surnames Cosby, Pigott, and St George.

Mrs Kelly's brothers and sister had the surnames Tighe, and Hamilton.

Elizabeth Wingfield and Caroline Kelly wrote memoirs interspersed with poems, and there are family letters. An unpublished poem by the children's aunt, the poet Mary Tighe, is in an appendix at the end of Part Three.

Rossana or Rossanagh House. The home of the Tighes in county Wicklow. The house was later reduced in size. (Reproduction, Desmond Guiness.)

Kellyville or Kellavil. The home of the Kellys and the Webbers near Athy. The house was later demolished. (Private collection, Australia.)

A Servant Girl with Bare Feet, 'January 1821'. Drawing by one of the older Kelly girls (private collection, Australia).

Drawing of an Unknown Man. Probably the girls' brother Tom. (Private collection, Australia.)

The Elderly Mrs Kelly and Mr Kelly. Drawings by Fanny Webber (nee Kelly) 1846.

The Early Years

The young Kelly sisters resided sometimes at Kellyville, near Athy, the home of their paternal grandfather while he was alive, and sometimes at Rossana, in County Wicklow, the ancient and beautiful abode of their maternal grandmother Mrs Tighe. There were seven children, and four were girls: Sally was born in 1803, Fanny in 1805, Elizabeth in 1807, and Caroline in 1816. The names of the older two were really Sarah and Frances; the younger two were often called Bessy and Cassy. They always lived as part of a larger family group.

A painting of the Kelly children playing in the drawing room at Rossana depicts the three oldest girls, with dark or golden-brown cropped hair, wearing white high-waisted Regency dresses, low cut and calf length, the short sleeves gathered at the top. There are books, folios of drawings, an organ, sculptured busts, and a dog. Outside the window, which has Grecian style columns and heavy, red curtains, sheep are grazing under large, leafy trees.

Caroline was an afterthought in the family, too young to be in the painting. When she was a child, the older children often considered her to be a bit in their way. She said, however, she was not the Cinderella of the family. She generally got what she wanted, and could not remember being punished. Once, for being wilful, she was taken to sit on her father's knee, where she fell asleep.

Mr Kelly was a nonconformist minister, who preached the Gospel in farm houses or halls, or wherever he could gather a congregation. For this he suffered disapprobation, and was banned from preaching in the churches. It was a time of religious revival. He believed that Christians were justified by faith alone, and that the authority for their beliefs and practice lay in the Bible. He wrote hymns, and the saying of prayers and the singing of hymns were regular practices of the family at home.

But Mrs Kelly chose to bring up the children in the Church of England, and Mr Kelly deferred to her wishes even though he had left that church. Mrs Kelly was simple and unpretentious in her piety; she abhorred cant of all kinds and only used religious language at appropriate times. She felt that the service in the established church was so beautiful and scriptural that it would be wrong to deprive her children of it.

Bessy remembered that when she was a small child the whole family went on a missionary journey to London. It was a serious undertaking with such a large family. They travelled slowly through Wales, stopping to see every object of interest, and collecting congregations to preach to. Mr Kelly was to preach a missionary sermon in London. Many people came to visit him. The Bible Society had just begun.

Educating the Children

Mrs Kelly was so well educated that she was often dissatisfied with governesses and teachers. She hired a governess to instruct her first daughter, Sally, but then found it did not suit the child's character, and decided not to persevere with it. So she undertook to educate the girls herself, with the help, now and then, of other teachers. She taught them to draw and paint, and to play the harp. She seldom even dined out at the time she was educating the children.

Mrs Kelly and her sister Mrs Hamilton were educated in that manner by their mother Mrs Tighe, mainly in the subjects of religion, dead and living languages, the best authors, writing, music, and art. Mrs Tighe had taken them to live for eight years, except for the holidays, in a small house in Harrow, England; at the same time, she was protecting her son from some of the dangers of Harrow School, which he attended.

Mr Kelly educated not only the boys, but all the children. He never wasted a minute, and regularly taught them dates and events in history at the breakfast table. He was a scholar in the Scriptures and languages; he studied the Scriptures in Arabic, Hebrew and Syriac. He was well read in politics, in which he took the Whig view, and in history and literature. He took a keen interest in science and mathematics.

However, the Kellys believed in a progressive education for children, in which they would learn by more natural and enjoyable methods than were usual in the schoolroom: in play, in conversation with their family and friends, and from nature in the outdoors. Bessy wrote later:

I do not think that it would be possible for happiness on earth to be greater than ours was, during our education. This is a time which most young people look back upon as one of toil and tyranny, from which they are delighted to escape when the governess takes her departure. But learning was made a pleasure to us. The sight of our beloved parents toiling to fulfil every duty towards us, to the utmost of their powers of mind and body, gave us a motive of self exertion which we could never have had under the teaching of others.

Although there was great care in the choice of companions for us, we were allowed to associate with those cousins who promoted improvement of every kind, which was the case with many. The mutual enjoyment we had from being together gave us a lawful stimulant for industry. Many a happy party we made together, each of us with a sketching bag over our shoulders, up the mountains or down the valleys, to the woods or to the sea, in search of subjects for our pencils. Mr Peter la Touche allowed us to spend days together at his shooting lodge, by the side of a beautiful lake. The Hamiltons, who were like one family with us, were our companions on these occasions. The brothers with guns and fishing rods, and we girls with sketch books and pencils, headed by our dear parents, used to set off with as much of joyousness and innocent lightheartedness as unrepressed youthful spirits could exhibit.

Our parents partook of our enjoyments and entered into them with a real zest, for our sakes. But it is remarkable that on these happy occasions, and upon all our journeys, our father never seemed to spend a moment upon mere recreation. He always carried a box with him containing his writing materials and a number of books, so that wherever he was, his studies were carried on as regularly as if he were in his own home. Nothing ever interfered with his hours of devotion and

Bible reading. His hymns were generally composed while walking with us; I have seen him constantly stopping to put down verses in a large pocket book which he always carried with him. His power of abstraction was very remarkable, but it appeared to him to be no difficulty to turn in a moment from the deepest subject of contemplation to play in a most lively manner with a child, and take an interest in a flower or drawing, or any subject in which his children were engaged.

Dancing, singing songs, and reading novels were decidedly prohibited in our education, but every other accomplishment might be cultivated to the highest we could attain to. I can from experience say that I found the value of those prohibitions: in securing a taste for the highest style of music, and in forming a habit of solid reading which can seldom be attained after the mind has become enervated by light and frivolous books, and a false view of what life ought to be, and the wrong motives for action.

When I have heard some friends express their feelings upon the subject of their upbringing, I have felt how grateful I should be for all that was done, not only for my happiness, but to draw out every right feeling, and repress every wrong, more by having an example set than by any compulsory measure.

And yet Caroline wrote, 'It was too desultory a life to be called a good education'. Her perspective was different because of the age gap.

Maria Spilsbury Taylor

The children's grandmother Mrs Tighe engaged an accomplished artist, Maria Spilsbury Taylor, to teach drawing and painting to the Kelly girls and their Hamilton cousins; she also taught them to play the piano and the organ. Mrs Taylor was the daughter of a Mr Spilsbury who had taught Mrs Kelly to draw in London before she married. When Mrs Taylor married and had children, the whole family stayed at Rossana. She painted individual portraits or group scenes of all the children. She painted little Caroline, with her golden-brown hair and blue eyes, carrying flowers.

Bessy wrote of the painting room at Rossana: 'It had a large, cheerful, sunny bow, and a closet filled with all the requisites for painting, modelling, carving, and any odd and dirty work in which we wished to expend our energies, and earnings, even a printing press and types. In short, it was exactly the room to form young minds to be busy and happy, and prevent a drawing room life of working worsted and light reading.'

The oldest girl, Sally, showed particular promise in art and music. She made drawings and washes in the fields of portraiture, landscape, everyday life, and copies of Renaissance paintings. The children collected drawings and engravings to work from: religious subjects, street scenes, rustic genre, romantic drawings of horses like those of Géricault, or naturalistic farm animals like those of Morland. They had books of small figures to copy and put in a work of landscape. One of them drew a servant girl with bare feet. One drew a little girl playing with a dog, which could be Caroline; she wore a long-sleeved dress with a ruff at the neck, and a white pinafore over it.

The Grandmother

The children went to Rossana for part of every year, and were welcomed at the door with a fond embrace from their small but stately grandmother, dressed in the black clothes of mourning. The sable garb and widow's cap, with a train flowing behind, enhanced the children's respect and admiration for her. This was the apparel she assumed for all the forty years remaining to her after the demise of her husband.

Mrs Tighe was a Methodist, and a friend of the Wesleys; she had sponsored John Wesley, the Methodist preacher, to come to Ireland to preach. She had established a training school for servants, who were mainly orphans, and was the guardian of some girls who were orphans. She also ran a Sunday school in her house. Only when Mrs Tighe was on her death-bed did Fanny take over the teaching of the Sunday school, using her grandmother's written notes.

'By Grace We Are Saved, and That not of Ourselves. It Is the Gift.' (The Reverend Thomas Kelly)

By the time the children were no longer in their infancy, except for Caroline, there was a great change and renewal in the Protestant church in Ireland, especially through the preaching of the Bishop of Cashel, and in the Bible Society in Wicklow. Mr Kelly was no longer an outcast for his religious preaching; instead, he was acclaimed as an orator of such eloquent and touching speeches that they made ladies cry. Old Mrs Fitzgerald said, 'He looked like an angel speaking from Heaven'. The three oldest girls attended religious breakfasts in the great hall at Rossana, which were held for the purpose of conversing on religious subjects. Hymns were sung and hearts were pledged to Jesus. Two ladies in Dublin, Miss Kiernan and Mrs Shirley, were the first to host these religious breakfasts.

Bessy was only fourteen when she was invited with her family to a religious breakfast to meet Lord Powerscourt, who had been greatly impressed by Mr Kelly's preaching. Powerscourt, the home of the Wingfields, was next door to Rossana. The three pretty Kelly girls sang their father's hymn, *We'll Sing of the Shepherd that Died*, which Sally accompanied on the organ.

English and continental travellers and missionaries, and pastors of the Swiss and French reformed churches, now came to visit them; the Sultan of Crimea was brought by Mr and Mrs John Synge. They were invited to breakfast, and the girls sang hymns for them. Their father was delighted to receive Christians of all denominations into his house, wrote Bessy, especially missionaries who had forsaken all to tell the glad tidings of salvation in the dark places of the earth. A hymn which showed how deeply he sympathised with them in their work and trials, began:

> *Is the name of Jesus precious,*
> *Does his love your spirits cheer,*
> *Do you find him kind and gracious,*
> *Still removing doubt and fear?*
> *Think that what he is to you,*
> *Such he'll be to others too.*

Caroline

Caroline slept in a long room upstairs at Rossana, called the library, which was used as her nursery. It had bookshelves all round it full of old books. The first thing she could remember was sitting in the nursery and saying, 'I am three years old today'. Her nurse, Hannah Boyle from Bristol, had been with them since Fanny was a baby, except for ten years when she was married. She would stay with them until she died. She was one of the old-fashioned family servants.

Caroline learnt to read when she was three years old, and Hannah taught her some spelling. She said she mainly learnt to spell by asking people how words were spelt, and picked up reading by reading over and over any books that came her way; one of them was Knox's *Elegant Extracts*, a book of poetry for young people. She was put on the table to read the newspaper aloud to Mr Kelly, very much to the amusement of his friends. Hannah and she accompanied Mr Kelly every fortnight on his visits to his church in Dublin.

Caroline was a lonely child whose friend, her own age, was her cousin Freddy Hamilton, or his sister who was four years older, when their two families stayed together at Rossana. Freddy took two lumps of sugar once when they were in a shop, and when they left, Caroline told her father what he did. Mr Kelly took them back to the shop, and made Freddy return the sugar. Freddy would always 'twit' her thereafter for being a tell-tale, Caroline wrote.

At last the children's grandmother died, and they witnessed death for the first time. It had a peculiarly solemnising effect as they were taken, one by one, to give her a last kiss. On the grey winter morning from upstairs they saw the black hearse, with plumes, mutes and outriders, followed by crowds of carriages, disappear among the tall trees as they ascended the avenue. The burial was at Glenealy where Mrs Tighe had built a church for her son. They mourned, wrote Bessy, but not as those without hope.

Leaving Rossana

Now they would have to leave Rossana, where the music of running water lulled them to sleep, and the shade of the chestnut bowers cooled them in the summer's heat. Bessy wrote that they 'ran from spot to spot to take a last look and gather a last relic of a leaf or flower from each long-loved childish haunt, sketching each peep of house and tree' that they would no longer call their own. They would no longer mount the sides of Carrick Muriley, and joyously and hungrily return to dinner in the cottage in Glenealy woods, or spend a day on the flat 'murrough' of Wicklow to bathe and enjoy the sea breezes.

The sisters liked to quote from their Aunt Hamilton's poem, written in the bow-room at Rossana the last time she inhabited it:

Friends once so dearly loved, I scarce can tell
Which of you yet survive, or where ye dwell.
Whether ye mourn like me, departed hours,
Recalling to your minds these chestnut bowers
And their loved mistress who, alas! no more
Shall welcome to her hospitable door,
Not the rich only, but the good and poor.
Chestnut revered! so lately wont to spread
O'er the clear stream, thy tall and vigorous head,
How many truant boys have gaily played,
Screened from detection's eye, beneath thy shade.

The girls' uncle, William Tighe, wrote a poem about the childish enjoyments in the river, and playing in the old yew tree.

Kellyville

The family now dwelt only at Kellyville, which was situated in a relatively flat and uninteresting landscape about four miles west of Athy. A curved driveway led to a plain-looking two-storey house with five windows frontage, which was extended at the back. Caroline could remember sleeping in her mother's room, in a little bed beside her. There was a long library, later used as the children's schoolroom.

The children's education continued at home. Mrs Kelly wanted to keep her daughters away from the society of the world, one in which ladies would often dine out and play cards till late at night. While she feared that they might grow up without acquaintances, she hoped a society would form that suited her ideas when they were ready to enter into it. The whole powers of her mind and body were exerted to inspire the girls with a love of useful employments which could make them independent of external circumstances. They saw their Cosby cousins at Stradbally Hall three miles away, almost daily, but only at the time allowed for recreation. All knew the hours for study, and that interruption was not permitted.

Their older brother, Tom, had already completed his degree at Trinity College, Dublin, and was learning to take charge of the estate. Caroline learnt to write from Bessy; Fanny taught her the piano; her mother taught her Latin, and her father a little logic. She said her mother taught her most things she knew. Mr Kelly got up at 7 am, and rang the prayer bell at 8.45 for prayers before breakfast. He spent at least six hours a day in study and devotion, and periods in teaching, listening to music, writing letters, and attending to business. Dinner was at 4 pm, and was usually mutton and potatoes, and a 'sweet thing'. Tea was at 7 pm, and family prayers at 10 pm, before bed.

Sometimes their St George cousins came to stay. Their mother, who had been Harriet Kelly, had died only a few years after marriage. One stormy night in winter when Fanny St George had whooping cough, some linen, put to air on a 'horse' in front of a fire, caught alight. Fanny Kelly noticed the smoke, and tried to drag Caroline out of her bed, but she only burrowed deeper into the bedclothes. Caroline was dreaming that a corner of the house blew over, and that someone was carrying her down the stairs. Fanny rushed down to where the family was at prayers. She quietly said, 'Papa, I think the house is on fire'. It was just in time to save the house, as there was little water.

Mrs Kelly was so taken up with the older girls that Mr Kelly took pity on Caroline, and often took her out to walk with him. One time when she went with him to Athy, a shopkeeper gave her some figs. She decided not to eat them until she got home, but on the way she could not help eating one. She then could not decide whether she had changed her mind, or broken a promise to herself. After tea, when Mrs Kelly had dropped off to sleep in her chair, and Caroline was sitting on a footstool at her feet, she woke her mother up to tell her how she had broken a promise. But she was not sure if her mother appreciated the admission, after being woken up.

Caroline, Hannah and Mr Kelly sometimes stayed in Dublin from Saturday to Monday. They would look in the bookshops; books were Caroline's companions. But she was too shy to give her name to Mr Curry in Sackville Street, who wished to make her a present of a book, and wanted to write her name in the front. She would go to hear her father preach at his chapel; on one occasion, she lay down on the church pew and fell asleep. Her father couldn't see her and suffered the greatest anxiety for the remainder of the address, thinking that she had wandered out.

The family rented a house in Dublin for some months every year so that the children could learn from the best masters; Caroline was learning Greek. A French lady, Madame de Bavière, stayed at Kellyville for a year so that they could all learn conversational French. Caroline had her first experience of working for charitable purposes at the age of eight. She made pincushions and needlebooks, and sold them to friends and visitors for half a crown in support of the Irish Society. At a later time Caroline went to a school in Dublin run by the Mademoiselles de Bavière. She said her sisters teased her about being sent to school.

Mr Kelly had written a book called *Andrew Dunn* about a child who was converted from the Catholic to the Protestant faith. Some Catholic women went to Aunt Hamilton's house and talked to her daughter about Catholicism, and the daughter lent them a copy of *Andrew Dunn*. She heard later that one of them had become a Protestant. This was not the end of the story. Mrs Kelly and the girls were walking in Dublin once, and they took shelter from rain in a Catholic chapel. They were surprised to find some children in a classroom who were reading a revised version of Mr Kelly's book. In the revised book Andrew Dunn was converted from the Protestant to the Catholic faith.

Sally

The oldest daughter, Sally, had grown up. She had dark blue eyes, black hair, a rather tall, plump but fine figure, and pretty hands and feet. She was greatly admired, an Irish beauty, and had caught the attention of young men. She never stepped from the carriage without all eyes gazing at her, wrote Bessy, which made her downcast eyelids cover more closely what others wished to see. All the girls painted and drew, and wrote poetry, but Sally was particularly talented and industrious. Their parents loved all the children equally, but had they been more proud of Sally, the girls declared, no jealousy would have been felt because she deserved it. Mrs Kelly often said that Sally's ideas were high, but that she far surpassed them. She was the idol of her parents.

Bessy wrote: 'Professional artists have said, had she been one of them they would have envied her, and musicians have said the same. Her teachers delighted to instruct her. Dear Papa used to visit her as a refreshment after teaching his boys, and gaze with pride and joy on her designs, sketched the evening before, and the following day wrought into a picture, and finished in a style peculiar to herself.'

Sally soon turned her talents to account and became very productive in making drawings to sell for the sake of feeding the hungry and clothing the naked. For that purpose, wrote Bessy, she did not scruple in spending a great deal of time at an occupation which otherwise she might have thought wrong. While finishing her designs she was mentally employed, and worked better, if Fanny or Bessy read to her and held discussions at the same time. With her sisters or cousins Sally was merry and witty, but otherwise her manners in company were retiring, and it arose from a genuine modesty and humility. Instead of being raised in her own estimation by praise, it seemed to give her pain.

She made a picture of the three oldest Kelly girls, in pencil and wash; herself as the artist, Fanny with their mother's harp, and Bessy holding a stringed instrument. The girls wore floor-length Regency dresses with puffed sleeves, and their long hair was drawn back and let to fall in elaborate curls. Sally drew other portraits.

'The Afflictions of the Lord's People Are Doubtless Intended by Him to Have a Salutary Effect Upon Their Minds.' (The Reverend Thomas Kelly)

The Kellys passed a more than usually cheerful winter, but Mrs Kelly often said, 'I should be too glad if I could stop time as it is, but I see a dark cloud hanging over us'. When Lady Powerscourt visited them, she said, 'How frightfully happy dear Mr Kelly is, so many years married and not one trial. When a blade is ripe, the Lord of the harvest will say to the reaper, "Thrust in thy sickle".' Many members of her family had died young. Bessy felt a cold shudder pass over her, as she thought of who was nearest being ripe.

In the midst of their happiness, Sally developed a cough that would not go away. At first no one paid much attention to it; they were all recovering from influenza, and there was no doctor within easy reach of Kellyville. Just at that time Mr Kelly purchased Rathmines Castle in Dublin so that they would be near the two younger boys, Edmund and William, who had started at Trinity College; and so that the girls, who were not to go into the world, might see their friends more often. It would be more satisfactory for Mr Kelly to hold his congregations there; he said, 'Let us have large rooms to hold a large congregation, not that we may have dancing, as some would think'. The oldest son, Tom, was to stay at Kellyville and farm.

It was then that they sought the attention of a physician for Sally, but it was too late. Her lungs were affected with tuberculosis, and there was no certain cure. It was not usual for people in their families to have tuberculosis, but an aunt, Mary Tighe, had died of it. Mary Tighe, who was a poet, used to visit the Kellys at home. She wrote for Sally:

Sweetest! if thy fairy hand
Culls for me the latest flowers...

May no tempest's sudden doom
Blast thy hope's fair nursery!

Mary Tighe may have infected Sally with tuberculosis.

Mrs Kelly was recommended to take her daughter on sea voyages for the summer, so they went on journeys to Clifton, to Cork, and to Scotland, and to visit the philanthropist and writer, Hannah More. After the summer, Sally was to be kept in a heated temperature, taking vapour baths. By the middle of the next winter, her condition had worsened. She sometimes made playful remarks to Bessy about how long her clothes would last. She was only twenty-six years old. Finally Mr Kelly understood her real danger, to which he had been blind because the progress of the disease had seemed so slight. Bessy wrote:

One night I met him coming from her room, with his hand stretched over his face and tears flowing fast. She had spoken to him herself, she had no longer a doubt, all restraint was gone. For a fortnight during which she grew weaker each day, she spoke to him freely and openly of her prospects through the merits of the atoning blood of Christ. For a time his grief seemed swallowed up in thankfulness. But the closing scene, how can I describe it? Papa had pictured a bright and glorious ending; he was not satisfied with what God had wrought. When bodily afflictions clouded sense, the agony of mind he suffered was beyond description.

I remained with her all the last night, as I was strong enough to lift her from the bed to the couch. It seemed as if the hitherto healthy frame was unwilling to part with the spirit. Once she threw her arms round my neck, and cried out, 'Oh that you may never suffer what I am suffering'. Consciousness seemed to decline as she grew weaker. I can see my father now, although so many years have passed, imploring for aid on his knees, with arms extended to heaven.

Fanny wrote the account of Sally's death:

After twenty-four hours of suffering we were all assembled round her bed. The breathing became less and less quick, till it ceased without a frown or look of pain upon that lovely brow. Mama raised her hand, and said with composure, 'This mortal shall put on immortality, this corruptible shall put on incorruption. She is the first fruits of our unceasing prayers; the Lord gave and the Lord hath taken away, shall we not give Him back His own?' Papa said, 'Is my lamb at rest?'. No doubt could be on the mind of any but that she was now safe, 'To be forever with her Saviour'.

Bessy continued:

That sorrowing father could not be comforted. Satan seemed to have pleasure in throwing doubts across his sensitive mind. He repeated over and over, while the psalm lay before him, 'Why art thou cast down?' Satan seemed to say, 'Thou hast comforted others, now comfort thyself'.

He had not known that his loved child was in the habit of expressing her thoughts and feelings in verse. This discovery brought comfort at last, as her hymns imparted feelings which could only have been shown by a true Christian. By degrees his hopes revived; all interest, however, in any of her occupations, which had afforded him such pleasure, appeared to be gone. The sound of music and the sight of drawing seemed to touch some chord from which he shrank in pain, and he was roused to greater holiness of life.

Bessy Marries

At that time, 1830, Bessy was already betrothed to William Wingfield, a minister in the Church of Ireland. He was the guardian of his nephew, the young Lord Powerscourt, whose parents had died. William and Bessy were to marry the same year. Fanny wrote a poem just before Sally's death, which also anticipated Bessy's leaving home:

Why doubly heaves my bosom so,
This half articulated groan,
Is it because my sister
And I shall soon be left alone?

Three hearts united long in love
Must soon endure the parting hour;
One for celestial courts above,
The other for a distant bower.

One bids a brother's heart rejoice,
And promises his days to bless,
The other waits her bridegroom's voice
Clad in a robe of righteousness.

My heart then contemplate their bliss,
And silence every rising sigh,
Learn too the chastening rod to kiss,
And in thy Saviour's love rely.

He also has a way for thee,
He has a work for thee to do,
And be it thine, whate'er it be,
To follow where he bids thee go.

'Tis now for thee in love to cheer
Thy parents as they journey on,

Thine to dispel each rising tear,
Then say not thou art left alone.

And still there is a prospect fair,
A silent hour when we shall meet,
For praises one, for other's prayer,
Low-bending at the Saviour's feet.

Fanny Marries

Two years after Bessy's marriage, Fanny married Thomas Webber, a friend of William Wingfield's, and also a minister of religion. The two men had rented a farmhouse together once near Castlemacadam, where Thomas was now the rector. They had met as students at Christ Church, Oxford. Thomas's father, Daniel, was a retired queen's counsel and a widower, and shared a house in Dublin with his widowed sister. He had once been a member of Parliament for Armagh.

Thomas's mother had died in recent time. She had often stayed alone with her two boys on the farm in County Sligo she inherited. Sometimes she attended dances on her own. She smoked the locally-grown drug, hemp. She had not had fine clothes.

Both Bessy's and Fanny's weddings were quiet and plain. On their honeymoons they went on tours of relatives, and made sketches. Fanny and Thomas went to live in a house, Cherrymount, at Avoca, County Wicklow, which they rented from the Misses Hardy. It was surrounded by a landscape of mountains, wooded valleys, and lakes. A miniature of Fanny displays her warm brown eyes, and brown hair in an elaborate coiffure. She wore a waisted, low cut dress with a belt, and wide puff sleeves.

William

Within a year of Fanny's marriage, her brother William died of tuberculosis before he could finish his university degree. He was only twenty-one years old. He had longed to visit Wales, so Mr and Mrs Kelly, Edmund, Caroline, and the nurse Hannah went with him on a trip to Wales, and he died at Bangor. Caroline wrote that at the foot of the Cross, where none are ever rejected, he recognized himself as a 'Hell-deserving' sinner. She wrote: 'I could never forget his angelic countenance that morning. He was speaking of his hopes and, calling Edmund and me, he said, "Come to Jesus, it is the only thing that can make you truly happy. What should I do without Jesus now?" My father read him a verse of a hymn of his own:

> *We hope to see His face*
> *With all the Saints above;*
> *To sing for ever of His grace,*
> *For ever of His love.*

William's countenance brightened as he said, "Glorious hope through Christ Jesus". In a moment he ceased to breathe, and was with the Saviour he loved.'

The Kellys sold Rathmines Castle after living there for five years, and returned to Kellyville with Caroline. Edmund was finishing his second degree, which was in medicine. He must have felt keenly the loss of William as a male companion near to his age. Caroline continued with her interest in charities. In the cholera epidemic, when they were still at

Rathmines, she had been the secretary of a committee for making collections to assist the sufferers. Mrs Kelly and Caroline became the main companions for each other. Mr Kelly wrote some verse in a light-hearted vein for Caroline, who was eighteen:

Cassy thinks Papa a poet,
Cassy much mistaken is,
Read these lines, and then you'll know it,
For, alas! these lines are his.

Hymns there are of his inditing,
This he owns, but what of this!
'Tis the subject, not the writing,
Gives them worth, and that's not his.

Could he do as Cassy asks him,
Would he put her off an hour?
But he blames her, when she tasks him
With a work beyond his power.

Fanny's and Bessy's Children

Fanny and Bessy now embarked on motherhood. Bessy's first child, called Elizabeth like her mother and grandmother, and nicknamed 'Bena', was born just before Fanny's wedding. As the time for the birth of her second child drew near, Bessy started to suffer from illness which was to dog her all her life. It was a rheumatic condition. Bessy, William and little Bena went to live in the Mediterranean, and a second daughter was born at Nice and died at a month old. There was much cholera about. They were to remain on the Continent for over two years.

Meanwhile, Fanny gave birth to her first child in Dublin, where she went for reliable care, and some help from Caroline, in her confinement. The baby would be called William Downes after the patron of his Webber grandfather, although they sometimes referred to him as 'little Dan'. Her husband Thomas wrote to her from his parish, which he could not leave at the time, with love and humour:

My dearest love,

I am very thankful for the good news in Cassy's note of today about yourself and dear Baby – Everything we have wished and prayed for – how thankful we should be – So you have 'eat a chicken' for dinner – is this literally true, or did Cassy mean only that you had eat your dinner of chicken? I suppose next week you will be able to manage a pair. I am glad you have begun to change your room – it will be cheerful for you – Write to me yourself, love, as soon as you safely can, and tell me all about the dear little Dan, and how your nursing goes on – I hope it has not caused any soreness – so you begin to think his hands pretty – God grant that they may be often held up in prayer, and then I shall think them beautiful.

May the Lord help, and bless, my precious wife is the prayer of her affectionate T W.

Bessy wrote Fanny a long letter from Rome, telling her about sketching the view from one of the seven hills, and of the wonder of walking amongst the ancient ruins. She was learning to paint in oils. She greatly admired the work of

Raphael, and hoped to copy a child from one of his paintings. She said she would rejoice to see Fanny's picture of her child. She went on excursions with Hannah Stuart (a Tighe cousin). A highlight was a trip to the catacombs, where, after walking through the dark and narrow underground passages, their group reached one of the little excavations that had served as a place of worship. They imagined how the dark passages had often resounded with the praises of him who had brought his persecuted followers out of darkness into his marvellous light. They could not help themselves but sing her father's hymn, 'Brother, thou art gone before us'.

Bessy said that her daughter Bena was delighted with St Peters, and told everyone she 'kissed Peter's toes'. The people looked at her more than at the sights. She told Fanny about a way to take plant cuttings that she had observed at Genoa, which might be useful for carnations, or the sweet-scented heath they found difficult to make grow. At Carrara, picking up pieces of marble, she had been affected by the wind. She was still suffering, and had since stayed indoors away from the cold. Her husband wrote in the same letter that Bessy was expecting a child again, and was in a better state of health than in the last pregnancy.

Later in 1835, all the Kelly family, except Fanny, were staying in Paris when Bessy gave birth to a son there, Richard. The Kellys went over in their own carriage. It was a joyous occasion. Edmund had recently finished his degree in medicine. While in Paris, Mr Kelly and Mr Wingfield held a drawing room conversational meeting for the study of the Bible every week, to which their friends, and many strangers, were invited. All the family attended Marbeuf Chapel, where Mr Lovatt officiated; he was a weekly attendant at their meetings. The Kelly young people saw much of their cousins the Pigotts (their mother was Mr Kelly's sister); and their cousin Hannah, with her husband Lord Stuart. Caroline had violin lessons from a Mr Osborne. While recovering from the birth, Bessy joined Caroline for lessons in lithography, so that they might learn how to print their own drawings.

Fanny wrote to congratulate Bessy. She said she was lonely in Wicklow without society or friends. 'My dearest Mama', she always began. She scolded her mother for not writing enough about everyone. She wanted to hear more about Bessy, and had forgotten to thank her for her letter and the gift of a table. She thanked William Wingfield for the basket hat he sent for little William, who was running about everywhere, constantly falling down and bumping his head. He put his hands together whenever she said 'Mama says', and always obeyed. She had a nurse to help with him. She asked anxiously after Edmund, who had a slight cough.

Fanny wrote again in April 1836. The Kelly family were still in Paris. But William Wingfield had taken up his position as vicar of Abbeyleix, and Fanny hoped that Bessy would be back in time for Fanny's second confinement. She was worried about the damage to the furniture she was looking after for William and Bessy; they knocked over the table and broke some china. The house that Lord Powerscourt was having built for them was not progressing; the architect said that the plans would have to be changed because they would not be able to build it for the money. She felt reassured about Edmund and hoped he would soon find some work to do.

Fanny's second son, Thomas, was born soon after she wrote. The Kellys were spending a month in London. Caroline came at last to see her new nephew. He had straight, dark brown hair and brown eyes. The older boy, Willy, trying to say Aunt Caroline, called her 'Aunt Can', and it became her name to all the nephews and nieces. She had returned to be bridesmaid at the marriage of their cousin Sally Hamilton, to Francis Howard. Their brother Edmund obtained a job in the post office.

From that time there was frequent travel between Kellyville and Abbeyleix (where the Wingfields lived), which were twelve Irish miles apart. Each family sent a carriage halfway, to Lamberton, and there was an exchange of passengers. Caroline attended the regular Bible study meetings held at Abbeyleix. The family had a great many pleasant friends, Caroline wrote.

Fanny still felt isolated in Wicklow. She made a drawing, with wash, of Willy and Tommy. The babies wore lace-frilled bonnets, and long white dresses with tucking, too small for a baby today. Fanny sewed the babies' clothes. A Webber cousin, Isabella, wrote to her from Dublin about her own baby, and hoped that Fanny's children would become friends with hers. Thomas Webber sometimes went on trips there associated with his work; he drove a phaeton with two horses. Isabella offered him a bed whenever he was on a trip to Dublin. She begged Fanny to come there too and make drawings of her baby.

Fanny and Thomas Webber and their family moved into their new house, Avoca Lodge, near to Castlemacadam, towards the end of 1837. It had been very cold. Caroline was spared by her parents to visit, so that she could help Fanny with nailing down carpets and putting up curtains. Fanny wrote to Bessy that 'the whole castle in the air is on the ground'. Caroline's cooking left much to be desired, she said. Thomas was setting up a Bible education society in Wicklow. They had a new nurse for the children. When the old nurse left, little Tommy said nothing for a while but, 'Mamon gone, mamon gone'. The new nurse, Sophy, was teaching Willy to recite hymns, and Tommy was saying the lines immediately after him. Fanny was looking forward to working in the garden.

A third son, Charley, was born to Fanny and Thomas in 1838. They kept a donkey to supply the babies with milk, and the little boys rode her. The donkey taught the boys to stick on when she hoisted her stern and tried to kick them off, but did not run away. When they used a switch to try and make her go, she often would not, and only tucked in her tail and put back her ears.

The Webber family owned a property, Leekfield, near Skreen, County Sligo, but the farmhouse had burnt down shortly after Thomas Webber's marriage. Thomas had a schoolhouse built at Farnharpy near Skreen, and was patron of the school.

Fanny Tries to Save Her Husband's Life

Fanny's husband, Thomas, had always been a nervous person whose health was delicate. His university studies were hampered, and examinations affected, by sickness and a nervous disposition. Now he was struck down with illness every winter, especially in some particularly cold and damp winters they were experiencing. His survival became so much a matter of concern that a warmer climate was recommended by his doctor.

In September 1839, Thomas and Fanny, with their five-year-old son Willy and Fanny's sister Caroline, set out on a journey which was to become nine months long, to seek a remedy. They followed the same route their family members had taken before, to Paris, Nice and Rome.

They had to leave behind the two younger sons, Tommy and Charley, aged three and one, and the nurse Sophy, with Mr and Mrs Kelly. They would stay in Dublin at first, then Kellyville. Mr Kelly was now seventy, and his wife not much less.

Fanny was not at all happy with the thought that her baby would not recognize her when she returned. She was apprehensive about travelling. She had never been out of Ireland. They were not on the Grand Tour. She had had to balance the welfare of her husband against the needs of their very young children.

The sisters and Mrs Kelly wrote letters to one another as a group, in which more than one person wrote on the same sheet of paper. They sent the letters to more than one person, as the letter was to be sent on from a first recipient to a second. The men often wrote short notes on the bottom of the letters.

Their letters from Nice, where they settled for four months, have many references to unusual weather for the time of year, and beggars. They heard about bad weather and much sickness in Ireland. Fanny worried that little children were at risk of their lives.

The Journey Begins

Caroline wrote to Mrs Kelly that they (Fanny, Mr Webber, Willy, and herself) arrived safely at Birmingham, and were not ship-wrecked. They were staying with their cousin Hannah Stuart, in the Malvern Hills. She had not realised there were such high mountains in England. They were walking up the hills every morning before breakfast, and walked to the top of the highest one with the assistance of a donkey. They sketched the old church, and attended the Sunday service. The deficiencies of the sermon made her appreciate the Irish preachers.

Fanny wrote that Hannah did a drawing of her and Willy. (Hannah had been Hannah Tighe, and learnt to draw like all the cousins). Willy was no trouble, and made some drawings too. Fanny heard much against over-feeding of children since being in England, and was more than ever convinced that under-feeding promoted health. She sent kisses for her precious ones, and a message to Tommy that she would send him letters. She was happy not to have them with her to be anxious about, because it would be too much to watch them. The present of an ink bottle from William Wingfield was of the greatest use to her, she said.

Fanny wrote again from Southampton, and the letter continued to Paris. They had the coach from Malvern to themselves, changed horses every ten miles, and had not the slightest accident. Willy had a whole seat to sleep on. They saw the pretty towns of Gloucester and Salisbury, and Fanny loved the beautifully cultivated plains, and the hedgerows. She was surprised how clean and trim the houses were; how picturesque the cottages covered with vines, but not in ruins, and never a dirty window. They were going to sketch Netley Abbey (a ruin) in the evening.

They had a gale and a crossing of sixteen hours in rough seas, and arrived at Le Havre 'through the tender mercy of our God who kept us safe', said Fanny. The custom house gave them no trouble, so they must have had honest faces, and dinner was ready at the table d'hôte. They met an American clergyman in the packet, who went with them to a French protestant church nearby, Bethel, to hear a good sermon.

Fanny wrote for Willy that he sent his love to Tommy; he hoped that he would take good care of the horse, and wanted to tell him he went 130 miles in one day. He sent his love to Bena, and begged to tell her that the packet from Dublin was called the Royal William and had been twice to America. She ought to make haste to learn French (the Wingfields had a French nurse). He told Dicky that he liked his country of birth, but thought the women in high caps very odd. He sent his love to his Kelly grandparents, and said that they were writing a journal every day.

Paris

It was a pleasant journey by steamboat to Paris, with picturesque scenery. Artists boarded the boat and offered pretty pencil drawings. Willy impressed the passengers with his own drawings, and they were astonished at his bare legs (which he could not understand). Caroline wanted to sketch the views, but the boat moved so quickly that it was impossible. Fanny was pained to think of Charley missing her, yet it was best for him to be quietly at home with the nurse. Children younger than Willy should not travel, she said, as they could not enjoy it.

Mr Webber, who was well, thought they should leave Paris by the following week because of the expense. They took a walk to show Fanny the Palais Royal, and they had met some Bligh relatives. They would go to the Musée de Neuilly, and to see the place the Kellys used to stay at, in the Avenue de Neuilly. A few days later, they were dead tired from walking on the rough streets. They went to the Jardin des Plantes and the Panthéon, and twice to the Louvre. They climbed to the Barrière de la Cloche to see the view at sunset.

Thomas wrote 'Dearest Mama' like the others, and signed himself 'Your affectionate son'. He said Fanny was very nervous at first. Whenever she wanted to tell them secrets, she spoke in French! He met some old friends, and he 'was not ashamed to introduce the wife that God has given me'. He visited the Rosins' school, and was asked to lecture to the boys. He wanted to know how the enlargement of his church was proceeding. He bought *The History of the Reformation* for Nice reading '(not meant for a pun)'.

Fanny wrote to 'Dearest Bessy', wishing to know whether their parents were really managing to take care of her children. She felt nervous about the separation, and the excitement of being in Paris magnified it; she would feel happier if she knew that the children were a real pleasure to them. Willy drew a picture, and fell asleep on the sofa beside her. They were living in five rooms, at six francs a day; their breakfast was one and a half francs, and their dinner two francs. They found a place where they could go for dinner at two o'clock, when hardly anyone was there, and get the best dinner 'for a French dinner'. The air was not wholesome, and the people looked pale. She drew pictures of Parisian clothes for little boys.

Thomas added a note asking Bessy what the weekly cost of the nurse Sophy and the children was, so that he could give that amount to Cassy for her upkeep, instead of Mr Kelly sending her his money. Cassy was such good company, and a help and a comfort. Fanny was not the most courageous of travellers, he said.

To Lyon

They arrived at Auxerre on a Sunday. Unable to find a church, they conducted one for themselves and two English ladies, whom they were obliged to take to Dijon. The road was thick with mud. On the way to Chalon Fanny noticed the plantation poplars trimmed up to the top, and made a sketch of them. The fields were green like spring and the sheep white, she said, not like the brown ones earlier, which were feeding on ploughed fields. She liked taking the steamboat again, amid beautiful scenery. She forgot to bring her small teapot, and often wished for it; they had not tasted tea since leaving England.

Mrs Kelly had sent a letter to Lyon. She took the boys to Sandymount with Sophy, and met with Bessy and Miss La Page. They walked on the beach and picked up shells. Tommy was sitting by her drawing ships; he was a most agreeable companion, and they had taken a walk in the Botanic Gardens. 'Bessy played Patrick's Day for him – little Irish boy!' Bena missed Willy very much.

Fanny wrote that she could not bear to think of Charley forgetting her. He was not to walk too much. She wanted them to teach him to say 'Papa' and 'Mama', and to write Tommy a prayer and tell him to be a good boy until she came back. She had been frightened that the horses would overturn the diligence (the public stagecoach), and had often wished to be on the road going home.

Nîmes

The travellers went to Nîmes because a community of 15,000 Protestants lived there, and they could see the antiquities. A thunderstorm, with torrents of rain, cleared late in the day; they managed to look at the Roman ruins and sketch for a short time before dinner. Thomas had met an old school friend at Avignon who asked them to dine early. French dinners lasted too long, said Fanny; she sent her usual kisses to her precious ones. Caroline wrote that the diligence had been excellent, the horses quiet, and she had sketched in it; she complained about bugs and mosquitoes. They would sail to Marseilles, and then go to Toulon for the night.

At Nice, there was a letter from Mrs Kelly. She said Tommy was sitting on his stool writing four letters. He never forgot any of his absent friends, and often asked if Willy would come back the next day. Charley was merry and lively; he had cut his eighth tooth, and ran about. Bessy came again with her children and Miss La Page; Bena was to start French and music. They went to the sea, and Charley was delighted with the ships, a hundred or more, from three masters to little boats. Tommy was pleased to see the place his parents sailed from. On the way back they had a thunderstorm. Aunt Hamilton asked them to bring their 'young' to Hamwood. From Hamwood, Aunt Hamilton wrote that Charley was her pet, and Tommy made a great friend of his cousin Frederick, though at first they were very shy.

The Sojourn at Nice

Caroline wrote to her mother from Nice just before Christmas. They were affronted that Bessy had not written for so long. It was constantly raining; not the usual climate of Nice for the season. But it was warm, and they seldom wished for a fire. There was no end of tea parties they had been asked to, and invitations for almost every evening. The parties were 'not very gay in the common sense of the term'. They could not explore the country as much as they would wish, because of the bad weather. They had made a pleasant excursion to Villa Franca, about three miles off, with the assistance of donkeys, but had not had time for sketching. It was hard in this dissipated place, Caroline said, to find time for anything. The family in Ireland would enjoy walking by the beautiful blue

Mediterranean, and exploring the hills. They hoped that Tom Kelly, their brother, would join them as he had said he would.

Fanny wrote that the rain caused great distress to the labourers, who would not work in rain like the Irish, but were begging the English for alms. She was making drawings of the children of Kate Stuart (a Wingfield relative), and Kate herself was learning to sketch. They met some families: among them were the Hares and the Pallisers; the Pallisers had a sickly child. They all held a reading meeting, and an evening party where a subject was discussed. Willy had a great many friends and went to school. He willingly got up an hour earlier to go on a donkey excursion up the winding paths in the hills.

Fanny heard that there were fogs and influenza in Dublin, and hoped her family would remain in the house. She had a presentiment of worse things to come, and dreadful illnesses that would harm delicate children. Charley should not go out for long, she said, and should always take much liquid. If Tommy was not well he should omit meat. 'Mr Webber' was much better than he would have been at home; he had been better travelling, and better than when he left Ireland. Fanny wanted Bessy to send her recipe for making bread, as some English people did not like the bread in Nice. But Fanny thought it excellent, and was going to learn how to make it.

Thomas wrote that Mr Hartley's preaching was very interesting (the Hartleys begged to be affectionately remembered). Fanny had drawn a portrait of Cassy. They had lovely weather again for boating and donkey riding. The doctor said they must leave by the beginning of March because of the winds. They should not go north so soon, but would go to Rome. He was reading *The Wonders of the World* to Willy.

'Does Tommy never ask for his papa?' he questioned plaintively.

Bessy wrote to Fanny shortly after, from Abbeyleix. Bena and Dicky had been very ill, Dicky in particular. He had an attack of inflammation on the lungs. Bena had a heavy, feverish cold, and was better now. Miss La Page was improving greatly in her teaching; Bena was learning geography and mathematics, and she read French as well as she read English. Dicky was wanting Tommy for a companion.

The weather in Ireland was very unpleasant, with severe frost and fog, cold rain, and much sickness everywhere. Bessy envied them their sunshine. She hoped they drew the fishermen on the shore, and took the view looking back upon Nice from the top of the hill on the way to Villa Franca. She was hard at work with her needle. The renovations to their house were proceeding; the masons and carpenters were still at work in the yard.

At the new year, Fanny wrote to her parents that Mr Webber had an attack of illness. Before his illness they went on long expeditions on the Genoa boat and to St André. Willy had a tumble off his donkey. He was speaking French with a Nicezard accent. They had a French master to help them progress, and to teach Caroline Italian. With Lady Nairn, they were working and drawing for the Protestant revival movement, Société Évangélique, one evening a week. Dr Harrington said it would be better for Mr Webber to travel.

Fanny wrote to Bessy that the drawing master who came once a week used to sketch with Bessy. They tried to make a sketch of Nice from the sea but, when the boatmen stopped rowing, the boat went up and down too much. It was comical to see on every Nicezard a Scotch shawl; Bessy's might have been the first one they saw. She wanted to know if the accounts of distress in Ireland were true. They heard of nothing but deluge, want of fuel, and typhus fever. 'Poor dear country, how I long to set my foot upon it again.' She hoped Bessy would let her know how their mother looked, and was, and that her dear ones did not make her too anxious.

Caroline accompanied a large party to Beaulieu; the group included a Miss Stuart and 'Emmeline, a daughter of some Lord Stanley'. They saw the great olive, and sat under the trees like gypsies. They discovered the spot where Bessy sketched a view, even the blue trees. They would not think the sky so blue, or the sun so bright, when they got home. They loved to see all the oranges. Caroline wrote to Bena, for Willy, that he had many drawings to show her. He was very fond of the waves on the shoreline, and often walked there. Sometimes he shot his bow just in the place she could see the boat in the picture on the writing paper.

Later in the month they received news of Bessy's giving birth safely to a second son, Edward. Fanny sent congratulations. She said that her husband had tried homeopathic plants under Dr Harrington, and was well again. To 'Brother Wingfield', Thomas wrote that he was going to preach in French to a congregation of French protestants, after the French master corrected the sermon and taught him how to pronounce it. He taught a class of gentlemen. He had his portrait drawn in sepia.

In February, Caroline wrote that they had had more rain, and a foretaste of the dust and cold winds that would come. They had been to Corsica, taking many pleasant expeditions up the hills. They went to Falicon with a small party, and saw the views, but did not get as far as the grotto. They dined with the Boileaus, who sent many kind remembrances to Bessy, and showed them the sketch she had drawn while staying with them.

They were becoming rather tired of the dissipation, Caroline said, and were relieved if they ever had an evening alone. Mrs Willis, who had a beautiful voice, sang a great many of Mr Kelly's hymns for them. Mr Webber was getting from Mr Hartley information useful for writing a report for the Continental Society. They had news of the Queen's marriage. The English were raising a subscription; the gay ones for a ball, and the good ones for something charitable. So far the ball was outstripping the other. They did not have enough news about Tom coming to stay with them, or about what Edmund was doing.

Fanny was glad that Grandfather Webber stayed a few days at Kellyville, and was pleased with the grandchildren, and the good care taken of them. She said she was ashamed of the way Willy ate; she wished Charley to be taught to eat slowly and chew his food properly, only small pieces at a time. She was still pained to think that Charley would turn away from her. She could not let Sophy go until he learnt to love his mother a little.

Miss Stanley wanted them to chaperone her back to London. Mr Webber had decided to let Fanny out of the carriage whenever she thought it dangerous. They were going to see curiosities that were dug out of the Roman ruins; Caroline would walk to the Sugarloaf, not to be outdone by Miss Stanley. They talked with a Mr Adean about the possibility of Edmund's getting a grant of land in Canada.

By early March, they anticipated travelling to Rome for three weeks, before starting the return journey. Tom Kelly had not arrived to accompany them. They were reading a Roman history to brush up on memory. The trees were just budding. Caroline could now walk miles without being in the least fatigued. They would be sorry to leave the many friends they had made.

To Rome

Their group took the coach to Ventimiglia, where they spent a Sunday. Mr Webber looked for some English to preach to, and they were surprised to make up a congregation of eleven people. It rained all the way to Genoa, where they walked round the palaces under umbrellas.

They missed the boat to Civita Vecchia, so they took a small steam packet, through wind and rough seas, to Leghorn. Well wrapped in winter clothes, they went to Pisa to see the leaning tower. Fanny thought the people looked Irish. She wished she was at home again; the rain had left Ireland, she said, and come to where they were instead.

Their arrival at Rome in April was later than they would have wished. It was now Holy Week, but they managed to find lodgings. Mr Webber became ill. They received a letter from

Mrs Kelly, who hoped they had not learnt bad manners on the Continent. Tom said he would be in Rome in May to bring them home. Aunt Hamilton wrote that her family were all in a state of dissipation. Bena sent a message to Willy that they had fun doing gymnastics in the garden. William Wingfield said that he had fears about warfare in every quarter of the globe, and that the potato crop would be extremely damaged.

In Rome, the family had the company of their friends from Nice: Miss Stanley, who was learning to sketch, and the Pallisers. Mr Webber was especially sick, but they found good doctors, and he was recovering. There was a delay. Tom Kelly did not come. Over the Splügen Pass into Switzerland, the party shared the very large carriage of Lord and Lady Mayo, and their eight children.

The Return

Caroline wrote from a steamboat on the Rhine, in early June. They did not tumble down any precipices in Switzerland, she said. They took a steamboat across the beautiful lake of Wallenstadt, and another up to Zurich. On the Rhine, there were picturesque castles and towns in the hills. It would be more agreeable, said Caroline, if the odious Germans did not smoke so much. Their pipes were never out of their mouths unless they were eating, and that took up no small part of the day. A German dinner was a trial of patience.

Fanny said that the Germans had more business and more eating than even the French. She had become very careless about seeing anything. They had loved Switzerland, and it was so clean. The Swiss cottages were pretty, with green lawns under romantic rocks and waterfalls. She tried to buy a watch in Switzerland for the children's nurse, Sophy, without success, and hoped to find one at Cologne. They were glad to hear that Edmund had at last found a job that suited him, and it was not so very far off, compared with going to the colonies. They hoped to see him in London. Mr Webber was a great deal better. The weather was hot and lovely, and Willy was brown. How would she make Charley love her again, she asked, and know that she was his mother?

From Antwerp they wrote again, catching up with a lost trunk. Miss Stanley had gone to Ghent with friends, and had sailed. They saw the only pleasing paintings of Rubens, in Fanny's view, 'The Crucifixion' and 'The Descent from the Cross'. The style of the others was too grotesque.

It was a calm passage of twenty-three hours across the Channel. Fanny wrote on the Thames as they were going to meet their brother Tom for lunch at the Tower. 'The care of our tender Father preserved us', she said. On arrival at Kingstown by the sea, they were overjoyed to see their parents and the little boys. Charley looked like a cherub with golden ringlets out of a picture by Correggio, said Caroline.

After the journey, the Webbers went back to live with all their family at Avoca Lodge in County Wicklow. Their son Charley was to keep Sophy as his nursemaid while he got to know and love his parents again. A fourth son, Francis, was born to them in 1841. And Bessy Wingfield had a daughter, Isabella, in 1843.

The oldest of the Kelly children, Tom, died in 1844. He had been injured by a blow to his liver as a youth, and it was thought he would be affected by it at a later age. He didn't marry. Tom was seventeen years older than Caroline, the youngest, and she felt she hardly knew him. Yet she wrote an obituary and a death scene for him, as fitting for the oldest son. He was a kind and generous brother; though he trained horses for the Curragh, he was never led into any vice. She included a poem written for Tom as a child, by their aunt Mary Tighe (which is in the appendix). After Tom's death, Mr Kelly left Tom's room in its original state and kept the door locked. It was the same room in which, fifty years before, the Lord had heard Mr Kelly's prayers about going into the ministry.

Thomas Webber Dies

Fanny's husband was ailing, and her attempts to shore up his health failed. He was at last incapacitated, and unable to continue his duties at Castlemacadam. His family and he moved to live at Kellyville, and he occupied the dining-room for the last months of his illness in the winter of 1844 and 1845. Thomas's father, Daniel, wrote a letter to his grandson Willy, at this time:

My very dear Willy,

I received your letter with great pleasure, caused very much by the good writing and good French in which you expressed yourself, but more a great deal from my love for the writer. I am glad that the bows and arrows are so pleasing to you and Tommy, and also that the cart and horse are amusing to Charley and Stumpy. Give the enclosed letter to your father. Tell him to direct to Post Office, Harrogate, as I have changed my hotel, and probably will not remain as long as the end of next week. When I have removed for any time, I will write again. I am so glad he feels happy at Kellyville.

Tell dear Mama that I saw Mrs Howard well at church this day, and that I have not seen a female here whose countenance was at once so intellectual and pleasing. She will explain to you what I mean by the first word, which will encourage you to become equally pleasing by improving your mind, and thus becoming sensible and amiable. Love to you all, and most kind compliments to Grandpapa and Grandmama and Aunt Can, also to Mr and Mrs Wingfield when you see them, with a kiss to little Eddy when he has recovered from his cow-pock, which, I am glad to learn, is not dangerous.

I remain, my dear Willy, very affectionate Grandfather D W Webber.

Thomas Webber was only forty-three years old when he died. He left Fanny a widow after thirteen years of marriage, with four children under the age of eleven to bring up.

Fanny kept in touch with the elderly Webber grandfather, who mainly resided in Dublin. She made a drawing of him in conversation with three of his grandsons, the little boys wearing tunics gathered at the waist like a frock, over their trousers. The Webber grandfather died two years after his son. Fanny drew a portrait of Mr Kelly, and one of Mrs Kelly; their sunken lips suggest that they had lost their teeth. She painted a scene of Mr Kelly teaching three of his Webber grandsons.

After Thomas Webber's passing, the dining-room he had inhabited at Kellyville became the schoolroom for the four Webber boys, and meals were served in the breakfast room.

They had a tutor, Mr Willey, as well as Mr Kelly, to educate them. Mr Kelly taught them Greek and geometry himself. He used Henry White's recent *Universal History* (1843) as a textbook. Mrs Kelly did all in her power to repeat the educational labour she had expended on her own children. The Kelly grandparents were to spend the last ten years of their lives helping to bring up and educate the boys. They saw three of them off to university.

Caroline was as yet resident at Kellyville. Not long after Thomas Webber's death, she went for a holiday with her sister Bessy Wingfield, and her family, to Wicklow. They rented a small, furnished house on the part of the seashore that they loved, called the Murrough, which was near to old friends and relatives. It was just a primitive little place, only suitable for sea-bathers to picnic in. They dined one night at Glanmore Castle with the Synges, and visited the Eccles of Cronroe (Harriet Eccles was a St George cousin). The Tighes of Rossana sent them vegetables; their girls came to bathe, and everyone danced in a ring in the sea.

Caroline's Work

The Irish Famine

Caroline started charity work when she was still a child. At the beginning of the great Irish famine of 1846 and 1847, she was staying in the Isle of Wight with the Wingfield family. She organized working parties to make clothes for poor people in Ireland, and large bales were sent over weekly for distribution. The Wingfields had gone to live at Ventnor in the Isle of Wight for the winter, in the milder climate, because Bessy's health was again a concern. Bessy and William now had another daughter, Emily. In 1847 their son Edward died, and the following year they had a fourth daughter, Fanny.

When Caroline returned to Kellyville, she arranged the sale of small knitted articles made by girls in the cottages nearby. She wanted to teach them some special kind of fancy work. She had heard of 'tatting' from a friend in the Isle of Wight, and acquired a small, worn sample of it, but she didn't know how to do it. Eventually she met a religious lady in Dublin, Mrs Chave, who learnt 'frivolité' at Boulogne, and taught it to her. Caroline practised by teaching it to Maria

Comerford, who had painted miniatures of members of their family.

Soon the daughters of labourers and small farmers around Kellyville were learning to do the work, and were selling clothes done by tatting for their own profit. Caroline provided the materials, sold the products (to her friends at first), managed the business and kept the accounts. Gradually the quality of the tatting improved, the patterns increased in variety and artistry, and the market was extended and grew into a cottage industry. When Caroline and Fanny went to the Great Exhibition in London in 1851, they were very proud to see the beautiful specimen of tatting made by the Kellyville girls, in the form of a shawl.

During twenty years Caroline paid between £4000 and £5000 for tatting to the country girls of the parish, all Roman Catholics. Their work was exhibited in Dublin in 1856, and again in London in 1862. After that point the industry waned because of change of fashion, and the emigration or marriage of the workers.

William Wingfield wrote a jocular poem, entitled 'Tatters versus Rags', about how Caroline looked at the time of the famine, ending it:

Long may she reign, the Queen of Tatters,
Not caring much who frowns or flatters,
While all around her good she scatters -
In Ballintubber.

In the potato famine more than a quarter of the Irish people died or emigrated. In the winter of 1847 and 1848, the famine was as bad as in the previous year. Mr Kelly sacrificed everything to alleviate the distress of his poorer neighbours. He no longer received any rent from his Galway estates; nevertheless, he mortgaged them heavily. He fed and clothed the people around Kellyville, and employed hundreds of men in sub-soiling the pasture fields. Perhaps he put in the lake at Kellyville at that time. He assisted families to emigrate to America. As a practical lesson, he gave his grandchildren the choice of doing without butter or sugar for a year, and the money so saved was used to help the starving.

Mr and Mrs Kelly lived less in the world than ever. They saw few people except for their nearest friends and relations, and their neighbours; they took the greatest pleasure in their grandchildren. Mr Kelly continued to write hymns, and wrote letters to his brethren. His sisters, Mrs Cosby and Miss Kelly, drove over nearly every day from Stradbally Hall to Kellyville.

Mr Kelly still attended to his congregations. He drove into Athy or rode a pony almost up to his death. When the railway to Athy opened, he used it. He went to Dublin every second Sunday to take services at the chapel he had built in Great George's Street. He left a short address, on those occasions, for one of his friends to read to the small congregation at Athy. He lectured for an hour before the church service at Ballintubbert, his local church, because he thought the preaching of the clergyman there was insufficient. However, Caroline wrote in her memoir, there was no ill-feeling or rivalry with the incumbent clergyman, who sometimes attended Mr Kelly's lecture.

He dressed in black and wore knee breeches, and an old-fashioned hat. He always lifted his hat to the smallest salute, said Caroline, and never allowed a beggar to go unhelped. He had a black pony, called Polly, tied behind his old barouche, wrote his grandson Tommy, and during long journeys he used to ride the pony for miles beside the carriage as a change, until he got tired of jogging. When he rose in the stirrups it was with a quaint motion, jerking his right arm up.

Bringing up the Boys

The Webber boys had riding lessons, and learnt to shoot. They had read about the American Indians and their equestrian exercises. So they rigged themselves out with feather head-dresses, tomahawks, and bows and arrows. They galloped around the fields on the black pony, hanging onto her mane or a surcingle which encompassed her waist, and screeching. They practised vaulting onto her back and clinging on one side, while they hurled javelins at a supposed enemy. A book that Tommy took delight in was T Williamson's *The Wild Sports of the East*; it was kept on a shelf and shown to the boys as a treat.

In 1851 Fanny, Caroline, and Tommy Webber went to see the Great Exhibition in London. They met with their cousins the Pigotts. In the winter, Fanny, Caroline, Charley Webber and the Wingfields stayed with their cousin Robert Tighe in Torquay. Robert Tighe had an open carriage and pair, and would take some of the party out driving every day. They went to the lectures of a local scientist, Dr Pengelly. Charley made a collection of seaweeds with help from the Misses Griffiths. Caroline formed a friendship with Miss Charlotte Elliott, the well-known writer of hymns; she composed a hymn especially for Caroline. The Pigotts paid a return visit to Ireland the following year. Salisbury Pigott had married Count Gustav Sayn Wittgenstein, and the Count, an admirer of Mr Kelly, sent him a German bible with woodcut illustrations in colour (Koberger, Nuremberg, 1483) as a gift.

For two or three years Fanny, Caroline and the Webber boys resided at Kellyville or Dublin, and the boys had tutors. One of the tutors was a Mr Caine. All the young people had long twilight walks with Caroline and Mr Caine, sometimes to the top of Cobbler's Castle. In the summer, Robert Tighe would take with him, as a travelling companion, one of the Webber boys or their cousin Dicky Wingfield. Charley Webber had his name down for the Royal Military Academy, Woolwich, and was offered a place when he had just turned sixteen. He attended the Dublin school of Dr Flynn in 1852, and Dr Bridgeman's preparatory school at Woolwich in 1853. Tommy had an offer from the Royal Military Academy too, but declined it. He went to Trinity College, Dublin, with Willy.

The Irish People

Caroline supported a small school near Kellyville, with a Catholic schoolmistress. Caroline wrote about the Irish people who lived near them at Kellyville, and for a considerable distance from it, especially of a character, Mary Grady:

Our relations with the poor were very intimate and cordial. All the Protestant farmers, most of whom bore English names, either attended the parish church at Ballintubbert, or went to Athy to Scotch or dissenting services. Many of these had attended my father's religious lectures and preachings. Our intercourse with the Roman Catholic tenant farmers and labourers was equally friendly in its character, and nothing could exceed their regard and affection for my father and all his family. Although the labourers' children attended a small school (which I supported), with a Roman Catholic schoolmistress, and although books of modern thought of all kinds were in use and in circulation amongst the people, there was never an idea of introducing religious controversy of any kind.

The neighbourly feeling subsisting between us and all these peasantry and our own dependents (workmen in the place) was a kind only to be met with elsewhere under similar conditions. One possible cause of discord, it should be observed, was absent, as my father was not the owner of the lands surrounding his demesne.

Amongst the poorest, there were several original characters, such as were to be met with only in the old-fashioned Irish country districts, before the days of railways and telegraphs. At the top of the 'Quarry' field resided a very old man, Paddy Fennan, and his wife. He remembered as a boy helping when the modern part of Kellyville House was built by my grandfather, Judge Kelly. The wife remembered being the housemaid during his life time, and used to say that the guests always left a shilling for the housemaid between the sheets when they were leaving. They were a very clean and tidy old couple, and Mrs Fennan's girdle cakes were much appreciated by the younger generation.

There were the blacksmith's family, the Murphys, and that of the carpenter, the Carberys. Old Dan Carbery was an excellent skilled mechanic, and his sons and grandsons still follow the trade, some of the latter in America. He dressed in the old-fashioned style, with knee breeches, knitted stockings, and blue cloth coat with brass buttons. There was a herdsman of the name of John Gorman, who was quite an authority. His favourite manner of drawing attention to any person or thing was, 'Look at that, now'. He was a most warm-hearted man, but endowed with the coarsest brogue I ever heard.

There was a little gamekeeper of the name of Tom Branigan, who was a good rabbit shot, and had a very dry manner. He was generally more silent than Irishmen of his kind. He married at an advanced age and, in consequence, as is the custom in Ireland, had on his wedding night to go through the ordeal of a great deal of what is called 'booing', accompanied by the blowing of horns. There were cottages belonging to families, such as the Whelans, and Regans, which, though constructed with thick walls of stone and clay, and thatched with straw, and having mud floors, were always clean and tidy, so that no one could object to visit or sit down in them.

An old man of the name of Tom Cushion, whose conversation we enjoyed, lived in a cottage on the road to

Athy. One day I was improving the occasion, as I thought, by talking to him on some instructive subject, when he remarked with a straight look, 'It's a murthering pity, Miss, that ye weren't male born'. Once I asked him to let me have a little gravel from his sand-pit for my garden; his answer, in the fullness of his heart, when I wanted to pay for it, was, 'Ye shall have it sponta-a-neous as the leaves grow on the trees'. He was one of the very few Roman Catholics of his position who read through his Bible continually, and talked freely about it.

A character who was well known in the whole countryside, and who rarely passed a week without being seen and given food at our door, was Mary Grady. She had married and had a large family, but the poor thing had a disordered brain, brought on through illness or disappointment. She lived with her husband, mother, and six children, in a cabin on the Ballyadams bog. The dwelling was of the poorest and most elementary description, and her husband was a day labourer. Although she was rarely at home, and spent all her days wandering over the country far and wide, the children grew up well and healthy.

On one occasion when I was talking to her, she said how fond the poor girls (to whom I gave tatting to do) were of me. 'Oh', I said (in joke), 'it is only for the money they get'. She responded: 'Die tomorrow, and see what a grand funeral ye'd have.' Her restlessness of brain forced her from house to house, and from town to town. Her life, which was passed in repartee and wild conversation, or altercation with those who laughed at her or pitied or disliked her, produced a flow of vigorous language, and filled her with a vast amount of local gossip, upon which she discoursed, or which she retailed, greatly to the amusement of the young and old of all ranks who *would listen to her. Her genius for quaint sayings and for coining quaint words and funny names was wonderful. For fully forty years she wandered over parts of Kildare and Queen's County. There were few houses of any kind where she was not pretty sure to get something to eat and, if it was a dinner, she especially enjoyed what she called the 'top finish', which in ordinary language is the sweet thing.*

Another local character was Larry Barry, the tailor, who had made clothes for five generations. He lived in a cabin, and kept one or two young men. He was very skilful, and could copy with accuracy the fit of garments made by the best London tailors.

Mr Kelly Dies

When all the family were in Dublin in the winter of 1854, Caroline collected clothes and blankets for the wives and families of the soldiers who were absent in the Crimean War. She was invited to distribute the contributions at the Palace of the Archbishop. Mr Kelly showed signs of failing. On one occasion he roused himself to look at his grandson Charley in the uniform of an officer of the Royal Engineers.

Mr Kelly died in 1855. His death scene was written by his son-in-law, William Wingfield, and was printed in Caroline's memoir. He was buried at Ballintubbert in a vault where his oldest son was laid before him. A large concourse of peasantry attended his funeral, besides friends, relations, and neighbours.

Mr Hall, the Presbyterian minister at Athy, gave a memorial sermon for Mr Kelly, which was printed as 'The

Memory of the Just'. The memory of the just was blessed, he said, and justified. The righteous gave other humans an idea of what a person could be, and spoke with 'the human voice divine'; they instilled a remembrance in ourselves, and would not be forgotten. Mr Kelly loved his country, Ireland, and he loved liberty; he had prayed most earnestly for all those who suffered for conscience' sake. He was a lover of literature and religion, and had published his 'Plea for Primitive Christianity', and 765 hymns, many of them with music he had composed. He was a follower of the Gospels. He had administered church ordinances without authority, but he was not a religious zealot without knowledge; he respected church practices. He believed in a 'primitive Church' of elders and deacons only, and that ordination was an appointment to office or trust, by the 'called, and chosen, and faithful'. He was a lover of Christ, and he knew, like the apostle Paul, that 'the love of Christ constraineth us'. He truly tried to live like Christ.

Bessy's Memoir Writing

The Wingfields still lived at Abbeyleix. For a number of years Bessy was an invalid. She wrote a memoir in the form of letters addressed to her oldest daughter, Bena. Her purpose was to tell her children how their grandparents and great-grandparents conducted their lives before the children's memory of them, and what their lives meant to them. They searched the Scriptures, like the Bereans of old, and were rich in faith and good works. Bessy was a chronicler of her family at a deeply emotional and religious level. Much of her writing was close to her death in 1856, not long after her father's, when she was forty-eight. She had five surviving children; the youngest one was eight then.

'I Must for Myself Cry Out, "My Leanness! My Leanness!".' (The Reverend Thomas Kelly)

Mr Kelly's father, who was a judge, wanted his son to go into the law profession. Bessy wrote:
There was a noise made in Dublin about a young man who had given up the world, its honours and pleasures, and had

become a preacher of the lowly and crucified Saviour. It was when he was studying in London that the Lord first sent an arrow into his heart. He was from childhood so perfectly moral, amiable, and upright, that his friends considered him a pattern of all that was good. So when he spoke of himself as a sinner, none could understand what he meant. But when the conscience is touched by the Spirit of God, all things are viewed from a different aspect. Now he saw himself as a Hell-deserving sinner under the wrath of an offended God. No words could express the depth of his anguish; he could see nothing but an eternity of misery before him. In vain he sought relief from the cold, dead preachers of salvation by good works; he often tried to drown his feelings by going more into society.

But the Lord had a great work for him to do, and sent probe after probe into the wounded conscience. He felt at times that he could neither eat, drink, nor sleep, till he had found peace with God. He sought after it by prayers and fasting, till his health began to give way. His great desire was to give up the Bar and go into the Church. But he knew not how to make such a proposal to his father, being aware how great his expectations were for his son had he continued in that profession.

He took his case to his best friend and counsellor, who had prepared his father's mind to receive the request favourably; his father had suffered in seeing his only son's health declining under a state of mind for which he, and the other members of his deeply affectionate family, could not account. The friend mentioned the subject of his entering the Church to his mother that she might break the news to his *father. One day when Mr Kelly was asking the Lord to settle this matter for him in whatever way was most for His Glory, there was a tap on the door, and his mother brought consent from his father.*

From that time the only desire of his heart was to tell to others the great and wonderful news of a free salvation offered to perishing sinners through the blood of Christ. Little did he imagine the opposition and persecution he was to undergo when he set out to follow in his Master's steps.

The Archbishop of Dublin banned Mr Kelly from preaching in Dublin. After Mr Kelly left the Church of England, the Archbishop of Tuam tried to persuade him with many arguments to return. The archbishop and Mr Kelly loved to hold conversations in which they both instructed each other, with humility. Bessy continued:

We can hardly believe a state of things such as then existed. The doctrine of justification by faith appeared to have been blotted out from the creed of the Church of Ireland. Mr Kelly stood almost alone to proclaim it, for which he became an outcast from society, and felt what it really was to be reproached for the name of Christ. Some of his old friends pitied him, but shrugged their shoulders in scorn and contempt. Some were angry, and cast him off altogether. Those who really loved him, deeply mourned.

Being by nature of a peculiarly tender and affectionate disposition, he keenly felt the unkindness of friends, but that was little to him compared with the necessity he felt was laid upon him to render his family miserable by his conduct. He felt a woe was upon him if he preached not the Gospel, and he must obey God rather than even his own father. This was a severe trial, as there could not have been a more excellent son, and the idol of his family.

To save his father from pain he used often to leave the house at four or five in the morning, and return before breakfast, having met a congregation, and preached in some of the farm houses. His father had actually forbidden him to preach at Ballintubbert in the church which he and his family attended, but the Lord acknowledged his work by the many souls that were given to him. He expressed the joy that was set before him in his hymn beginning:

And art thou gracious Master gone,
A mansion to prepare for me,
Shall I behold thee on thy throne,
And there forever sit with thee?
Then let the world approve or blame,
I'll triumph in thy glorious name.

Should I to gain the world's applause,
Or to escape its harmless frown,
Refuse to countenance thy cause
And make thy people's lot my own?
What shame would fill me in that day
When Thou thy glory will display.

And what is man, or what his smile,
The terror of his anger, what?
Like grass he flourishes a while,
But soon his place shall know him not.
Through fear of such an one shall I
The Lord of heaven and earth deny?

He offered to give up his inheritance rather than cease to do the work that opened for him in every surrounding town and village. I remember Miss Kiernan said, his was a deep calling, for he had a great work to do. He needed all the sufferings, the relief from which produced a love which burned with increasing brightness to the end of his long and arduous labours in his Master's cause.

Bessy wrote about how Mr Kelly met his future wife at the house of a mutual friend in Dublin, Mrs Shirley. Elizabeth Tighe thought Mr Kelly was too merry for a religious man, and wore too bright colours in his waistcoats, although she was fashionably dressed herself, with long auburn-brown curls tumbling down from under her white cap. But she was humble, retiring and sincere, devoted to the study of the Bible and accustomed to the company of holy men and women. She had been educated by her mother from the age of seven in a little schoolroom, together with her sister. It formed in her a contemplative habit of mind, and an indifference to worldly things. She had a religious bent from a young age.

In the holidays at Rossana, she was like a bird let loose from its cage, as she climbed the mountains and ranged uncontrolled through woods and valleys, listening to the murmur of the dashing waters and the warbling of birds. But she was meek and resigned to the will of God, as to her mother. She was truthful and upright in conduct, with a fineness of feeling and taste, which helped her to meet the difficulties of the positions in which she was often placed; positions which made her actions misunderstood by some people. She had the deep humility that always accompanies knowledge of higher things, and she often said, 'A woman can never know more than enough to make her lament her own ignorance of all that might be known'. Mr Kelly remarked, 'If anybody ever got a wife from the Lord, I did.'

The Tighe family members had a tradition of doing good works; one of them was the founder of the House of Refuge, another the founder of the Orphan School. Mrs Shirley's grand-daughters carried on this tradition; one visited the poor and preached in jails, another ran an establishment for old servants who were passed labour (the Retreat), and a third ran a school to train girls for service. Mrs Tighe would have envisaged her daughter taking on this kind of role. She admired greatly the lives of Madame Chantal and Madame Guyon, whose writings were lent to her once by a Roman Catholic lady.

When Mr Kelly married Elizabeth Tighe, his family hoped that the marriage would make him give up what they considered oddities, and that his wife would influence him to cease from itinerant preaching. But she would not, and dared not, interfere. She knew who had given him the commission to go and preach the Gospel to every person. Instead of being a hindrance, she travelled with him from place to place, wherever a congregation was offered to him. Whether they lodged in a castle or a cottage, it was all the same to her, when she was with him. His preaching was exceedingly admired; crowds came to hear him in Dublin, and wherever he preached.

At the end of five years it was only the happy event of the birth of a son that kept Mrs Kelly from many of the preaching excursions. Still, they went together on an expedition to

Edinburgh to visit Mr Robert Haldane, whose work in Scotland, with that of his brother James, was similar to that of Mr Kelly in Ireland. They remained there a month; the custom was to meet in the evening and have conversations at early suppers. Mr Kelly took a lively interest in the plan adopted by the Haldanes for educating young men to preach on the Continent. Mr Kelly was one of the first on the committee of the Hibernian Bible Society.

Bessy Wingfield wrote: 'It has always pained me to hear my father spoken of as a dissenter; his spirit was unlike the sectarian spirit so often to be met with under that denomination. Though his followers might peculiarly claim him as their own, he was in reality the property of the whole Christian church.'

'The Believer's Love of the Saviour Is Liable to Variations; It May, from Being Warm, "Wax Cold".' (The Reverend Thomas Kelly)

While Mr Kelly was abandoned by most of his friends, Lady Roden, along with her step-daughters, always took his part. When Lord Roden lamented that such a promising young man should go mad, his wife replied, 'I hope he may bite my son'. Lady Roden would often sit in the jail at Dundalk reading the Bible to the prisoners. At the time the religious breakfasts were begun in County Wicklow, many people were astonished to see Lord Powerscourt (Richard Wingfield) attending with breathless delight. How did the change come about?

He had been a despiser and scorner of the followers of a crucified Saviour, but now he was a humble and self-abased learner at the foot of the Cross. His wife, who was the Rodens' daughter, had died mourning the loss of their firstborn child, which was caused by her sitting on its damp grave. Her deeply afflicted husband was brought to a knowledge of the Saviour, who alone was able to comfort him, by Mr Daly, the bishop of Cashel. Lord Powerscourt died too, not long after his wife.

His younger brother, Edward Wingfield, fell in love with the Rodens' niece (known for her gaiety and love of dancing) after she fell down a precipice and shattered her leg. Their conversation now turned to the things of God, a subject new and attractive to both. An attachment was formed that soon ended in their being married. But Edward was carried beyond his strength in his zeal to serve God. In his ministry he engaged in difficult and controversial sermons, and travelled continually in his work as secretary to the Bible Society. In addition, he managed a large property, and was guardian to his brother's two children as well as his own three boys. Like his brother, he died at the age of thirty-three.

So it was that Bessy's husband, William Wingfield, the youngest brother, became guardian to his orphaned nephew, the young Lord Powerscourt, who was only a child. The grief sustained by the family because of all the losses was best reflected in a poem by Theodosia Wingfield, the step-mother of the young Lord Powerscourt and his sister. The poem began:

Jesus, my sorrow lies too deep

For human sympathy,
It knows not how to tell itself
To any but to thee.

Theodosia had been widowed after a year of marriage. She carried on the tradition of Christian assemblies, and invited Christians from all denominations and countries to the family seat of Powerscourt. She said, 'Your parents alone fulfil God's intentions in families'. Bessy idolised her; she was Bessy's dearest friend. Theodosia and her two step-children died in their thirties, before Bessy died.

Bessy wrote of a viewpoint that she shared with her father: 'It gave him satisfaction to think that his family was the first one in Ireland to throw off the yoke of Popery, forced on them by England when it found a happy, civilized, learned and religious people, in a country long known as the Island of Saints. I pray that it may be so again.' She expressed this in a poem, which she wrote for a poetry competition she organised for the New Year of 1849. The last two verses were:

Erin, my country, my voice will I raise
To join with the seraphs in hallowed praise;
Saints again shall adore thee, rejoice once more,
Superstition and darkness shall fly from thy shore.

Once the pride of the nation, the joy of the world,
The Banners of Truth first by thee were unfurled;
England, oh England, to thy shame be it spoken,

Thou has leagued with the beast, and thy faith hast thou broken.

Finally, Bessy said that Caroline had been a comfort, from childhood, to every member of the family.

When Bessy died at forty-eight, she left five children. Her oldest child, Bena, married soon afterwards. Her son, Richard, would marry and have two children, before dying at the tender age of thirty-five. Her daughter Isabella would marry Robert Webber, a first cousin of Fanny Webber's boys, and have five children.

Then Mrs Kelly died the year after her daughter Bessy, having seen four of her children predecease her. Mr and Mrs Kelly had lived to their mid-eighties.

Fanny and Caroline Continue Life's Journey

Now there were only Fanny, Edmund, and Caroline. Fanny, not Edmund, inherited Kellyville. Her youngest child was still a schoolboy. Caroline lived with them. Fanny didn't have the support of a husband, and couldn't earn an income, but Edmund would be expected to have a job. The Wingfield children were supported by their father, who continued on until the age of eighty. In 1858, Fanny and Caroline had a holiday at Torquay with Robert Tighe, who took them on driving excursions into Devonshire. They returned for the wedding of Bena Wingfield and Henry Colley.

After all the deaths, Caroline was in her early forties. In contrast to her cousin of the same age, Freddy Hamilton, who married and started a family at this time, she was unlikely to find a marriage partner. Maybe she didn't want to marry. She had a very full life in her family. She was a practical person, and had a career working in and organizing charities. She was still managing to run the tatting business. An old Irish man and family friend once said to her, 'It's a murthering pity, Miss, that ye weren't male born'. The girls would have done as well at university as their brothers, if they'd been allowed to go to university at that time, and could have had professions.

Caroline was destined to be a kindly aunt, Aunt Can, to her nine nieces and nephews and, since she had so long a course, their children.

Edmund

What had happened to Edmund Kelly? Throughout the letters there were many anxious enquiries about his health and job prospects. After finishing a medical degree he worked in a post office. Mr Kelly enquired of an influential cousin about a preferment for Edmund in the courts of law or in the colonies, but the answer was not encouraging. Possibly he had a job near London. Caroline had little to say about him in her memoir.

Bessy Wingfield had written for her children in her memoir that they 'could not judge of what Mrs Kelly once was, not having known her till sorrow had broken her spirit, and deep-seated grief had bowed her down. It was not that three of her loved ones had gone before, and would be the first at Heaven's gate to receive her. No, of them she could speak and rejoice that they were beyond the reach of suffering and sorrow. But she mourned the hopeless illness of her second son, who had given every promise that health and talent could do that he would rise high in his profession, and be an honour to his family.' However, patient submission was Mrs Kelly's peculiar character; she would say, 'It is the Lord, let him do as seemeth him good'.

Edmund suffered from a depression or melancholia, and could not get started in a profession. He had studied medicine, but medicine had not saved the members of his family. He had seen their illness and death, and it affected his sensitive nature. It was hard for the boys to emulate the example set by their father. Yet Edmund continued to exist until 1870. Although little is known about him, he went to England and became a lawyer. There is some evidence that he lived with a widow who had children.

None of the three Kelly sons married and had children. They were in the most senior line of Kellys who could trace their descent from the warrior Maine Mor in the fourth century AD. Did this line of descent end? Maybe it didn't. It is not known if Judge Thomas Kelly's older brothers, John and Ulick Kelly of Galway, married or had children. Bessy Wingfield wrote that Judge Kelly's oldest brother 'wasted' a very large property, the sale of which was the cause of the youngest Kelly's going to the Bar. Judge Kelly said that he would never purchase any of that property himself, as people might think the cunning lawyer had got it from his brother. He left Fedane, County Galway, to take up residence near Athy.

A Mr Kelly of Dublin believes he is a descendant of this family. A DNA test shows that he has a significant relationship to the Kellys of Galway. He inherited documents linking his ancestor, Joseph Kelly, who lived in the nineteenth century, to Kellyville. He has a painting of the landscape at Kellyville by Thomas W Webber. So Fanny and her children kept in contact with this branch of the Kelly family.

Fanny lived until 1877. She continued to draw and paint. When her son Thomas and his wife visited from India in 1871, she drew a portrait of their first child, Oswald, who was thirteen months old.

The Webbers' bungalow at Hoshangabad, Central Provinces, India, 1870. Matilda Webber with baby, servants, horse and carriage. (Photo album in British Library)

Matilda Webber sitting on an elephant. This elephant was lent to the Duke of Edinburgh for the Great Hunt of 1870. (Photo album in British Library)

Bhootia woman 1870s (Photo album in British Library).

Fanny's Sons

Fanny's son Thomas had travelled when young in America, where he rode broncos in the Rocky Mountains. In 1860 he went to India, sailing round the Cape of Good Hope, to build roads. One of the first was the road up to the new hill station of Naini Tal. He became a forest surveyor in the Indian Forest Department, under Dietrich Brandis, and then was made deputy conservator of forests in the Central Provinces and Gorakhpur.

He took photographs, mainly of forest trees, which show him camping and travelling in the bush, and meeting the local people. He journeyed into Nepal and Tibet. He claimed to be in the first group of Europeans to cross the Gurla Range north of the Himalayas, and reach the sources of the great river Brahmaputra, and in the second group to visit Lake Manasarowar. He made sketches on the way, including ones of Gurla Mandhata, and Mount Kailas. On leave in 1868 and 1869, he studied in Hanover the subject of conservation of forests. In 1902 he was to publish a book, *The Forests of Upper India and Their Inhabitants*.

Thomas married his relative Matilda Barstow, at Garrow Hill, York. (They were both descendants of Colonel John Irwin of Tanrago, County Sligo.) Matilda visited Ireland, before going to India with him. Only two years later, Thomas gave up his work in India because of his wife's ill health, and they returned to Ireland. Their second son died; they had a daughter in 1874. Before she died, Fanny had acquired a few grandchildren to be interested in.

Fanny's son Charles fought in the Indian Mutiny, along with Dicky Wingfield, and was one of the leaders of the escalading party at the storming of Jhansi. Thomas Webber wrote: 'The walls of the ancient fortress of Jhansi were thirty feet high all round the city. An eye-witness, Major Baillie, said that the young subaltern of the Royal Engineers who was first over the parapet, using his revolver and sword to good purpose, was my brother.' This was at the height of British militarism in the late nineteenth century.

Returning to England, Charles Webber married Alice Hanbury-Tracy, and their four children were born before Fanny died. For some years he was an instructor in military surveying at Woolwich, and he took up the study of the electric telegraph, and its military applications. He then served in the Austro-Prussian Campaign, in Zululand, Natal, Transvaal, Egypt, and the Nile expedition. He retired with the rank of major-general. He founded the Society of Telegraph Engineers and Electricians, which became the Institute of Electrical Engineers, of which he was one of the first presidents. He was a chairman and managing director of manufacturing firms, including London electric light and power companies. According to his nephew Oswald Webber, he installed the lighting for the Tower of London, and was consulting electrical engineer to the London Tube Railways. Two of his sons would settle in South Africa.

Fanny's oldest son, William, married Anna King, widow of the Earl of Kingston, in 1873, and he resided with her at Mitchelstown Castle. About half their income was used up in paying off a mortgage. They did not have children. (Their story was written by Mark Bence-Jones, in *Life in an Irish*

Country House, 1996.) Fanny's youngest son, Francis, may have been less robust than her other three boys. He served in the army, and married a widow, Mary Tottenham (née Crofton), but did not have children, and died at the age of forty-seven.

Because William had gone to live at Mitchelstown Castle, Thomas and Matilda Webber inherited Kellyville, where they had sometimes stayed when Fanny was still alive. Thomas worked as an agent. Matilda gave birth to a second daughter.

Caroline Kelly was the residuary legatee of her cousin Robert Tighe in 1873. She moved to a house at Monkstown, Dublin, in 1878, after Fanny died. She wrote a letter to Matilda:

2 Eaton Square, Monkstown, Co Dublin.

Dearest Tillie – Of course you had better use whatever linen there is as if it was your own – and cut-up old cloths etc. I know most of them were very old – except some good large ones for the dining-room table – the 'lovely dear old damask' which must be 100 years old – I left quite separate – as I knew how much you respected old damask and I think it ought to be an heirloom – but I fear some of it is very ragged – and would be much the better for your clever fingers and some darning cotton. When you have a little time on your hands, you must be extremely busy – I know how hard I found it to get settled even in this small house – I shall be delighted to go to see you – when you get more settled and when I am not engaged here – I shall love to see your improvements – I am afraid I am a born Radical – as I do like changes of furniture etc – though not like that dreadful Parnell and Co.

Thomas Webber was a keen shot and rider to hounds like his brothers, and used a muzzle-loading sporting rifle and gun. He visited America again, in 1886, for a bison hunt. His policy was to shoot only a few adult male animals; he gave the skins of two Indian wild dogs to the Natural History Museum, Dublin.

Caroline was a regular guest of her nephew William at Mitchelstown Castle, where they played classical music after dinner, even when she was in her eighties. She played the violin, and he the cello, and sometimes there was a visitor who could accompany them on the piano. As Caroline had painted, (and written poems too), like the other Kelly girls, she might have sketched and painted with Thomas Webber, who was a prolific landscape artist, when she visited him. Thomas painted a copy of Romney's portrait of Thomas's grandmother Elizabeth Tighe, just as Elizabeth (Mrs Kelly), or one of her daughters, had painted a copy of Romney's portrait of John Wesley, the Methodist preacher.

Sometimes Thomas's little son, Oswald, went and stayed with Caroline in Dublin. Oswald trained with the Royal Engineers; in the 1890s he sailed around the world with the navy, and worked on submarines in Hong Kong. Caroline wrote letters to Oswald when he was fighting in the Boer War, to which he had gone with a horse given to him by his Uncle William. Oswald was building, with Lord Kitchener, camps in which Boer women and children would be interned. He wanted to know if he had, as a child, caused Caroline any trouble.

Caroline's Memoir

Caroline wrote her memoir in 1901 and 1902, with a bit of arm-twisting from Charley Webber, who helped her, and styled himself as the editor. She had collected notes that needed putting together before they were lost or dispersed. There were poems written by family members, death scenes, genealogical information, newspaper cuttings, and detailed accounts of friends, relations, and the Irish people who lived near Kellyville. Some notes were jotted down during her conversations with Charley. They set it in a story of Caroline's life, which she referred to as recollections by 'Aunt Can' which were not worth recording. There is little in it for the period after 1860; it was about her life as a member of the Kelly family. A photo on the title page shows a good-looking elderly lady in a mob-cap.

Caroline died in 1906 when she was nearly ninety. She had outlived half her nephews and nieces: Bena Colley, Dick Wingfield, Charley and Francis Webber. By the time she died, Caroline was a great-aunt many times over, and even a great, great-aunt.

Appendix to Part Three

A Poem by Mary Tighe

Caroline Kelly included in her memoir an unpublished poem written by the poet Mary Tighe, for her nephew Tom Kelly, in 1803 when he was four years old:

How bright is the sky and how clear is its blue,
When the light-giving sun all unclouded I view,
But though glorious and dazzling the sun that I see –
'Twas my Father in Heaven that made it for me.

How sweet is the earth and how green are its bowers,
How rich are its fruits and how fragrant its flowers;
How pleasant to think of each object I see –
'Twas my Father in Heaven that made it for me.

How kind is my mother, how fond of her boy,
In her eyes I can read that I am her joy;
But though dearest and fondest and kindest she be –
'Twas my Father in Heaven that gave her to me.

PART FOUR

MY MOTHER, JOAN WEBBER

Characters, for reference:
Joan Webber, née Wilkinson, and her husband William Webber.
Their children, Dorothy, Sylvia, and Margaret.
Joan's parents, the Revd Christopher Wilkinson and his wife Florence.
Dorothy Wilkinson, Joan's sister.
Marjorie and Tom Miles: Marjorie was Joan's sister.
Joy and Hume Chidson: Joy was Joan's sister.
Amah.

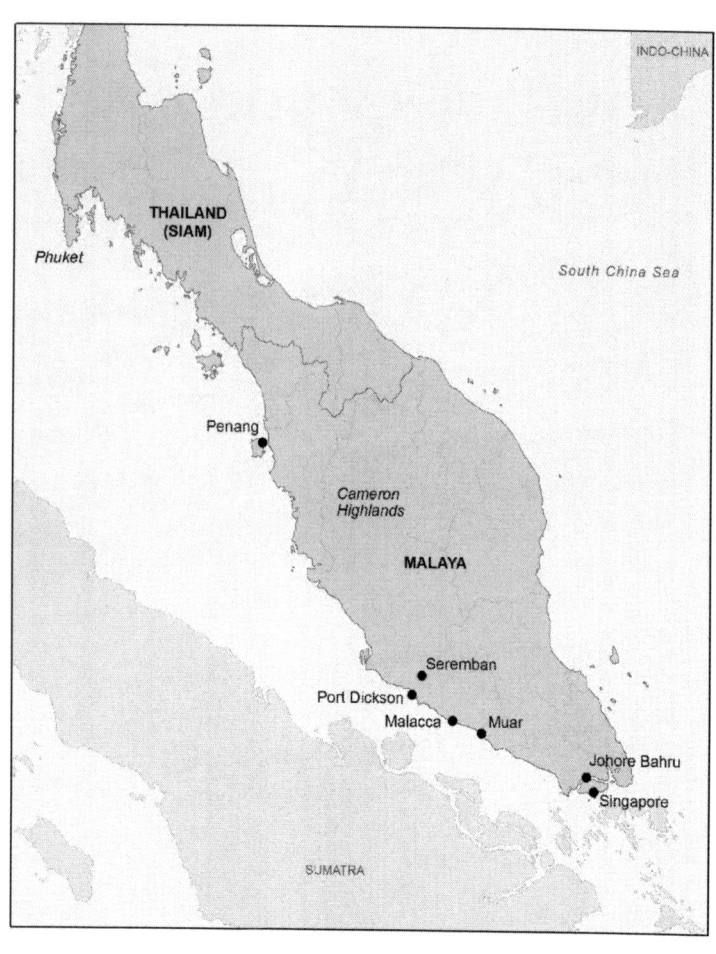

Southern Thailand and Malaya.

The Wilkinson Family. In the centre are the Revd Christopher Wilkinson, his wife Florence, and their youngest child, Joan. Otherwise, left to right are Marjorie, Cuthbert, Joyce, Dorothy, and John. (Private collection, Australia.)

*Joan Webber, nee Wilkinson.
(Private collection, Australia.)*

*William Webber.
(Private collection, Australia.)*

House at Jorak Estate, Muar, Johore, Malaya.

Joan Webber, in floral dress, teacher at the Government English Preparatory School, Muar, in 1940. The other teachers shown are Mrs Betty Milne, and Inche Yusoff Tajudin. (Private collection, Australia.)

Sylvia Webber and Amah. (Private collection, Australia.)

An Independent Woman

Joan Webber and her three daughters escaped from Malaya early in 1942, just as Japanese forces overran that country from the north with unanticipated speed. Two of the daughters were taken to Australia by ship in the care of a friend; I was one of the daughters. Joan remained behind, expecting to give birth imminently; she sent some letters to her sisters in Sydney. One of the letters was written from India, where Joan and her two-week-old baby had reached a temporary safety. She wrote *The Last Two Months in Malaya*, the story of the escape. I will return to this story.

Joan taught English in Malaya (now Malaysia) at Penang in the north, and at Muar. She married a rubber planter, William Webber, who was the manager of Jorak Estate, near Muar. They were going about their daily lives on the rubber plantation with their two children, aged seven and four, and the third expected soon, when William was mobilized for military action. He was a trained volunteer in the civil defence forces. He would become a prisoner for a time, and the family would be fragmented. The people who worked on the estate,

Malays, Chinese and Tamils, had to manage to live, for the duration of the war, under Japanese occupation.

Joan, as Joan Wilkinson, left Australia for Malaya in 1929, thirteen years before these events, to stay with a sister. She had three sisters and two brothers. There was a chain of events in her family. One of the sisters married a man who worked in the dredging of tin in Thailand (then Siam), and she went to live with him in southern Thailand after the First World War. Another sister went to stay with her and, after a time, met and married a British lawyer in Penang, northern Malaya. A brother who had been educated in England, and had a technical training in engineering, went to work in Malaya as a result of the same family connection. They were like camp followers. The other brother, because he felt he was English, joined the British army. By 1929 one sister, who was a headmistress, remained in Australia.

The Wilkinson Family

The Wilkinson family had arrived in Tasmania forty years earlier, from Yorkshire. In the nineteenth century, four generations of Wilkinsons were vicars of Ellerton and Bubwith, East Yorkshire villages. They had no wealth or land; their asset was their education. Now the Reverend Christopher Wilkinson and his wife Florence found opportunity in the new world of the British empire. Florence's guardian for most of her life, Aunt Shann, who was to have accompanied them, died shortly before they left. The children, the three of them, remembered saying a sad goodbye to their elderly grandparents, who would die within a couple of years of their departure.

The family had a rough trip in a steamer with sails; the sails added to her speed. The little boys gleefully explored the out-of-bounds boat deck and engine room, with their mother in hot pursuit, while their father was overcome by seasickness. In his *Whitaker's Almanack* for 1888 the Reverend Wilkinson wrote down the ports of call, between 2 April and 23 May, until they arrived at Formby. Formby was later named Devonport.

At first the Wilkinsons lived in a vicarage near a beach, at Emu Bay (now Burnie), where they kept farm animals and had a flower and vegetable garden. The children collected shells, climbed the red rocks and caught fish stranded in rock pools by the receding tide. They played and fought in a bush paddock at the back of the house. Soon there were two more children. Joan wrote later about a photograph which displayed 'one boy on a horse's back, another on the gate, the girl Dorothy posing proudly in front of the cow and calf with a basket of grain for the fowls, and the mother seated inappropriately in the midst of the farmyard life, with a long-clothed baby girl on her knee, and Fraulein standing behind'. They had a German nanny.

After a few years, the Reverend Wilkinson was appointed headmaster of Launceston Church Grammar School, a boys' school. He made a collection of stone implements from the camps of Tasmanian aborigines and sent it to the British Museum. Mrs Wilkinson met her father, Frank Shann, again; he had gone to Melbourne and left her with her Aunt Shann when she was three years old, after his wife died of tuberculosis. Now he had a new family.

Joan

Joan was born in 1901, the youngest child of the Wilkinsons, and seven years younger than her nearest sibling. She was often lonely; she was excluded by the older children, who formed a group. Her mother was too busy being house manager and matron to school boarders to give her much time and attention. Her mother did the house-keeping, looked after sick boys, and made clothes for the children. She was always running up and down the stairs, trying to be like a mother to everyone. The schoolboys delighted in tweaking Joan's long, brown plaits when no one was looking. They teased her about her second name, Theodosia, which was revealed in saying the catechism.

The Wilkinson children, including the girls, were educated at the boys' grammar school. At the age of twelve or thirteen, the oldest girl and one boy were sent to boarding school in Yorkshire, staying with an uncle and aunt there in the school holidays. The childless aunt was unkind to them; at a later time she showed kindness to the other Wilkinson son, so perhaps she just didn't understand how to treat children. The uncle died.

The oldest daughter, Dorothy, returned from England when she finished school. Dorothy and Joan often went in the dog cart with their father when he gave services in the bush. Joan remembered how they giggled and laughed, and their father chuckled in his beard, and they all sang *'Daisy, Daisy, give me your answer, do'* and other songs, on the duller stretches of road. In church their father played the hymns on a wheezy harmonium. The country folk liked best gathering outside after the service to share their joys and sorrows, and the news of the crops. The Wilkinsons were invited to a large meal in a farmhouse. They took home with them raspberries, damsons and mushrooms, growing wild. They picked sweet briar, with its hips and haws, to use for decoration in the drawing room, amongst the old Spode china, Edwardian peacock feathers and yellow satin tea-cosy, as Joan wrote in her reminiscences.

The oldest daughter liked doing the housework, and cooking and making jam, as well as teaching. She was almost a stranger in her family, and had left her friends behind in England. Now she turned away a suitor. She decided to study at university in Melbourne.

By the time she reached secondary school, Joan was able to attend the newly opened girls' branch of the Launceston Church Grammar School, where her oldest sister was now the head. Joan had been to school in Melbourne for a year when her sister was studying and teaching there, but she was made to return to show that the girls' school in Launceston was satisfactory for her family. Some of the girls teased Joan about her sister being the head, and it hurt Joan's relationships, both with the sister and the girls. She was a good student, who enjoyed swimming and playing hockey. She used to bicycle to the Mole Creek caves, a round trip of 100 miles. As it was the time of the First World War, the boys' section of the grammar school was short of male teachers, so one of Joan's sisters taught classes there. Another sister was running an old people's home.

Joan's oldest sister was eighteen years her senior and was more like a second mother to her. She paid Joan's living expenses when Joan went to university, at the cost of half her salary. Joan trained to be a physical education teacher for a time, and then took an honours degree in English. It wasn't compulsory any more at Melbourne to take maths, Latin and Greek in the first year of an Arts degree, as it had been with her sister. Joan became a teacher at private girls' schools in New South Wales. She loved quoting from Shakespeare, and *Alice's Adventures in Wonderland*. She wrote poems, and published a couple of them in a newspaper.

She had some male admirers in her twenties. She refers, in a note, to someone who wrote stories with her, and another person who had a picture painted for her. She was engaged to a man who became a bishop, but she broke off the engagement. It was because she felt he loved God more than her. She became an agnostic then. She went to England with a woman friend. They travelled round by bicycle, staying in pubs, and surviving on bread and cheese and similar rations. She taught there for a few months, but returned to Australia when her mother became ill.

While Joan was busily engaged with her life in this way, her family made some changes. The Reverend and Mrs Wilkinson had retired in 1918 to live on an orchard a short distance out of Launceston. They were taking care of the school-aged son of one of their daughters (now Marjorie Miles, living in Thailand) and her first husband; her first husband had died of tuberculosis. The little grandson rode to the grammar school every weekday on his pony. When the oldest Wilkinson daughter, Dorothy, became a headmistress in

Sydney, she was made guardian to the boy (her nephew), who moved with her to a boarding school there. He often spent weekends with her at the school premises where she resided, and school holidays with her in holiday cottages which parents of her pupils lent to them, when not in use.

The Wilkinson grandparents decided to change their situation completely. They sold their orchard and went to live in Sydney, and another daughter went away, to stay with her sister in Thailand. The elderly couple could not afford to buy a house, but rented their accommodation for the remainder of their lives. In this way they were close to any family members they still had in Australia. They could spend time with their grandson.

The Miles Family

British people who lived in the Far East frequently had children in boarding school in their countries of origin, as they considered there was no suitable education in the places where they were located. They took regular periods of leave, about six months every three or four years, to return (by ship) to England or Australia or other countries the British inhabited. It was often regarded as necessary for their health. The Miles family in southern Thailand lived in this manner and were soon to send a second son to boarding school in Sydney. Their children were born in the hospital at Penang. They went to boarding school at the age of seven or eight years.

Then, in 1929, the Miles family bought a home in Sydney, which became a nucleus and refuge for the whole extended family. Whenever any relatives found themselves temporarily without any particular lodgings, as they frequently did, or were on leave, they could stay at Hillwood, in Wahroonga. The family referred to it as a house that expanded like elastic. It was a large rambling house with verandahs, on a few acres, with stables and sheds. It was not really in a suburb then, but in the bush. Some of the children went to a school they called the 'bush' school. The family had grown to six children. They had a pony. For a few years they still lived partly in Thailand, and at times needed someone to mind the house. When he became ill in 1929, the Reverend Christopher Wilkinson went to Hillwood with his wife, and he died there.

After her father's death, Joan, who had been teaching in Sydney, decided to make a change in her life. She would visit her relatives in Malaya. She took testimonials with her, intending to work as a teacher. A family friend, the Reverend Nugent Kelly, described her as intellectual, of good character, and as having a scholarly knowledge of literature. There were others in a similar vein. Some of the references attested to her ability in teaching. One Violet Hancock, a state school teacher who had once taught at the grammar school, commented that 'Happy in the possession of English parents, and brought up in a cultured English home, Joan was safeguarded from the ugly twang and speech rampant on the mainland of Australia'. This English accent was in great demand in schools both in Australia and Malaya.

Penang

In Penang, Joan boarded for a while at the home of her sister Joy, who had married Hume Chidson. Joan obtained employment at the St George's Anglo-Chinese girls' school, which she would hold for almost four years. She was not a trained teacher like her oldest sister, but she had about five years' teaching experience. Starting at thirty British pounds a month, she became head of secondary school English, in which the girls sat for the Junior and Senior Cambridge certificates. She had a Miles relative who was involved in the Turf Club, and she rode race horses there as a hobby. She bought a car. Young men were interested in her. She was a tall, good-looking woman, with olive skin and long brown hair plaited over her head.

Joan had idolized her father and her oldest sister, Dorothy. Her sister wrote a poem about their father when he died:

> *Each age has its Christophers. While some on burning wheels*
> *Elijah-like speed up to God, others in waters fierce*
> *Nigh lose themselves. In saintly days*
> *The Christ-child came to Christopher; but how*
> *He later went to meet his Lord is veiled.*
> *And thus the legend stands that all may know,*
> *Through bearing others' burdens comes the Christ.*

She had written many poems that were lost or thrown away. Joan wrote to the sister about a window she imagined in a church, portraying their father as Saint Christopher, with 'A furry thing or two in his arms as well as the Child, or perhaps a maggy perched on his shoulder. A gum tree growing on one side of the river, and an oak on the other, and as many plants and animals as could be jumbled in. Underneath, that verse from *The Ancient Mariner*, "He prayeth best, who loveth best all things both great and small".'

Her sister sent her pictures of koalas and rock drawings for her pupils. ('Please, Miss Wilkinson, will you tell us about the Australian native people?' they asked.) By this time, Joan had saved the money to pay back her sister for her university education. She asked her sister to send her paisley shawl, a book of ballads and *Peter Pan*, her diary and old letters, and to burn her love letters.

Joan might have visited her sister Marjorie, who had gone back to Thailand with her husband and their three youngest children, and was living on the island of Phuket. She might have met with them in Penang. But the economic depression temporarily ended the Miles family's prospects in tin-mining. They returned to their home in Sydney, where, for a few years, they had a hard struggle to make ends meet.

Joan enjoyed her life in Penang. She wrote about the local people, and about a Siamese play she saw:

A 'Special Engagement'

In Penang, moonlit nights are pure magic. It is impossible to stay indoors. Driving about on such nights, I stumbled upon things: A Malay 'ronggeng', in which two dancing girls sang in strident voices as their feet wove intricate patterns on the ground, while rows of men watched solemnly, one after another getting up to show his skill by dancing opposite the girls and following their steps. Or through the open doorway of a Chinese house I saw yellow-robed Buddhist priests chanting, before an altar, prayers for the repose of a soul.

But the night I saw the Siamese players it was as if I had stepped back in time to see a medieval village play. It was late, and my friend and I were driving home, but we stopped when we saw the crowd. A rough shelter and exposure had been made in a grassy space, and the performance, and even the audience proper, were hidden from us by the solid wall of people that stood around it. Then above their heads we caught a glimpse of tall gilt head-dresses. 'Siamese players', said my companion. 'Have you got any money?' We were looking doubtfully at the few cents we could muster when a Chinese man spoke to us in English. 'You would like to see?' he asked. 'No, no! Free show. Go in. I will get some chairs.' He said his household was celebrating a 'special engagement'.

It was the interval. A mass of bright-eyed boys wriggled expectantly on their stomachs as they lay under a small stage built on one side, which was used as a wardrobe. Presently the players, who had been squatting in a circle, got to their feet for the next act. Their leader had an ugly, humorous face. He put on the towering Siamese head-dress, gilt, with curious peaks and decoration rising to a spike in the centre. His troupe of men and boys fell in behind.

They were all elaborately dressed; head-dresses, heavily beaded collars, and coats of bright colours wired at the edge into quaint upward curves, like those seen on the eaves of Chinese temples. They wore 'panungs', pieces of cloth curiously twisted to look like shortened baggy trousers. They began swaying in a file to the slow rhythm of their own singing. But they were dancing not so much with their feet as with their hands. Arms rose and fell in sinuous motion, wrists turned and bent, fingers writhed, significant to the very tip, expressing languor, sensuality, scorn, mockery, laughter, mischief, all by turns.

The chanting and dancing were only a prelude. Soon the play began. The dialogue was at times Chinese, Siamese and

Malay. The last was the only language we could follow, but their actions spoke plainly enough. It was a courtship. One of the men represented the village maiden, prinking and preening before her lover's visit. His 'hair', a long piece of silk of vivid peacock blue, he smoothed round the front of his head, combing it vigorously with a piece of wood, and kicking out the end which entangled his feet. He twisted it into a 'bun' behind, and the audience, who were mainly Chinese women, called out that it was lop-sided. Undismayed, he complacently surveyed his handiwork in a round brass tray, adding finishing touches, little pats and smoothings. He did not forget to scrutinize his back hair, using two trays. The hero entered, and the courtship proceeded.

After a while, the couple made a runaway match. They then returned with their infant child to ask forgiveness of an angry father. The child was a swathed log of wood. At last the grandfather's heart was softened. He took the baby in his arms rather clumsily. A woman in the audience told him how to hold it. He retorted, smiling, raised a laugh, and took her advice. But he was astonished to discover that his grandson had a wooden face. However, he saw the joke. So did the audience; two little Malay girls near me were giggling ecstatically. We gathered that he would not withdraw his forgiveness, if the young couple would promise to produce a real baby in good time.

William Webber

Joan's sister Joy Chidson, with her husband and their baby, moved from Penang to live further south, near Muar. They rented a house at first on a very large rubber estate, Craigielea.

Such large estates sometimes had bungalows to spare for people to rent, perhaps because someone was on leave. After a while they got to know a young English bachelor, William Webber, who was the manager on a smaller rubber estate adjoining theirs. They often invited him to come over for dinner. When they moved again to live in Muar, they asked him to call in and see them when he was in town. He did. So Joan was to meet William when she came down to stay with her sister in the school holidays, just as that sister had met her future husband through another sister.

William Webber left England for Malaya in 1926, at the age of eighteen, to work for Singapore Para Rubber Estates. He was a typical private school recruit of good social background. He had been educated at secondary school level at Dartmouth Naval College, but he was found to be too near-sighted to work for the navy at sea, which was what he wanted to do. He studied engineering at university in London for one year, and gave it up. He spent a year on a large rubber estate near Seremban learning the ropes before being appointed as assistant to the manager at Jorak, about ten miles from Muar. The young assistants mainly supervised weeding, and calculated the pay for the coolies (workers). He was like the man in the song I learnt as a child:

Satu orang pergi,	(One man went to mow,
Pergi potong lalang,	Went to mow a meadow,
Satu orang sama anjing	One man and his dog
Pergi potong lalang.	Went to mow a meadow.)

William was slim and handsome. With his straight black hair, Roman nose and suntan he could almost have been mistaken for an Indian. He rode a motorized bicycle which he often fell off because of the rough state of the roads; the roads were built at a slightly lower level at the sides, which was hazardous. He carried a gun, and sometimes shot wild pigs, deer, squirrels, iguanas, cats, and green pigeons. He wore all-white tropical attire, with shorts, and long socks up to the knees; after hours, he changed into a sarong, and the short, sleeveless Malay jacket. Occasionally, a cobra got into the bath through the water pipes, and had to be removed. There was no electricity, but he had a wind-up gramophone for entertainment. Lying in bed, he listened to the barking of frogs, and the clucking noises of nightjars and the little lizards that ran around the walls.

He described his job, in letters to his mother, as a gentleman's occupation. But some of the gentlemen could not stand the climate, the living conditions and the monotony, and drank a great deal of alcohol; some of them eventually gave up and went home. William could work hard and was a stayer; he was capable of learning the job and of running an estate. The 'tote', he called it. The planter had to plant trees, manage the coolies, and tend to the care of both of them. Natural good health and the ability to withstand diseases and insects were par for the course. In that climate scratches and bites could turn into ulcers. William had come down with dengue fever once.

Jorak was 1700 acres in a long strip, about five miles long. It was a mixture of old and new rubber trees and of flat land, jungle and swamps, hills and mountains. Inhabiting the jungle were tigers, panthers, elephants, monkeys, and snakes, which emerged into the more open land from time to time. The property was thought to have been a misjudged purchase by the company because it was too marginal in productivity. The labour force consisted of 180 Tamil Indians, 120 Javanese, and 60 Chinese. Each ethnic group of coolies tapped the rubber from the trees in its own area; only the Javanese could cope with the swamps, where malaria was highly prevalent. William was assigned to supervise the Tamil group. He wrote to his mother that he had started to learn Malay, which was an easy language, but Tamil was difficult.

The coolies were accommodated in long huts, or lines, divided into sections for families, which were maintained by the planters. The tappers were free to move and take advantage of better pay on another estate at any time, and managers were also free to lay them off. Taking up another row of lines were the office, the dispensary, the rubber store and packing shed, and conductor's and clerk's quarters. Also on site were a factory for making the rubber sap into latex sheets, and a smoke house for smoking them. While William's pay was thirty-four British pounds a month, his servants' pay was one tenth of that. This was such a princely life for Tamils that they were flocking to Malaya. Yet William could barely save anything out of his salary.

The social life of the planters and their families revolved around clubs which had been set up on particular estates. There were clubs at Lanodron and Nordonal, two parts of an old estate established about thirty-five years earlier, which were situated on either side of the Muar River, near Muar. The manager had a charming Irish wife from Dublin who ran popular tennis tournaments, dances and parties. Otherwise, there was the Muar Club, for Europeans only, more frequented by government officials, whom William thought mean and narrow-minded. The club provided golf, tennis, clay pigeon shooting, billiards, pool, pontoon, bridge, refreshments and dancing. Sometimes teams were organised for rugger and cricket. The Muar Rest House catered for dinners.

As he came to know the local crowd, William was invited to dinner parties at people's homes, and he often played bridge or billiards long into the evening. He joined the Johore Volunteer Engineers, a section of the civil defence forces, and did special training with them. He kept in touch with world affairs through reading: his parents sent him the *Times*, the *Spectator*, *Punch*, and the *Illustrated London News*, and William subscribed to *Scientific American*, the Institute of Electrical Engineers' journal, and *Blackwood's Magazine*. There was a local lending library.

William anticipated making a fortune in twenty years, and then retiring. Two years on he earned more and owned a new Morris saloon car. Now there was talk of professional standards in rubber planting which would require planters to sit exams in such subjects as languages, book-keeping, and plant biology, but William was assured that if he continued with the same company they wouldn't press it. All this was to be shelved because of the world-wide economic depression of the 1930s.

At the end of 1929, after a four-year stint and only a brief holiday in Calcutta to see his brother, an engineer, William was due for the usual six months' leave on full pay. He returned to England to visit his parents, who had a permanent home at last after leading a wandering life for many years.

When William went back to Malaya in 1930, managers and others senior to him, with two or three times his salary, were being sacked. Suddenly he found himself solely in charge of Jorak, apart from the help of a weekly visit from a company overseer. With a salary of forty-two pounds a month, but no family to support, he still had his head above water. He had proved himself in the job and was virtually the manager, at twenty-three years of age. He ran the whole estate on his own, living in the one good bungalow, and that's what he preferred to do.

A Love Affair

Joan and William fell in love at the dance in the Muar Club for the new year of 1933. Joan was staying with her sister in Muar for the school holidays. Joan went to William's house one time, and they danced there alone. He proposed to her, and she accepted. He thought she had been in love with him a little earlier. Joan returned to her teaching job in Penang.

William's mother had died the previous year, and he had been lonely and despondent. He tuned in through the shortwave radio every evening to music from London, or Bandung, Java, and wrote letters to Joan, just as he had to his mother ever since he had been at boarding school. Only his letters remain.

It had all happened suddenly at a time when each of them had another admirer in tow. They needed to be on their own somewhere. They were planning a short vacation at Fraser's Hill, a rest house in the high country where Europeans could escape from the intense tropical heat. The couple did not want the gossiping, narrow-minded people in Muar to know of their affair. They exchanged photos by post; they had mostly seen each other in the dark. Joan was hesitant to send photos of her that William mightn't like. He liked them, and selected one to send his father. He added, 'It does rather advertize your proportions. You might have put the belt a bit lower down, and not quite so tight.' His particular worry was that he wouldn't feel like talking to her at breakfast.

William described himself as a materialist, and said that English literature was not his strength. He was not intimidated by her. Joan said she had an inferiority complex. She was worried about her age, because she was a few years older than he was. William's father had commented on it, but it didn't matter to William. He described his family, the Rudstons, on his mother's side, as snobs with little sense of humour, and his Rudston aunt as a hypocrite; saccharine, insincere and sarcastic. 'May her fig leaf wither', he remarked. The Webbers had a broad and sometimes vulgar sense of humour, and the two sides hated each other.

William continued to lead his usual bachelor life, a fairly innocent one. It involved drinking alcohol in company and dancing with the women, whenever there was an opportunity. There weren't many single women. He went to Singapore and Malacca, now and again, to visit friends. He had servants: a cook, a 'boy' to clean the house and wait at table, and the *tukang ayer* (water workman) who washed his clothes and carried hot bath water upstairs. Sometimes he had a syce (a chauffeur) to drive the car. Joan said he was too thin; 'Wore to a shadder', she declared, affecting a dialect.

William said he was not much given to writing love letters. He wrote about his work. Joan sent him the *New Statesman* to read; he sent her the *Spectator* so that she could compare their political stance. He wrote about how he was painting and repairing the house in his spare time. She advised him about colour schemes: she liked white, cream, brown, and green. His car was being overhauled. Joan wanted to discuss her past love affairs to avoid misunderstandings, but William was singularly uninterested in them. He had trouble with his dresser (an Indian medical assistant), and had to hire a new one. He was fixing up his second car, an old one he used for driving around the estate; his office was over three miles from the bungalow.

He wanted to stay in a hotel in Penang for a weekend so he could see her, and they could go dancing. Joan said she hadn't been well, and she thought she might have dengue fever. She had had a fever at an earlier time. Now William had a cold that he couldn't shake off. His radio and gramophone were not working properly. Joan had been writing to him about theories that had interested her at university, such as those of Freud and the idea of repression. At last, he said that he realized he was ignoring her dissertations on subjects he knew nothing about. He remarked good-humouredly that she would soon make him feel inferior.

They had their holiday together, and she visited Jorak again. Then they were satisfied to announce their engagement to their families. She still had a fever; it was undulant fever, caused by drinking untreated milk. She might have to go back to Australia to recover. He was still having problems with his car. He had trouble with his 'boy' and had to get a new one. He kept reassuring her and expressing affection and constancy. Joan's health improved. They spent a weekend at Penang Hill, and were looking forward to getting married in November; 'spliced', he called it. Joan rested at the hill station for most of her school holidays.

William cemented underneath his house, projecting the floor out under the verandahs to form a terrace. He removed two of the pillars holding up the house to make a space in the centre, and put in an overhead beam instead. He installed an electric light plant for the evenings, a WC, and curtains. He acquired an air-cooled kerosene refrigerator to replace the twice-weekly delivery of ice; most of the food was delivered by Singapore Cold Storage. The stove and water heater were run on solid fuel (any wood lying about). There was no telephone, and they had to make their arrangements by telegram. Joan was impressed by his installing the electric light.

Marriage

Joan gave up her teaching job, at forty-two pounds a month, and brought her car with her to William's place. Her expectation was to be his companion, and to have children. They would be married in Seremban, where Joan's brother and his wife lived. Joan's mother was coming from Australia to stay in Seremban. William's brother was coming from England to stay with him at Jorak. They are all in the wedding photo, along with Joan's brother-in-law Hume (her sister Joy had not yet returned from a trip to England). The honeymoon was a fortnight's holiday in Hong Kong; Joan bought a long, red brocade dress, with a Chinese style of collar, and cloth buttons done up down the front with cloth loops.

The house at Jorak had a sitting room, dining room, two large bedrooms, a bathroom, and wide verandahs. William called the sitting room the 'mosquito' room because it was wired to keep out mosquitoes. The beds had mosquito nets over them. A long covered walkway led to the kitchen and servants' quarters at the back. The lower storey, which William had created by cementing the floor, would, in the future, be divided into rooms.

Joan and William's first daughter, Dorothy, was born the following year while they were on leave in England. They were staying with William's relations. When the baby was due they asked for it to be brought on by balloon induction because William had to be back at work, and wanted to be present for the birth. Within a week of the birth William was on a ship returning to Malaya. Joan was left in England with William's father and his new wife. Joan and the baby had jaundice, and Joan also had haemorrhoids, difficulty with breast feeding, and an unpleasant nurse to contend with. The induction had upset her; it was a procedure that held some dangers and had not been medically necessary. It would be three months before Joan and the baby joined William again.

In reasonably comfortable conditions, they lived the 'pukka sahib' life, with Malay servants, and a Chinese amah to look after the child. But the bungalow at Jorak was situated too close to the area with swamps and mosquitoes. After a while, William contracted malaria. Joan was not feeling well either and she had become very thin. They decided that Joan, together with Dorothy, who was almost two, should go to Sydney for a spell. It would be five months before they returned. There was no shortage of places to stay and people to see. Joan's mother was renting a house not far from Hillwood where Joan's sister still lived with her family. Joan's brother and his wife had left Malaya and were also settled in Sydney. There was her sister, the headmistress, to visit.

The elderly mother, since her husband's death, had been on extended trips to England, Malaya, and Tasmania. It probably fell upon one of the family members to arrange new accommodation for her each time she came back. Not long after Joan's visit her mother became ill. She died at Hillwood.

While Joan was absent in Sydney, William continued to have bouts of malaria. He had a lot of work to do, and was taking quinine. He was building a garage with two rooms behind it, after which he would fill in the walls and windows for the ground floor of the house. He got back into the rounds of his bachelor life. In particular, he was having a good time with a lady friend who lived at Malacca, by the sea; her husband was away in Sumatra. She had started it by inviting him to a party at which, as it transpired, he was the only guest. They went out to dine and to see films. Then William had an accident in his car and cracked his kneecap; the car could not be repaired. After that he wasn't so mobile. He had trouble with a tiger: one of the Tamils, carrying no gun, chased it because it had taken his dog! William put a door on the house to prevent the tiger from bounding up the stairs in the night.

In that same year, 1936, William was earning seventy British pounds a month in salary and commission, as a manager. He put in a cost-of-living statement to his firm for himself, his wife and one child, for a raise to one hundred pounds a month; by the end of the year he was getting it. One third of his expenditures covered food, clothes and household goods, including alcohol and cigarettes. Energy costs were a mere one pound a month for fuel and upkeep of lamps and the kerosene refrigerator.

The remaining two thirds of his costs fall into four equal categories, each equivalent to one sixth of his total pay:

1) Servants' pay: one cook, one boy, one amah, laundry contract, part-time syce (chauffeur), and part-time gardeners.

2) Car costs for two cars; one is used only on the estate and does not require registration.

3) Insurances: medical, dental, and necessary savings for fares.

4) Entertainments, etc: home entertaining; short holidays; radio, gramophone and photography; books and newspapers; stationery and postage; games, recreations, films, refreshments, dinners; and membership of the Muar Club, the Muar Golf and Tennis Club, and the Malacca Swimming Club.

As soon as Joan returned from Australia, she became pregnant again, just as she had straight after her marriage. The baby, Sylvia, was born in Singapore. Joan hired a new amah to look after the children. On the Webbers' next leave the amah travelled with them to England as a nanny. William's father died before they reached him. He was the last parent of William and Joan to die.

Boarding School

When Joan and William's daughter Dorothy was only five years old, she was sent to boarding school at Tanglin in the Cameron Highlands, Malaya. There was no local school considered suitable. This would have seemed quite normal to William because his brother and he were sent to boarding schools in England at a similar age.

The Webbers had been landowners in Ireland. William's father, Oswald, was in the army, and then worked as an electrical engineer at the Dublin post office. He rejoined the British army in the First World War, probably in order to retire with a better pension; he was seconded to the Dublin post office to continue in the same job. After the uprising of 1916, he was in great danger from the IRA, and he and his wife changed their address in Dublin from time to time. Whenever the IRA cut the telegraph wires, it was Oswald's job to reconnect them. For their safety, the boys often spent their school holidays in hotels at Bournemouth and the like, with their mother or their Rudston aunt. William couldn't invite his school friends to stay in the holidays, because he virtually did not have a home. (His father would sell the family property, Kellyville.)

I digress further: The Webbers migrated to Ireland in 1625 around the beginning of the British Empire, a time of great expansion across the globe of population and trade. Joan and

William lived in the demise of that empire. Generations of Webbers were mercenary soldiers, fighting in foreign countries, perhaps never to return. It was a typical occupation. The lands they held in Ireland were not sufficient to support all the sons in a family. For large amounts of time, a wife and her children were separated from the man of the household, who came home when he could. But the wife and children stayed together.

In the later part of the British Empire women were more likely to accompany their husbands to foreign lands, or to meet them there; it was the children who had separate lives in boarding schools, probably in a different country. The British had a tradition, centuries old, of sending young boys to boarding school.

This context helps to explain how it was that young English 'orphans' were sent to institutions in Australia, or that Australian aboriginal children were taken from their mothers and placed in institutions at a young age. On this subject, John Bowlby, the author of *Child Care and the Growth of Love*, has stated that children under the age of twelve, especially the younger ones, may suffer mental harm by being sent to boarding school. I have included in an appendix at the end, on this subject, the experiences of my Wilkinson ancestor of the eighteenth century who went to boarding school for fifteen years, which must be the longest time anyone did.

The Escape from Malaya

In 1940 and early 1941, Joan was teaching in Muar at the Government English Preparatory School (for Malay boys), and at the Sultan Abu Bakar Girls' School. She took over as temporary headmistress from a friend, Mrs Betty Milne. Joan's second child was three years old and could be left at Jorak with the amah. Not long after this spell of teaching, Joan was pregnant again. The family often went down to the beach at Malacca, about fifty miles away, where Joan's sister Joy Chidson, and her lawyer husband, Hume, now lived. The two Webber girls played with their three cousins.

The war in Europe seemed far away. Even in October 1941, Joan and William thought a 'Jap scare' had passed, and were planning their leave in Australia for the following year. But in December the Japanese attacked Pearl Harbour in the Pacific and started to bomb Singapore, and everything changed for William and Joan. By then Joy Chidson had taken her children to a safe haven in Sydney. However, the British were still complacent, and did not believe that Singapore was about to fall, as it did, on 15 February 1942.

William had trained in civil defence with the Johore Volunteer Engineers. When his unit was mobilized early in December 1941, Joan was a month or so away from giving birth to her third child. She was forty years old now. Her doctor had prescribed a mixture to calm her nerves about two months previously, but she began to feel unwell. She wrote to her sisters in Sydney:

I began to have most alarming symptoms: loss of memory, black-outs of sight, staggering, falling, drowsiness, giddiness, complete inability to think consecutively, incoherent speech, inability to write a letter that meant anything. Dr Crawford, when told of this, merely remarked that he thought I was looking better when he last saw me. William diagnosed it, quite by accident, from his planters' notebook, having stumbled on a paragraph entitled 'Henbane or Hyacymus poisoning'.

Joan stopped taking the medication and gradually recovered from the symptoms. But that wasn't all. In November their oldest child, Dorothy, aged seven, was sent home from boarding school early because she had been in contact with a child who had polio. She had signs of illness and was put into hospital, but, as it turned out, she had pyelitis and roundworms. She continued to be ill up to Christmas, so that they sometimes thought she might have dengue fever.

Under these conditions, it took Joan a couple of days to pack her husband's clothes, equipment and first aid supplies, for mobilization. The gear had to be in three separate bundles for different purposes, and she kept having to repack it because she'd put things in the wrong bundles. William, in the meantime, had to deliver to each member of his section a secret word, via trunk calls, and give orders to his employees for the running of the estate while he was away. Finally, he assembled his section in Muar, and got them in buses and cars to their war station in South Johore, where they would be attached, as sappers, to the AIF (Australian Imperial Forces). He would write letters home.

After seeing him off, Joan went home to black out the bungalow. It was an almost impossible task in a house built with wide openings for coolness. 'The only thing to do', she wrote, 'was to curtain our sitting-room windows well, and to use heavily shaded oil lamps instead of electric light. It was appallingly hot and stuffy. We had our evening meal before dark, and only used a darkened torch in the bedrooms.'

She invited another planter's wife and her two children to come and stay with her. They had been left in a very lonely place on Craigielea Estate without car or telephone. They had recently arrived from Indo-China. 'Her children were the two most spoilt and mismanaged brats I have ever seen,' wrote Joan, 'and her amah made trouble with my servants. I dashed about settling children's quarrels at the front of the house, and amahs' quarrels at the back, and did all the work.'

By Christmas, Joan was staying at night in Muar town with her friend Mrs Harley Clarke, a doctor. If Joan were to start labour in the middle of the night, it would be almost impossible, with the car headlights blacked out, to get down the very steep, winding road from the bungalow and the four miles of narrow track to the main road. But the children were thought to be safer on the rubber estate than in town.

Mrs Harley Clarke was in charge of reorganizing the Muar hospital on a war-time basis to receive war casualties. She advised Joan, because of the pregnancy, not to take a ship to Australia yet. After packing for William, Joan's body was swollen with fluid; the baby might have come on early and things might have gone wrong. They still didn't know if there would actually be a war in Malaya.

Joan heard about a ship two days before Christmas, when the state of affairs was beginning to look bad. The ship was going to take women and children to Australia. She was on the phone about it, in between packing, for the whole of the following week. She spent Christmas Day in the company of five children. She had brought from Muar the only child of her friend Mrs Meldrum in order to give Mrs Meldrum a chance to finish packing. She hoped that her children might be able to travel to Australia with Mrs Meldrum.

Meanwhile, the planter's wife who was staying with Joan went to Singapore to obtain passports and book passages for all their children. Amah went too, to see if she could travel with them, only to find that this wasn't allowed. Mrs Meldrum, on the other hand, was told that she could only go if she took more than one child, so it was decided that she would take Joan's two under her wing as well.

Joan continued to pack most of Christmas Day. Everyone had Christmas pudding, with enough ten cent pieces in it to go around. Dorothy said that her younger sister had chewed a glass ornament from the Christmas tree. Joan was frantic, but luckily she found that the doctor was on the neighbouring estate. Finally she heard that the bookings had been made. She wrote later, in January, to her sisters; 'Dear family', she called them, expecting the letter to be passed around:

A better advertized sailing you couldn't imagine, owing to the travel agent (Thomas Cook) making everyone ring them up every day to find out when the ship was going! This in a land riddled with fifth column, and the wires urgently needed by the army. I well felt I might be sending my children to their deaths. At last, the Governor walked into Cook's (much too late), and handed the whole thing over to the P & O shipping company and the navy, who soon got the people to Singapore and the ship off.

Dorothy was pretty much war-shocked before she left (she was really scared, and knew too much about it), me affecting her, I expect, very largely. 'Mummy, why does your face go like that? I can't bear it.' Well, I couldn't bear it either. I did try not to show things. They are better away from me too. My heart was bleeding for old poker-face, tender heart Sylvia, only just four, going off to a strange land without either her mother or her beloved amah. She's been most pugnacious about the Japs (when she's remembered them), her tough guy pose.

She hoped that the children would be good, and not a bother. She wrote that Sylvia sometimes still wet her bed, and that she couldn't help it. It was no good ticking her off about it, as it could cause psychological damage. Dorothy she regarded as a little paragon of virtue. She hoped that Dorothy would be able to go to day school, and live 'at home'.

The Children Leave

The children were instructed to go to Singapore on 30 December to catch the *Orion*. Amah went with them. They had to wait while bombing took place on two nights, and the ship left a day late, on 1 January. William managed to get leave to join Amah and see them off. On board, Mrs Meldrum had the Webber children moved to a cabin next to hers.

The ship reached Perth safely in less than a week, and continued to Melbourne, where Mrs Meldrum and the children disembarked. Mrs Meldrum's home town was Geelong nearby, but everyone took a train to Sydney, and surprised Joan's sister Dorothy by suddenly turning up at her school. Without much ado, she put them in a taxi and dispatched them to her sister's place at Hillwood, in Wahroonga. The children were to stay with an aunt who was a complete stranger to them. Marjorie Miles's husband and three sons were away at the war; her husband was a veteran of the First World War. Her three younger children, all girls, made their little cousins very welcome. Mrs Meldrum and her daughter rested some days before returning to Melbourne.

Joan's sister Marjorie wrote to Joan twice in January from Hillwood:

It's ages since I've written, but not for want of thinking. You have been on our minds all the time, and in your great anxiety you have had our sympathy. Now we have your darling children, what a joy, not only to have them, but to be doing something for you. What a heartbreak it was to part from them in those circumstances we know, and with what thankfulness you rejoiced when you knew they were safe in Australia. You certainly couldn't have found anyone better than Mrs Meldrum to bring them, from what I saw of her and the children. They are wonderfully fit, and so good, and their clothes arrived clean and everything just as it would have been with you, and an amah thrown in.

She said Sylvia felt flabby at first, as if she had lost weight on the voyage, but had firmed up and put on weight. Their Doctor Susie was treating Dorothy for pyelitis. Her daughter was doing everything for the children, but would not be their slave; Marjorie recalled how she herself used to say 'Dar-la id my slave' as a child, about her oldest sister. Her husband Tom, who had a posting with the Australian Army 300 miles away, had asked to be moved closer to Sydney so that he could get home every week to look after his 'two wives and three families' (the Mileses, Chidsons, and Webbers).

Tom Miles was anxious about his brother and his family too; they had moved down from Penang to Singapore. His brother was seen at the Singapore racecourse telling the coolies how to cut the hedge.

Joan's Escape

Joan was still staying in Muar town with Mrs Harley Clarke, the doctor, at least at night. By degrees she gathered together from Jorak and packed the household effects she thought she could save from the Japanese, such as the family silverware. She wrote, 'I was just about all in. I had legs like bolsters, and a heart just about thudding itself out of my old skin and bones.' In a letter to her sisters, dated 9 January, she said that Mrs Harley Clarke advised her to try and get to Singapore. 'I must have a comfortable car and someone with me in case I pup en route. But I don't suppose I shall. My babies are such stickers! I am most horribly boong oop wi' elephant, so it shouldn't be much longer.' A reconnaissance plane came over once when she was out walking, and she had to get into a ditch. Muar had the same air raid alarms as Singapore, and everyone had to put out lights.

Joan decided to go and stay with friends at Johore Bahru, just across the straits from Singapore. She heard that her brother-in-law Hume Chidson had evacuated himself and his lawyer's office files from Malacca, and was travelling to Singapore. Hume had been retired from the volunteers with a heart condition. (Like Marjorie's husband Tom, he had fought in the First World War.) Joan wrote to her sisters:

Hume left me with a message to telephone the chief police officer in Malacca. After I had spoken my piece, this man asked me when I was leaving Muar. I said, 'Monday morning'. He said, 'Um-m, well, I think you may just be in time', and strongly advised me to leave sooner. So I got in touch with Hume, whom I knew was spending the night at Batu Pahat, thirty miles south, and he said he would wait for me and see me safely through. My hostess came in just then and said she had been told to evacuate the hospital to Batu Pahat, behind the next big river, the next morning. It was hoped to hold the Japs at either Muar River or Batu Pahat.

I hired a car and dashed out to the estate. While I packed William's clothes, a Chinese packer hastily stowed our china and glass in boxes, and I locked them away. I might have saved myself the trouble, as anyone could have broken into the weatherboard house. I tried to find William's stamp collection, but brought the wrong box. I meant to bring the dog in to be destroyed, but could not find him as I was leaving. I was miserable about it, but then I was glad, as he might be there to be company for William.

I called at the office on my way out to say goodbye to the Indian clerk and the Indian dresser. They had been very decent and helpful to me after William went away. They stood one on either side of the car and looked at me dumbly, and I felt a swine. My children were safe and I was getting away, but they had to stay there with their wives and children, and take what came.

Joan left the next morning accompanied by Amah, and stacked up with the family silver and oddments she hoped to save. (She learnt later that Muar was bombed that very day.) She met Hume at Batu Pahat, and he drove down behind her to see that she was safe and sound. They passed a big column of Indian troops heading north. At the home of her friends at Johore Bahru she witnessed a dogfight over the straits. After one night there, a cold she had caught turned into bronchitis and she was taken to the hospital at Johore Bahru.

They kept me in bed a fortnight to cure the bronchitis, and rest a groggy heart. I also had a severe sinusitis which kept me awake nights putting ice on my face. But I dare say it prevented my thinking too much about William, or listening for the planes roaring overhead on their way to bomb Singapore 120 miles away.

I had a visit from William during this time, the first I'd seen him since mobilization. He was as thin as a rake and had much work, little sleep, meals when possible, but he was fit. It was hell having no air support. They lay out in the rubber all day being bombed, and got up at night-fall, without sleep, to do their work. They had no answer to it, but casualties were few; none in William's corps. My guess is that they were finishing the defences on the Mersing road that they, the Johore Volunteer Engineers, had already begun earlier. The fifth column was working well and every time an AIF headquarters moved, they had bombs next day. The letters AIF were often found cut in chalky soil with a huge arrow pointing in the appropriate direction. I myself saw someone signalling with a lamp from one of the hospital windows.

On 21 January, Joan, still in hospital at Johore Bahru, wrote to her sisters that she was having intermittent labour pains. She had nearly recovered from her cold and sinusitis. The swelling in her legs that could have made trouble for her was gone, and her heart was steady. Joan was able to instruct her bank, the Muar Bank, to send some money to Australia. (The bank offices had closed down in Muar, but had opened up after a few days in makeshift premises at Johore Bahru.)

On 25 January, all the patients were suddenly evacuated by ambulance to Singapore General Hospital. It was close to the docks, where most of the bombing was taking place. Joan experienced her first air raid that night. She was in the upstairs section with postnatal mothers whose babies were at least three days old, and women in the early stages of labour. They had to come down to the ground floor when the alarm sounded, some of them carrying babies. In the downstairs rooms were the women whose babies were only a day or two old, two in a room. The lower storey of the hospital had blast-proof walls.

Her Baby Is Born

At last her baby arrived. Joan wrote:

Margaret didn't seem to mind how many bombs fell, or how often I dashed up and down the stairs. But at last on 30 January she looked life in the face. It wasn't the sort of life I'd have chosen for her, but the Japs did take the afternoon off, and let us sleep that night as well.

When the alarm sounded, amahs and nurses flew to shut the window shutters on verandahs and in rooms. They, or the mothers, lifted the babies' cribs out of their stands and put them under the beds. Then everyone got under beds, tables, and couches. I dragged the pillows off the bed and stacked them around Margaret, putting one on top of her. The nearest bomb fell about a hundred yards away. I found the noise of the incendiaries coming down the most frightening.

I was worried about William, as a sapper from the Johore Volunteer Engineers (in to see his wife) reported that most of the corps had crossed to Singapore Island, but that William and some of his section had been sent up country on a last job. We knew there was very little 'country' left. How glad I was when William walked in next morning! He had returned the evening before. When he reached camp he received a note from me telling him about some luggage I'd had to leave behind in Johore Bahru. He got straight back into his car to go and fetch it, but found they were about to dynamite the causeway. He must have been one of the last to cross.

Earlier, they had been sent to blow up the railway bridge at Kulai in South Johore. The Japs were only a mile or two away. They placed their charges in position and were just about to blow the bridge, when a message came from the railway authorities that they must have a train over it first, going north. William ordered the detonators removed. He was then told he must remove all explosives, which was nonsense. As it was an order, he had to do it. They then had to leave, as the Japs were practically on them. So they pitched the charges in the river and came away. It looked very like a bit of fifth column on the part of the railway people.

The causeway across the straits was dynamited, on 31 January, by the British. There was a last-minute evacuation of women and children to England by ship, but Joan and her baby were not ready to leave yet. Joan's brother-in-law Hume spent most of his time, in the first week of Margaret's life, sitting on the doorstep of the P & O shipping company trying to get them a passage out. People still had to go through the process of booking passages and having their passports stamped. William took time off to see Joan. She wrote later:

I saw William three times in the week after Margaret was born, though I think he did without his sleep to come and see me. They were set to work the very night they crossed to Singapore Island to begin the defences on the north where the Japs were bound to attack. The Australians had been very much cut up in the fighting at Muar. They were given a section of coast opposite Johore Bahru where the Japanese were now in possession. They had far too few troops to hold such a big sector. I could see William was worried, but I did not realise how bad things were. We were being filled up with 'pep' talk in the newspapers. I suppose the Governor had to justify his refusal to get the women and children out of Malaya earlier.

On 8 February, Joan and her baby boarded the French troopship *Felix Roussel* with a companion, Hume's sister-in-law Mab, along with other women and children. Once the ship had disembarked its troops and taken on board the new passengers, it did not delay departure to replenish its provisions. Had it delayed, it might have become a burning wreck like other ships in the harbour. It had already been hit by bombs three times, but had not sustained serious damage. It was bound for Bombay.

Mab had been waiting for her husband, who was in the British Army, to arrive from Shanghai. But now it was best for her to leave. Hume would wait for him. Mab had said to Hume, 'Look after Chid for me', and he replied, 'I'd never forget my little brother'. Mab was company for Joan, and Joan needed her support. The food on the ship was poor and meagre. Joan was unable to breastfeed the baby, but a doctor saw that she received sufficient supplies of powdered milk and boiled water. The baby sucked hard on her thumb.

On reaching Bombay, they heard about the capitulation of Singapore. The Japanese had landed on Singapore Island the very evening the *Felix Roussel* had left. Joan wrote to her sisters, 'Hume did such a lot to help me get away, as I couldn't hustle for myself. It must have been very difficult for him with no car, and the P & O office moved out of town. I hope he realised how much I appreciated it.' A kind English family (the Baldwins) billeted Joan and her baby. Their host was the harbour master and could advise about shipping. Mab was housed with the army wives.

Joan received an allowance deducted from William's army pay. She was fatalistic about whether her husband or she would survive, but she wanted to get to Australia by ship as soon as possible. She wrote, 'I ought to be looking after my children, and not leaving it to my family'. Mab and she were nervous about the prospect of the voyage. One ship, after taking on a full load of passengers, was sunk in the Bay of Bengal. Another's port of embarkation was bombed.

Joan worked on making financial arrangements for her two children in Australia. She advised her sisters about schools and clothes. She thought she would be able to get a job teaching, and pay one of her nieces to look after the children.

Joan's baby was strong and vigorous, but Joan realized that a regular life jacket would not hold up a baby's head, so she adapted one by sewing more kapok-filled sections to it. She might have begun it on the *Felix Roussel*. She tested it on her baby in the bath water. She made a wristband for the baby with the name and address of her oldest sister inscribed on a metal plaque, in case the baby was rescued from the water without her mother.

Mab, Joan and Joan's baby obtained passages on the troopship *Dominion Monarch*, which was taking soldiers from the Middle East back to Australia and New Zealand. The ship was a converted passenger liner, painted entirely grey, which could carry more than 3,000 troops. It picked up thirty-six civilian passengers in Bombay and Colombo. The only signs of enemy presence were some Japanese high-flying dirigible balloons observed on 19 May. The ship arrived safely at Fremantle on 26 May, and continued around the Southern Ocean.

When the *Dominion Monarch* reached Sydney Heads on 2 June, 1942, it was in the middle of a period of Japanese submarine attacks on the east coast of Australia, which were aimed at coastal shipping. Two days previously Japanese submarines had sunk a ship in Sydney Harbour. On 3 June more ships just outside Sydney were sunk or damaged. Because of alarms and warnings, the *Dominion Monarch* was made to circle around outside the Heads for two or three hours before it was allowed to enter the harbour. It berthed safely.

Not long after her arrival, Joan received a postcard from William informing her that he was a prisoner of war. Hume Chidson, Hume's brother, and Tom Miles's brother were also taken prisoner. They would all survive.

My Childhood With Joan, or Without Her

I didn't spend much time with my mother, even as a child, but still she was controlling my life. I have few memories of being in Malaya. But from the time I arrived in Sydney at the age of four, I have many memories. My childhood was affected by war, separation, and being sent to boarding school.

I remember, before the war, watching Amah write Chinese characters with a bamboo brush she dipped in black ink. She wore black, smoothly ironed trousers, and a white shirt, and her hair was pulled back in a bun. I fell out of bed in the night, and Amah came with the sound of her bare feet on the wooden floor, and put me back on the mattress with my arms around the bolster. I was trying to bathe the kittens; they didn't like it, and scratched and mewed. Someone said to me, in Malay, *'Banyau jahat, jaga bibir'* ('Very naughty, mind what you say'). I was sitting on the stairs, looking down through the dining room at the people in the sitting room behind the mosquito wire. I kissed my father goodnight, and his moustache prickled me.

Hillwood

When I was just four years old, I arrived, with my sister, at my aunt's home, Hillwood, in Sydney. My aunt had red hair like me. I ran down the lawn with her youngest child, who was fourteen; she was holding on to her bicycle. My sister and I had our beds in the sleep-out, which was part of a verandah that had been closed in, and she had her own room that I could see into through glass. Mine was the bit that went around the corner of the verandah, with little louvre windows in it. At night I could hear my cousins whispering on their verandah bed. I could see and hear the tops of the gum trees waving in the wind and talking to one another.

The house was very large. There was a long, dark passage in the middle which led to all the rooms. Around the verandah way, I could walk out of the bathroom into the open sleep-out of one of my cousins, which had a mosquito net over the bed, and was off the bedroom of another cousin. Then I could go through my sleep-out onto the long, open back verandah, and come into the house again at the passage or the kitchen. There was a pantry off the kitchen, and I could climb through a window in the pantry, and reach another long verandah, which was closed in with wire. I could go in again at the dining room or the sitting room to the front hall and the front porch. My aunt kept the sitting room closed most of the time. It was fun to play hide-and-seek in the house.

My sister and I usually played in the wired-in verandah off the dining room. She had a doll called Pat, and I had my pink teddy. We had some doll's clothes, and a doll's pram.

There weren't many toys. We had old comics to read, and a book, *Little Black Sambo*. We played a game, roulette.

I would lie in the bath in a daydream, waiting for Amah to come and dress and feed me. She always did everything for me, and I only did things for her. One of my cousins had to come and get me out of the bath so that the family could use the bathroom and have dinner.

My aunt had two black cats called Fatty and Big Puss. Big Puss caught mice, while Fatty just lay around on laps, purring. When we had dinner at night in the dining room, my aunt sat at the head of the table with Fatty draped round her shoulders like a fox stole. One time I ate all my spinach so I would be strong like Popeye. I got down from the table and pushed my aunt sideways in her chair, holding onto the arms of the chair until the cat had to jump out of the way, and my aunt put out her hand onto the floor, and said, 'Ooh, you are strong!'. She had a lady called Olive who came to do housework, and she looked just like Popeye's wife.

At one end of the dining room there was an open fire in the corner which we sat round after dinner. My mother had sent a letter from India which my aunt read out aloud. My mother complained about her eyesight; she said that she needed new glasses. I cried because I thought she was going blind. I had a boil on my arm and had to be given castor oil. My aunt forced it down my throat with orange juice, while I screamed and cried.

My uncle and three boy cousins came back from the war sometimes. My uncle came more often, because he was working in Australia. If I took too long to finish my dinner, my uncle would say to me, 'Think of the starving children in Europe', and I would reply, 'Well, send it to them then, Uncle'. My aunt was always making things to send to the soldiers; she baked them fruit cakes, and knitted them woollen socks.

My uncle used to call me 'Goldilocks', and recite the poem, *Who is Sylvia?* I sat on his lap while he read to me from *The Sentimental Bloke*, which was illustrated with nude cupids, and from *Gulliver's Travels*. I remember the picture of Gulliver being tied down to the ground by Lilliputians, and my uncle's warnings about the yahoos of the world. There was a dark box-room off the hall, with a cord to pull for the light to come on, and it was full of old magazines: *National Geographic*, *Punch*, The Bulletin, and *The Illustrated London News*. I enjoyed looking at them, asked what the captions said.

My aunt often worked in the kitchen, where we had breakfast and lunch. I liked eating her porridge with clotted cream and brown sugar, scrambled eggs with Vegemite, and peanut butter sandwiches. She baked oatmeal biscuits and cornflakes crackles. She kept about thirty chickens in a wired pen, and we collected the eggs together; she gave some away, or sold them cheaply to neighbours. There was Cushy the cow, who had to be milked by her if uncle was away. I tried milking her, in her little shed, gently squeezing and pulling her teats while she ate some hay. Her head was held by a wooden bar, and one back leg was tied with rope so she couldn't kick.

My aunt made butter, cream, ice cream, and cheese. She separated the clotted cream, and churned the butter and rolled it into little pats. She hung the curd up in muslin bags to drip, to turn it into cheese. She grew vegetables in the garden, and had many fruit trees. She made jam. In the laundry she boiled the clothes in a copper, and wrung them out through a mangle. A cousin made my sister some school clothes on the treadle sewing machine. My sister handed down her old clothes to me.

There was a large garden of lawns and garden beds to look after and weed, and a grass tennis court. On the other side of the tennis court was the bush paddock where the cow lived. All the children learnt to ride two-wheeler bikes on the tennis court. The cousins sometimes held tennis parties. The lawns had to be mown, even the grass steps. There were lawn mowers without motors. The court had to be rolled and marked. The gravel driveway was raked every Sunday before church. We looked for ticks in the little dog, an Australian terrier, and took them out. Everyone was very busy.

When the weather became colder my aunt took me to sleep in a bed in her bedroom. I remember dreams I had, and hallucinations, but not frightening ones. I saw a guardian angel who said to me, but not in speech, 'I am watching over you'. On another occasion the three bears were standing at the foot of my bed. Father Bear had a blue coat. In the early hours of dawn everything returned to normal with the clip-clop of the milkman's horse coming up the hill.

My sister went to school with the cousins. One of my cousins took me to nursery school on the back of her bike. After that I went to nursery school by myself, on a bus. I had a tricycle which I rode down the street near the house, and I held my feet up so that the pedals went round very fast.

My Mother Arrives

My mother arrived with her baby. She put the wicker basket holding the baby onto the dining table, and everyone stood around the table and looked at the baby. I stood at the opposite end of the table, staring at them. I felt as though a very long time had passed since I last saw my mother, and that I was living in another world. I felt jealous of the baby. She was a competitor for my mother's attention.

My mother and the baby stayed in the sitting room at my aunt's house, and we all remained there for a few more months. My mother was like a shadowy figure in the background. She made one of the cousins help her with the baby; the cousin didn't like doing it. The cot with the baby in it usually stood in the hallway. I glowered at the baby, and pulled her fingers away from the cot rails so that she sat down. Later, the baby played in a pen in the dining room, and learnt to stand up and walk around it.

The time had come for my mother to stop treating her sister's house as her home, and to claim her own family. We moved into a rented house nearer Wahroonga railway station, where the shops were. I was sorry to leave my aunt and uncle, with whom I had been so happy. I was to go to school soon at the Wahroonga Preparatory School. It was not far away and I could walk there.

My younger sister and I were often sick. We had croup and bronchitis. I had to stay in hospital until I'd recovered from illness sufficiently to have my tonsils and adenoids removed. I had pneumonia one time, and missed a whole term of school because of a raised temperature. I didn't mind it at all. My mother found me things to do and make. I made nasturtium leaf sandwiches, and scent from rose petals. A possum lived in the roof, with a baby on her back, and I fed them bread. I caught butterflies with a net and put them under the meat-safe cover while, in the kitchen, flies laid eggs in the cold meat.

We moved to a nicer house and garden at Braeside Street. We loved playing in the mango tree. There was a large main bedroom with an alcove for a baby's cot, and a sunny nursery off it, which led into the garden. Sometimes I slept in the bedroom when I was ill, and sometimes in the nursery. My older sister had a bedroom to herself, which she always did, wherever we lived. The nursery was full of books, and toys too, that my mother bought.

I got used to being at home, sick in bed, and reading books. Once I had mustard applied to my back and chest, which burnt. Another time I chewed on the thermometer to see what would happen. After the pieces of glass were taken out of my mouth, I was made to swallow cotton wool and bread. My mother brought me hot lemon and honey drinks, and a steam bath for the face made with Fryer's balsam, with a towel to put over my head.

I had nightmares, and I would scream in the night and wake my mother. She would go out into the garden to look behind the bushes, and come back to tell me there was no one there. The nightmares were about a monster man who was coming to hurt me, and I had to learn to fly in my dreams in order to escape from him. I used to hear a lion roaring in the corner of the room. Sometimes I lay awake at night, pressed against the wall, terrified, with my heart pounding.

These war years were the only extensive period my sisters and I spent together in our childhood; the six months when our father returned from the war was the longest time we spent together as a family. My younger sister walked around the street asking strange men if they were her father. She always wore overalls, and wanted to be a boy. The three of us played a game in which I was the mother, and my older sister was my high-spirited, often disobedient child, whom I had to discipline. I'm sure she thought it up as relief from always having to be the responsible one. She would run away and play with the other sister, whom we pretended to be a boy called Roddy from next door.

I was badly behaved about going to school. We now lived farther away, and I had to walk to the corner and catch a bus. I spent too long walking round and round the room testing my shoelaces to get the same tightness, and my mother would push me out of the house and lock the doors. I'd bang on all the doors and scream. I missed the bus sometimes, but I was happy to walk for a change. I would arrive at school about the time of the mid-morning break, and the teacher would keep me in at lunch hour to do the work I had missed. I didn't care, as I didn't want to play with the children every lunch hour. The school could do nothing about the situation, because they didn't believe in caning girls.

My mother only had to look after the house and her children, but she had been used to having servants. She had a kind lady called Mrs Mullins come to do housework and to mind us regularly so that she could go shopping. Mrs Mullins was a barrel-shaped person, who dressed in floral print frocks and had stout legs that ended with a pair of blue-veined feet in Roman sandals. When she sat in a chair, her tummy heaved up so that she tilted backwards, and then the chair creaked ominously. My mother, looking worried because the chair might break, would say, 'Oh dear, Mrs Mullins, I think you've got the wonky chair again', which always seemed to be the one she had. When she drank her tea the cup had to go on such a long journey that it usually dripped down her front on the way. Yet she hardly ate a thing, and whenever my mother offered her more, she said, 'No thank you, Mrs Webber, I've done nicely, thank you'.

I played doctors and nurses with two girls in our street, in the bushes, until our curiosity was satisfied about our body parts. I had a special friend, a boy. One day he was hanging by his legs from the mango tree when I was watering the garden with a hose, and I aimed the water onto his face. He didn't turn his face away from the stream of water. I suddenly realized that he couldn't, and I turned the hose to one side. He got himself down and, looking shaken, went home immediately. He didn't come round to play so often after that.

I made a kite for my little sister, with a long tail of rags and paper tied with string. We tried to fly it in the street, and it became tangled in the electricity wires, and hung there disconsolately for weeks. Once I was left behind when the family walked over to a friend's place for afternoon tea. So I dressed deliberately in bad taste, with colours that clashed, and turned up late on my own, looking like 'Orphan Annie', or so my mother would have thought. By the time I was seven, I did not believe in God. God was something grown-ups made up, I told my mother, like Father Christmas.

When my father came back from the war, he was a total stranger to my little sister, who was three years old. We went to the railway station to meet him; my mother cried out his name and ran through the barrier. There he was, a thin man holding a kit bag, walking down the platform. We then spent six months together as a complete family. He built a cage for the white mice my older sister wanted to have. I used to love sitting on his knee. He spanked me once for being naughty; the only time anyone did. He had a huge scar from knee to ankle on one of his legs from an ulcer which had healed. After his leave, he said, he would have to go straight back to his job in Malaya. My mother and little sister were to follow him later.

Our Uncle Hume came back from the war too, and lived for a short time more. He was a very funny man who said things like, 'If I unscrew your navel, your backside will fall off'. I felt quite alarmed at first, when he said it to me.

Boarding School

When I was eight years old, I was sent to a girls' boarding school in Australia, in the country. My older sister was to finish her final year in primary school at the day school she attended, and would go to the boarding school for her secondary education. I did not want to go to boarding school. I did not want my father to go away. My mother took me to the school on the train. She had afternoon tea with the teachers while I played rounders with some children. When it was time for my mother to leave, she started to come across to where I was playing with the children but, before she reached me, I called out, 'Goodbye', and waved her away. So she just continued walking to the railway station. I wasn't going to show her any emotion. Probably she was glad not to have me at home causing problems with my bad behaviour.

My father wrote about me in letters he sent to my mother on his way back to Malaya; letters I read as an adult: 'When you've got Sylvia off to boarding school you ought to have a somewhat easier time in the house, and Margaret will be less demanding without me there.' 'I'm glad Sylvia took to boarding school so easily, but I can quite imagine her being "hard-boiled" about it.' 'If she can work off her energy on games, her emotions will get a rest.'

I didn't have bronchitis at boarding school. I had been given copious amounts of cod liver oil, until the doctor at last decided that instead of curing my bronchitis it was causing it, and ceased to prescribe it. The nightmares left me too, except for one which was about the dropping of an atomic bomb. As in the worst nightmares I had, I was lying in the same bed in the same place so that I thought it was real; it seemed like a dream state between sleeping and waking. The bomb had been dropped, there was a flash of light, and I was dying. I'd struggle to wake up and stay alive.

At boarding school it was compulsory to write letters to our parents. The rough copies of our letters were read and corrected by a teacher. When I made a complaint about a teacher, I was told to remove it from the letter. Because of this censorship, nobody could criticise the teachers.

All the children were either 'popular', or 'unpopular'. As I wasn't popular, I must have been the other. I wasn't teased by the children, although I dreaded it might happen. They gave me a nickname which I never used outside the boarding school. For my birthday my parents sent me some presents, and a birthday cake that I could share with some friends. Life at boarding school was like a completely different world.

When my older sister joined me at boarding school, she was situated in the senior school buildings, and I rarely saw her. I remained at boarding school for ten years. For three of these years, when I was aged nine, ten, and eleven, I only saw my parents and younger sister for a month in the Christmas holidays. My younger sister returned to Malaya with our mother, and when she reached the age of six she was sent to boarding school there. Our mother occupied herself in Muar with coaching Malay, Indian and Chinese girls in English for the Cambridge entrance exams.

Auntie Marj

In these years, my older sister and I spent the two shorter holidays of the year, in May and September, at Hillwood with our Auntie Marj and Uncle Tom. They were good, kind people, who did more for our mother than she deserved. My aunt believed in mind over matter and she always said, 'There's no such word as "can't".' She didn't believe in taking medicine for illness if possible, as she thought that illness was mostly caused by the mental state of the person and their lifestyle. She had a small glass of brandy and warm milk before she went to bed, as a sleeping draught. She told me to sweep the dust under the carpet, if pressed for time. She called me 'Dearie'. She had a somewhat acerbic nature, and would say to me, 'If you go on making that face, the wind might change, and you'll be stuck with it for ever'. She knew how to discipline me.

Auntie Joy, who was a widow by this time, was a gentle, light-hearted person, but stoical and self-reliant, and she had a good sense of humour. (My father once wrote of her that she was a person 'who could mix with all sections of any community'.) Over the years, she did voluntary work for the Chinese community in Sydney. She lived nearby with her three children.

In our holidays we spent a number of days at Palm Beach, where I got badly sunburnt, 'burnt to a chip', or at a horse-riding place at Burragorang Valley. Or we stayed in the Blue Mountains, where I remember fighting the bushfires. On a few occasions we went to Luna Park, or to Disney or Laurel and Hardy films, or to stage shows like *Annie Get Your Gun*. I rode my sister's bike with one of my cousins to 'Hole-in-the-Rock', a picnic place on a creek. There was a long road called Eastern Road from Turramurra to Wahroonga, two stations away, which two of my aunts' houses were close to, and I used to walk the distance between them. The road went up and down hills. One of my cousins liked to drive a car along it without turning on the engine, coasting down a hill and hoping the speed would carry the car up the next one. Usually she had to turn on the engine just before the top.

My aunt and uncle allowed me to have a dog, a kelpie, which was ill-advised, as I was mostly away at boarding school. They had to look after the dog, which was a bother, as he loved to chase cars. The aunts came to visit my sister and me at boarding school on some of the special visiting weekends, and brought a picnic lunch. For their social life at home, they often played bridge with friends and neighbours. There was always a card table that could be folded up and put away, or used for other purposes. At Christmas there was a family gathering at Hillwood to which everyone was invited, and we sat on folding chairs and cushions on the wide front lawn, under the shade of the gum trees. It was the Wilkinsons who were the nucleus of the family group, and their relatives; even my uncle in the British Army, 'the Brigadier', would turn up.

Malaya

For two of the long Christmas holidays, in this period of time, my older sister and I saw our parents and younger sister for a month in Malaya. This was the only time we saw them in the year. We flew to Perth to take a ship to Singapore, because it was cheaper to go by ship. The ship was for school children, most of whom attended Perth schools. (The ship also loaded livestock.) It was fun to be on the ship, with organized games, and sneaking in to the evening dance for older children. We larked about in cabins and out-of-bounds places, and held battles with catapults and water pistols. One battle-axe matron was in charge, constantly on the prowl to catch children who were making trouble or were not in bed. At last we reached Singapore where our parents and little sister came to meet us.

It was at the height of the 'Emergency' in Malaya, when there were Chinese communist guerillas in the jungle who might attack our house on the rubber estate at any time. They had recently struck and killed a man at Craigielea next door. The house precinct had a trip-wire, with tin cans tied to it, surrounding it. There were guard posts around the precinct, at intervals, connected to the house by phone. At regular times, day or night, phone contact was made between the house and the guards in the guard posts. Occasionally there was a false alarm when wild pigs ran into the trip-wire. We had two Scottish soldiers, Seaforth Highlanders who had come from Palestine, boarding in the downstairs bedroom. The garage with two attached rooms, which my father had built once, housed ten Malay special constables who guarded the estate. They appeared at set times, armed, for drill, and marched down the road for a distance.

The constables, with rifles cocked and pointing out of the window, sat at our sides in the back of the car when we went to Muar. They had hand grenades on the shelf behind our heads, my sister told me later.

My older sister and I were driven to Muar to have some frilly dresses fitted by the Chinese tailor. Our mother bought us Malay enamelled bracelets, reed baskets for our sewing things, and Chinese embroidered slippers. Some beggars asked us for money; one was a child whose legs were deformed, and our mother said his parents had maimed him deliberately. When we got home, the 'boy' struck the gong and said, *'Makan siap'*, and we had curry for dinner. My father said it was good to have curry and tea in the tropics. I wondered why as I watched the sweat trickle down the contours of his face and drip from his nose and chin. At night the 'boy' poured the bath water into a giant pot for a bath. Little lizards ran around the walls, calling out, 'Chi cha!'. We named them chi-chas.

I liked the early mornings, when we got up at five o'clock, the coolest time of the day. We had the first breakfast on the upstairs verandah, where there was a rattan table and chairs. The 'boy' brought us tea and tropical fruit on a tray. We watched the sun rise over the trees and listened to the noises of the jungle. I loved eating rambutans, mangosteens, and the tropical grapefruit, pummelo. In our garden we grew mangos and papayas; sometimes our father shot them down with a gun. One morning we found that a snake had got into a cage that hung on the terrace with a little bird in it; the snake had eaten the bird and then could not get out of the cage because of the bulge in its belly, so it had to wait there until the bird was digested.

I took photos with an old Box Brownie camera someone had given me. One was of the cook, his wife, and the 'boy'. I have written their names on the back: Ibrahim, Tama, Yatim. The cook's wife did the washing, ironing, and washing up. There is a photo of Corporal Yusof holding his rifle, and Abdul's wife and little daughter standing in front of latex sheets, the daughter dressed only in underpants.

We remained in the bungalow over Christmas and New Year; then our mother took the children down to the beach at Malacca and Port Dickson until it was time for packing up to leave. Our father came for weekends. He took my older sister out sailing in a yacht. I got stung by a jellyfish. We played mah-jong in the evenings.

Amah

My mother gave me a gold brooch that had been sent for me by Amah. It was made up of the word 'Goodluck'. I was very touched by the gift. I thought that Amah had gone to China after last seeing me on the wharf at Singapore when I was four, and had sent the brooch from China.

Now, on the ship returning to Australia, I saw the full moon through the porthole of the cabin. Amah's face was like the moon, pearly and shining. Her features were faint, unchanging shadows on the face, just like the moon's. The porthole framed a bit of black night which was the hair around her head, pulled back in a bun. She was looking down at her reflection in the calm tropical sea. She was always there. I had missed her.

My parents were thinking of starting a new life in Tasmania, so in one Christmas holiday, all of my family visited Tasmania together. We had a tent by the beach. We collected oysters and ate them. A cow sat on our tent in the night. We stayed with a family on a farm, and did fruit-picking.

In 1950, our father decided to leave Malaya for ever. He travelled in England for six months, visiting his relatives and talking over the possibility of working there. It didn't look promising.

I Repeat the Class

The previous year, at boarding school, I had finished primary school. Then the school decided that I should repeat the last year of primary school because, they said, I was not mature enough for my age. I couldn't understand it; no one explained it to me. I worked out, from the exam results, that I was one of the top three students in the class I was in. I was usually well-behaved. I went to the teacher responsible for it and pleaded to be allowed to go up with my class to the secondary school, but to no avail. I begged my parents to overrule it, but they had hardly been involved in my life of late, and they accepted the judgement made by the school. I felt I had no power; no one was on my side. I would be totally cut off from the children I knew, who would be located in different buildings. I didn't forgive my mother for this betrayal of my trust.

When I went back to school after the Christmas holidays I felt humiliated by my position, and guarded towards the new group of children I had been put down with. I plunged into dismay and suffering. All my consciousness changed at that time and, from being a relatively unselfconscious, playful child, I became a withdrawn adolescent. I know now I was in a state of grief. I saw the other children as if through the wrong end of a telescope, so that they were very small and far away, down a tunnel. The children thought I lived in Tasmania, but I had no connection with it; they had no idea what my life was like. As I had done the schoolwork before, I was often sent out of class to paint pictures on my own; on the walls, in the outdoors.

My parents were in the process of leaving Malaya. My mother was staying at Hillwood, and wrote about me to my father. I had started the school holidays earlier than my sister, because of an outbreak of scabies in the junior school. My mother wrote that she thought the school was right to make me repeat a year. She said:

Sylvia was a little brick about washing up till Dorothy came down. Then she sat back. She is incapable yet of more than spasmodic efforts. When she and Dorothy were to go on the 8.40 bus for a dentist appointment, she missed it because nothing on earth would make her get on with dressing and breakfast. So Dorothy had to go on alone and I, who was not going in till later, had to fly into my clothes and get a taxi, because Sylvia had no idea how to get from Town Hall Station to the surgery. I said to her in the train, 'This is why you couldn't be put up into the senior school'. She said, 'Oh, I don't do things like this at school'. I said, 'Don't you?', and she just looked rueful and didn't answer.

When I read this letter later in my life, I saw my mother as a punitive person who had lost contact with her child. I remember in the train she pointed out 'NSW' in the sign for the government railways as standing for 'Naughty Sylvia Webber'. She thought she should halve my pocket money. For all her Freudian theory about not causing psychological damage, she had omitted the effect of her own absence. She had not been present in my life for most of the last three years; she had earned no authority as a carer. She had been like an only child, expecting others to wait on her, and doing nothing back for anyone. She wrote at the end of the holidays:

Sylvia had a very dull holiday as usual, as she won't play with the local children.

She was in such a state about going back to school that she came rushing down the steps to the taxi, without coat or hat. Her garters fell off as she ran, as she had made them too big. She went back for her coat and forgot her bag, then got that, and left her flannel behind. She does so hate boarding school.

I hated boarding school because I'd had to repeat the year. Naturally, in the holidays, I didn't play with local children I didn't know.

The children at the boarding school were partly from the families of graziers who lived on large sheep properties, and partly from city families, especially the socialites. As my family didn't belong to either of these groups, I came to have a rather stereotyped idea about their lives, from which I felt excluded, in any case. The socialites ate out at Princes or Romanos. I was invited once to have lunch with a school friend at one of these places. My aunt wouldn't let me wear a velvet dress that had been one of her children's, because it had a little mark on it that wouldn't come out. I threw a tantrum. I had to wear my summer party frock with a winter coat and stockings.

I liked the country families better; they were more casual and warm-hearted. I learnt about rural life and language from their children, who knocked about with the workmen and helped with shearing, droving, lamb-marking, and rabbiting. I knew of men who did lamb-marking with their teeth.

When we went to live in Tasmania, my older sister and I would no longer spend holidays with our aunt and uncle in Sydney. My younger sister would go to a state school where, at first, the children said, 'you talk funny', and threw stones at her when she was walking home from school.

Joan and William Settle in Tasmania

In 1950, Joan and William bought a weatherboard house at Devonport, in Tasmania, which was called Formby once, and was where my grandfather had arrived from England. Our house was actually in East Devonport on the east side of the Mersey River (where the ferry docks nowadays) which was formerly called Torquay. The house was on a large block of land with a view, and old fruit trees. It wouldn't have cost a great deal, and I know my father paid for it in cash. He said that he never borrowed money or paid interest on anything.

Some of the money may have come from the Rudstons, his mother's family. At the time my father was freed from the prisoner-of-war camp in 1945, the Rudston inheritance was disputed in the high court in England by his brother, who lost the case. Five-sevenths of the money was awarded to a woman in America with whom the last male Rudston of Hayton had lived; the remainder was divided between my father and his brother, the only descendants.

My father found a job in a hardware firm, doing the accounts. He then did the office work in a crop-dusting business. (He mixed the chemicals, and it harmed him.) Later he joined a small group of business people and gradually took over the stockbroking work. My mother taught English to migrants. She held social gatherings for them, and helped to establish them in a new country. Joan and William made a success of the new life they developed in their forties. William never faltered in his role as the bread winner.

My mother had a potential relationship to people in northern Tasmania through her family's past involvement in the Launceston Church Grammar School. Tasmanians, not being a large population, tended to discuss people in terms of whom they were related to, and my mother could take part in these conversations from remembering the names of boys in the school. She would meet up with some of them. My parents joined clubs and societies; my mother had an active life in local politics in support of the conservative side. It was my mother's job to write to us at boarding school; couples sometimes have such divisions of labour. She often wrote in the middle of the night, because when the wind changed to the east she woke up.

In our school holidays we met families who had children our age. They were friendly country people who asked us to outings, parties and dances. My mother organised social occasions for us, to reciprocate. She had a good repertoire of party games. We played tennis, had picnics at the beach, went bushwalking with the field naturalists, or participated in adult education groups. I went rowing and fishing on the river with a friend. I remember particularly the netting parties in which a group of us would wade out in the river with a net at night to catch fish, and were enveloped in phosphorescent light down to our feet. We had a bonfire on the beach afterwards.

My parents allowed me to own a horse, which they then had to look after most of the time, and it rolled on my mother once. I galloped for miles along the beach. Sometimes we went to plays in the repertory society that my father acted in, or films. Because of the efforts by my mother, I developed a sense of being part of a society and I met different kinds of people. We had one life for the school holidays, and a different life at school. My mother did actually look sad when we left at the end of the holidays; she was almost in tears.

My parents maintained a good vegetable garden, mainly due to my father's efforts. They grew berries suited to the cool Tasmanian climate, which we ate with cream, and the odd caterpillar. My mother bottled fruit and vegetables, and made jam. She had some strange cooking habits like rolling the sausages in egg and flour, or frying stale scones to eat with golden syrup. She made an English version of 'nasi goreng' with croutons and fried sultanas in it. She hated breakfast cereals, which she said were like cardboard, and complained that the bread wasn't truly 'brown', but had been dyed. She made cooked breakfasts, old-fashioned puddings, ice-cream, chutney, tomato sauce, and ginger beer. Our cutlery was the family silver my father inherited, and we had to use it properly: fish knives and forks with the fish, a butter knife for the butter. Table manners mattered.

My father had various hobbies over a period of time. He kept Rhode Island Red chickens; the eggs were sent from New Zealand and hatched in an incubator. A cousin in England sent him cuttings of evergreen poplars in a small box marked 'pencils', which he grew in a corner of the garden. He went prospecting for nickel with a man who used a divining rod. They found nickel deposits in sand, and he converted an old washing machine to separate the minerals. But it turned out that mining it wasn't a commercial proposition.

My father would shut himself into his study, with a bottle of a sweet liqueur called Strega, to do office work. Sometimes he worked on his Rudston family papers. I believe the papers connected him to a past that was part of him, and that he wanted to be a part of, and that it was psychologically supportive to him. He had fought for the British Crown. On the few occasions that he talked about his mother (who had been Annie Rudston) he seemed to become uncharacteristically emotional, almost angry. She had died too young of breast cancer when he was in Malaya, and he hadn't come to terms with it. He tried to find a reason for cancer in its electrical potential, which could be treated with radiotherapy. He wrote letters and papers about his theory to some doctors and researchers, who replied in a serious vein, thinking he was a research student.

Secondary School

Boarding school was like a prison. Up to the time of repeating the class I had largely adapted to, and accepted my situation. Now I felt I had been wronged, and punished unjustly. I was living a false life, struggling to be who I was against the circumstances. I had to protect myself by having a reserve towards the outer world, and keep my spirit alive against the forces that were trying to control me. I looked forward to the holidays, but my mother and I always fell out with each other, and I was soon longing to be free of her as well. I would have to wait until I was grown up to start my own life.

At school there was a structure of endless bells, prayers and hymns, and other regular routines that were imposed from morning till night. I had to find little pockets of freedom in it. I gradually dropped subjects so that I could have 'spare periods'. In these I was allowed to read in the reference library, or practise music. (I took, unnecessarily, both piano and violin as extra subjects.) Sport, in which I was supposed to have 'school spirit', was played every day, and I hated it. However, as the teams were posted with two or three children as extras, I frequently absented myself. I was usually painting or weaving in the art and craft rooms, or just thinking to myself in the dormitory, which was out of bounds at that time of day. I rarely attended a class in a classroom without a book to read 'behind the desk', as it was called. In that way I read one novel a week on loan from the fiction library.

I dropped science after the first year of secondary school. At the end of the second year I was finished with geography. After the third year I dispensed with Latin. Maths was intolerable; trigonometry, boring. In the face of parental opposition to my dropping the subject, I deliberately failed all the maths exams in the fourth year. The examination subjects I still had were English, history, art, and French, a foreign language being compulsory. Luckily, we were offered economics for the last two years of school, and I was enthusiastic, and took it up. In the last year I had to enrol in geography again, as it was usual to sit six subjects. Meanwhile, in the spare periods I spent in the reference library, I read Marx, British Fabian Socialism, historians of the French Revolution, and works of literature. My reading Marx had inspired my interest in economics.

I seemed to protest against the coercive forces by being almost, but not quite, late for meals. The staff were preparing to enter the dining room after the second bell, when the children were supposed to be already in the room. Just at that moment they would see me running round the corner of the garden beds, and would delay their entry. A teacher would call out, 'Sylvia Webber, last as usual!'. On one or two occasions they walked in and shut the door. I was obliged to go then to the high table, after Grace was said, and apologize to the head. A punishment might be to eat in silence; such things were enforced by prefects. My older sister, still a paragon of virtue, became a prefect, and was often head of her form. I hoped that I would not be made a prefect or head of a form.

In the middle of my secondary school years, feeling rebellion and despair about most things, I wanted to leave the boarding school and go to the high school at Devonport where my parents lived. My father would not hear of it. In fact, my parents planned to send my younger sister to the same boarding school, in case she felt that a privilege had been denied to her that had been granted to her sisters.

Sometimes during that year I would sit on a second floor parapet in the dormitory, at a time of day when it was prohibited to be there, and I would look down onto the concrete below and think of throwing myself over. I didn't reach the point of pain at which it could have happened. I always imagined that people would come and find me dead on the concrete, and they would say, 'Poor Sylvia, nobody loved her'. In doing that, even if only in my mind, they gave me a shred of sympathy that helped me to hang on to life.

My Mother

At home in the holidays my mother could never seem to get to the end of the housework. I always felt burdened by it, and guilty of not having helped enough. She had to do more cooking than usual; then there was all the washing-up. There was always ironing waiting to be done. My mother was tired by the afternoon and had to put her feet up because her ankles were swollen. She said that I looked like the wreck of the Hesperus, and that my bedroom was a chamber of horrors. I escaped by taking a book to read under some bushes; we had a good supply of World Books she subscribed to. When buying dress material in a shop my mother embarrassed me by taking the roll out into the street to see the colours better in daylight.

My mother manipulated us to make us feel guilty. She had an indirect manner of speaking which played on the emotions, like 'Would you mind walking down to the shops for some butter?', which was really an order. If I did it, it meant that I didn't mind, when I did. She didn't organize the shopping properly. So sometimes I answered her rudely, 'Yes, I would mind', which forced her to give the order and show herself in her true colours. I liked people to be direct, and call a spade, a spade. My father would just say, 'Look, we need some more butter', like someone passing on information to the one who was in charge, as he didn't consider it to be his job to get it, when he was at work all day. My mother was so flustered by dinner time with all the people in the house that she occasionally dropped the pressure cooker, which was going off full steam; or she almost did. It was frightening.

I had very ambivalent feelings about my parents. My mother started the day with a running commentary, at the breakfast table, on the news she was reading in the local daily newspaper. She made critical remarks to discredit anyone who was in a political party that was not the one she voted for. She even derided them for their spoken accent; she regaled us with the story about the English visitor who, on listening to the Australian Parliament on radio, thought it was a parody of parliament. She attacked me for my Australian accent as well, so then I made it broader.

My mother hated the Labor Party (so to speak), and of course she hated communists, but she couldn't stand Americans as well. My mother made herself appear to be superior to everyone. At that time, I was moving towards the radical left. When I told my parents that the workers should run factories and share the profits, they cried out in dismay, 'But you are a communist!'. I often found that we were talking at cross purposes: I discussed the distribution of wealth, and my mother thought I meant giving money away in the street to the needy.

My mother liked having arguments, but these invariably turned into heated altercations. If I told her, in the middle of it, that I was happy to debate a point but not to fight about it, that made her angry. She tried to challenge me to arguments that seemed to be hopeless or unwinnable, like why a work of modern art could not have just as well been painted by a chimpanzee. I think she considered it good training for me, as Amah had often said I ought to be a lawyer. (I had argued with her a lot when I was three.) When the argument became unbearable to my mother she would end it by saying, 'I am older than you, and I know better', or, 'Don't be rude to your elders'.

The way she was, hurt my soul. She was so domineering and prickly. My mother didn't understand art. I was always drawing horses, and I showed her a drawing I did of a beautiful ideal horse, and all she could say was that the neck was too long. In naturalistic terms, it was. My older sister was a very tactful person, like a diplomat; perhaps that was her way of coping. Once when my sister had gone overseas after leaving school, I said that she would soon be home to pour oil on the troubled waters; this put my mother into a huff.

Sometimes, as a teenager, I could not stand my family. I remember my father talking interminably at lunch about the mining industry, and no-one else could join in the discussion. I suddenly burst into tears and ran out of the room, and locked myself in the bedroom, crying inconsolably. My mother came after me, beating on the door, and saying, 'Unlock the door, your sister wants to come in'. I had to share a bedroom with my younger sister. We had drawn an imaginary line down the centre of the room and I had to walk across her half to reach mine. My sister often would not get up in the morning, and my mother would pull the bedclothes off her. She told me to do it once; after that I refused to do it.

One time I hated my mother so much that, standing in the kitchen, I had a strong desire to pick up a carving knife that was lying on the table, and stab her with it. I told her I had no respect for my father. She told him, and then told me that he was very hurt and couldn't understand why I had said it. Of course, I said it to hurt him.

When I finished school I had a rocky road ahead at times. But I always felt I was living my own true life, however much it fell short of anyone's standards. I held a variety of jobs and attended courses. If I visited my parents, I quarrelled with my mother after a few days. When my father asked why I had stayed so long outside in a car with a boy after dancing at the pub, I told him he could 'think the worst', to stop him enquiring about it. I didn't show my parents the love poems I wrote, which were imaginary, because of what they would think. Between their minds and mine, it seemed, there was a great gulf.

Joan; Me

I worked my way through an arts degree in Melbourne, sharing a group house near the campus. My older sister married, and was finishing her degree in architecture at the same time as she had a small child crawling around her feet. It was liberating to be at university, and the experience replaced a past I had left behind.

The times were 'a-changing'; I had been waiting to step into that time when it arrived. It was the time of existentialism, the French 'New Wave' films of Truffaut and Godard, the protest songs of Joan Baez, and folk-singing in cellar joints. I had a beatnik image, and for many years I often dressed in black jumper and pants, duffle coat and desert boots. I saw films by Jean Cocteau, Ingmar Bergman, Cacoyannis, Satyajit Ray, Kurosawa, Fellini and Antonioni, and I went to the Melbourne Film Festival. I read the novels of Camus, Kafka and Sartre. I went bush-walking.

Inhabiting a suburb with Italians and Greeks near the university, I felt my identity was part of a multicultural society. Like my neighbours, I had come to live in Australia without having roots there. The cosmopolitan influences, like the films, released me from a too narrowly Australian outlook.

I married John Passioura, a post-graduate science student, whose father was a Greek who had escaped from Smyrna when the Turks burnt out the Greeks in 1922. The Passiouras would buy sandwich shops, run them for a few years and then sell them, and sojourn in Greece with their extended family for many months. (They had a hard slog through the years of the Depression to reach that point.)

In 1963 my husband and I went overseas for three years. John did research in Scotland and Holland. That was the time of the Beatles, and Carnaby Street fashions; mini-skirts and bouffant hairstyles. We travelled in Europe, and stayed with Greek relatives in Athens and Mytilene.

When I returned to Australia, I went to see my parents for a few days while my husband organized a house for us to rent in Canberra. I had a toddler under two years old and was seven months pregnant. I became ill. My parents found the toddler very difficult. My mother didn't like her walking round holding a drinking mug (one with a lid and spout), even though she had shut us into the kitchen and back entrance. My daughter put her hand on my father's knee as he sat at the kitchen table, and he said 'Hello' in a funny kind of voice, and looked around anxiously to see who was taking care of the child. It was beyond him to pick her up, or play with her, or anything else. I had a panic attack in the bedroom, saying, 'I am not free, I am not free'. I left as soon as possible.

My husband and I bought a small house in Canberra which we intended immediately to extend. The shares my husband had bought with savings from a student grant skyrocketed in the stock market boom of that time, so that most of our house was paid for in cash. For a few years I led a very domestic existence out of necessity. My husband's parents often stayed with us. They would arrange their day to be out and about, and would cook the dinner and retire to bed early. 'Papou' was a very good cook.

I wrote to my parents intermittently to tell them what the children were doing, and I went to Tasmania to see them about once every two years. My children called my mother 'the granny with the raspberries', as they often picked them. My parents built a little beach house on the estuary of a river, only twenty minutes' drive from where they lived. It was in bushland, and had one room downstairs, with beds behind a curtain, and one attic room upstairs for visitors, a lean-to kitchen, outside toilet, and a small water tank. There was a local shop. We washed ourselves by swimming, and if everything became too primitive we went home. My older sister would go there with her children too, or I would stay with her in Melbourne on the way.

By 1969 I started to find casual work, and relief teaching. My two aunts in Sydney came to visit. I showed them the newly opened National Botanic Gardens. My children were fascinated by my Auntie Marj being able to remove her wooden leg, which she demonstrated. She had lost her own leg to cancer. On another occasion, my Auntie Marj and Uncle Tom held a dinner at the Commonwealth Club in Canberra for their relatives. These included two Shann relatives; one of them was the of Foreign Affairs, and the other was married to the head of Defence. My younger sister, who had moved to Canberra, argued against the Americans going into Cambodia; she had been out marching all day on that issue. It was at the time of the moratorium rallies against the Vietnam War. My aunt talked about Han Suyin, whom she greatly admired, and who was her authority on China.

In 1971 my husband took sabbatical leave in Cambridge, and during this time I was involved in the Women's Liberation movement. A major activity was to protest to the Department of Social Security about their spying on single mothers receiving the pension; the purpose of the spying was to see if the mothers were cohabiting with men. We participated in large political meetings and small consciousness-raising groups, and gave talks at schools and colleges. Some of the women experimented with living in a commune (a heterosexual one). The men had to do a share of housework and child care, and have sex with all the women. Another concern of the group was about the practices of psychiatry.

Meanwhile, my husband was unable to use a reference library for half the year because he hadn't brought the correct letter of recommendation with him. He was invited to some college dinners with men dressed in gowns. The speeches in the Cambridge Union that year were made by Germaine Greer and Arianna Stassinopoulos. I was looking after my children, so I couldn't attend them. (I had to debate against Arianna once at Selwyn College, on 'liberation versus emancipation', because another person was sick.) My husband used to play with Germaine in the streets of Melbourne when they were five and six years old; he cut off her plaits once during their play.

When I returned to Canberra I studied for a diploma of education. There was radical change in education towards 'free, progressive' schooling, and a similar change in people's relationships. My daughter went to a school of the 'Summerhill' kind (but not a boarding school), the Association for Modern Education (AME) school. I helped to set up the School Without Walls, which was for older children; after that, a learning exchange, based on the ideas of the de-schoolers. My daughter said later that I sent my children to progressive schools because of an over-reaction to having been sent to boarding school myself.

Problems

My marriage fell apart. I had previously become depressed from feeling trapped at home with two young children. I only rated myself at just a pass mark in teaching and raising children. I developed a nervous tension which was caused by my taking a number of anti-depressant tablets with a bottle of red wine. I had to take medication for the nervous tension. Sometimes I have been teetering too close to a cliff at the edge of an abyss.

I left my family home and continued to teach at the technical college. My children lived partly with me and partly with their father. My younger sister's marriage broke up before mine, and she was working as a taxi-driver. My parents thought that when my sister's marriage ended, it was her fault;

when they heard about my break-up, they thought it was their fault; and when my older sister's marriage came apart much later, my parents decided philosophically that it was all due to the nature of the modern world. I had relationships, which my parents couldn't bear; they would say, 'Why don't you get married?'. The situation for women was difficult, in these circumstances, because they didn't marry a younger person who was unencumbered, as men tended to do.

My mother came to stay with me once after I had separated from my husband. My children probably drove her mad with their wildness, as they loved jumping on the bean bags, and such things. I said to her with an awkwardness one can have about emotions, 'I don't approve of how I was brought up as a child', and she said, 'I feel guilty'. That was all the conversation we had about the matter; it had nowhere further to go. She left shortly after.

My mother invited my children to stay in the summer. I did not think it a good idea for them to go on their own. My mother found she couldn't cope with having the two of them, and an old school friend of mine kindly offered to have my son to stay at the beach with her family. My father, although he had retired, probably escaped to work every day, and didn't help. My mother then developed low blood pressure and became depressed; after a few months, she had electric shock treatment. I didn't hear about this for a long time as it was something my parents didn't talk about, because of the stigma. The treatment caused her to have some memory loss for a year.

A couple of years later I sought the help of a Jungian psycho-analyst for myself. Psychotherapy cured the nervous tension I had had for a few years, which no medicine or transcendental meditation could cure. I regarded it as a miracle. The things that are mental can cure the things that are physical, and vice versa. I took no drugs, but cried copiously at home as I worked through my past life at an emotional level. I grieved the loss of my parents to me as a child, and other losses in my life. I told my parents about this experience. I didn't go to visit them so much any more.

I went to the two alternative lifestyle festivals that were held near Canberra. The alternative lifestyle movement came to Australia in the early 1970s, about ten years after it started in America. A large number of young people left places like Sydney to practise an alternative lifestyle in the far north coastal region of New South Wales. At one of the festivals, a guru said that I had a rosy glow around me, but black spots inside. I thought his analysis was remarkable, and agreed with it. I would try to blend the two colours.

My younger sister went to live in northern New South Wales with the alternative lifestyle people, and my parents did not hear from her for many years. Her partner and she bought a few acres of land, partly rainforest with a creek, built a house themselves, and grew their own fruit and vegetables. By degrees, they set up a native plant nursery. They did not have electricity or other services. By the time they parted company about ten years later, their land had increased tenfold in value. With her half of the assets, my sister was able to buy a small house in a country town, where she brought up her daughter.

Infrequently, my parents took trips to England. Two of my father's aunts, widows on the Webber side of his family, were still alive when they went in 1974. My father's brother sojourned in Australia, and the two brothers travelled around together. My mother didn't like the brother to stay long in her house, because she had to do all the extra work.

I went camping in Tasmania in 1979 with my partner and his children, and we dropped by to say 'Hello' to my parents, on the way to put up the tents. My father opened the door and was surprised to see me with a man and two children he didn't know. He said, 'You can't come in here'. My father had just had all his teeth taken out. When my mother heard my voice, from somewhere in the house, she called out for me to come in. So I alone stayed a few hours. At that time my mother would not normally see people, but she was very sweet to me. She had had a severe depression, and electric shock treatment again. In a state of apparent catatonia once, she broke her silence to talk to a Lithuanian doctor who tended to her; perhaps she was reminded of the migrants she used to teach and help. She kept a lot of pills in a cupboard, and my father took the opportunity to throw them away.

My older sister was in touch with our parents by phone; she saw them often, and was helpful to them about illnesses, moving house, and sorting out household effects. She was a model person in many ways. Like many women who have children, she completed a second degree after an absence from the workforce. At that time, university education was free of charge. She had a full-time career as a social worker for twenty years; I only worked part-time, on average. But siblings want to be different from one another. Our parents approved of my older sister, and partly approved of me. I only communicated with my parents by letter, which I was used to doing from the age of eight. This expressed, for me, the distance I felt from them, and wanted to feel.

Joan's Retirement

A few years later I saw my parents at a smaller house and garden that they had moved to. I drove down to Melbourne past bushfires, and left my old car at the airport. My father was doing the shopping, cooking and housework, and he still had the energy to grow some vegetables. My mother had retired from those things, and had found refuge in her bedroom. She had probably had enough of living with her husband. I would have a conversation with her in the bedroom, now and again, during the visit. She complained a good deal: the noise of the trains where they now resided woke her up in the middle of the night. She read library books constantly; the books at the local library had little marks in them made by borrowers to record whether they had previously read the book.

I sat and talked with my father most of the day; we both had an ability for it, and he had become better able to communicate. He was working to conserve native plant species in Tasmania. We climbed a mountain to see a place where there were native orchids, my father with a stick in one hand and his camera slung around his neck. (My father helped to save a little park where wild orchids grow, Somerset Park, from being made into a car park.)

At the airport, as I was leaving, my father happened to see a lady he knew, and they started a conversation. His disloyalty to me, in the circumstances, annoyed me, and I cut short their chat with a few words. I turned to my father to say, 'Goodbye' and, just at the moment I had to depart, I posed this question about my mother: 'Why was she so negative?'. I left him standing there with his mouth open in surprise; I knew he couldn't answer it.

I went to Sydney for the ninetieth birthday of my Auntie Joy soon after. I now completely took myself by surprise by going into a state of grief about my Auntie Marj, who had died ten years earlier. I had seen her a year before she died, but no one had told me about her death for many months after it occurred. So I mourned her loss then; not just her death, but her loss to me when I was a child, and her disappearance from my life. I had come, sometimes, to grieve on special days like my birthday, or Christmas Day.

In 1985 I went overseas for eighteen months, living on the rent of my house in Canberra. I travelled around Europe, partly by bicycle, and mostly staying in camping grounds and youth hostels. While I journeyed in China, I was always seeing Amah, as it were, an elderly lady dressed in black trousers and a white shirt, with her hair drawn back in a bun, looking after her grandchild on the street.

When I saw my parents again they were very welcoming. My mother had osteoporosis, and had shrunk down four inches without bending over a great deal. My father was still my mother's carer, but he would soon put her in an old people's home as he could no longer cope with her needs. She broke her wrist one time, and he could not manage her in the bath. He was now ill himself.

He died as I was driving down from Canberra another time, before I could reach him. It was just after the stock market crash. My niece had arranged for my mother to be taken to see him before he died. My sister Dorothy and I went over to clean up the house, and my sister found a little diagrammatic drawing our father had made of the underside of a woman's body. I thought it was the answer to my question at the airport a few years earlier, 'Why was she so negative?'. The reason was, at least partly, that he had not pleased her sexually.

I visited my mother on two more occasions, staying a few days. She was nice to me and talked quite readily, and enjoyed telling me about her early life. She had her own room, in the old people's home, with a view of Mount Roland. She couldn't abide being called 'Darling' by the staff and was known as 'Mrs Webber'. They had to give her a bath twice a week as she refused to use a shower, being unaccustomed to it.

I saw her for the last time at her ninetieth birthday. She slipped and broke her hip some months before, running to get her library book. She recovered enough to walk with a walking frame. My older sister had phoned the nursing home to find out how she was after the operation, and was told that, when asked, 'Are you all right, Mrs Webber?', she replied by reciting the limerick 'There was an old man of Madrid'. My mother had a penchant for 'dirty' limericks, which were passed on in her family.

She had only just woken up when I came into the room, and she said, 'Who are you?'. She then remembered who I was, and said, 'What took you so long?'. It was eighteen months since I had seen her, which I didn't regard as being very long. I arranged for her to have a birthday cake and a present. In the morning she was particularly alert, and sat in a chair by her bed reading the newspaper and telling me what she thought of the politicians, just like old times.

During our discussions she said, 'You had better stay here with me', and I gathered from it that she thought she would die soon. I explained that I could not stay, and reminded her that my younger sister was coming to visit in a little while. Of course, she made me feel guilty because I had taken so long to come and then couldn't stay. Once she said to me, 'We did love you, dear'. I could not reply to that, but looked at her with a warm and kindly expression. Because of everything that had happened in my childhood, her words were not adequate, but I realised that it was the best that she could do.

Later in the day, she said, 'I had three robust daughters. Dorothy was good, Sylvia was naughty, and Margaret was—' 'I don't want to hear what Margaret was', I said, thinking that it would be derogatory, so she stopped speaking. I will never know what Margaret was. (Parents often refer to their grown-up children as if they were still children.)

Towards the end of the day my mother's mind would deteriorate. At dusk, when I was leaving, she told me her oldest sister would get me a taxi. This sister and all my mother's family members were portrayed in photos facing her along a shelf across the wall. I gave her a kiss and said goodbye, knowing I would not see her again.

My sister Dorothy was the last of us to see her. I had been in touch with the old people's home, and I knew that my mother had not eaten for a few days, and was now declining to drink. She was refusing in a very definite manner, by pressing her lips together and pushing the cup away. Two days later when my sister spent a weekend with her, she was unable to speak. My sister took a collection of old letters to read to her. As my sister was leaving, my mother roused herself and said, with great effort, 'Thank you'. She died the following morning. She had partly caused her own death. She was not taking medicine for any illness. It seemed she'd decided not to live any more.

The Jewel Queen

After my mother died, I had a particular kind of nightmare intermittently for months. It was about jewellery that had been left to me. In the dreams I sold it or gave it away, or lost it or it was broken, or stolen. In most of the circumstances I was careless and therefore greatly to blame; I had to suffer guilt for what I had done. My mother actually gave her real jewellery to the three of us at an earlier time; it wasn't a large amount and I sold some that I didn't like. My father had given her jewellery because that was his desire. She wasn't really a kind of woman who would want to wear jewellery a lot; she was a woman who was more like a man.

In my nightmares I kept inventing new jewellery which I imagined in colour and fine detail. I was usually going on a journey, or packing up to move, or even flying to outer space, but by the end some jewellery, or sometimes small ornaments or pieces of silverware, were missing. I suffered guilt during the day as a result of the dreams, as I partly believed the imagined jewellery was real. I could not bear to look at my existing jewellery to see if any was missing; in fact, I had forgotten what there was. At last I wrote a poem about my mother, called *The Jewel Queen*, which helped the dreams to leave me. In the poem she was really more like the evil queen. She had been given the jewels as a token of love, but she did not pass on love to her children, but only jewels. In this way she passed on a curse.

My mother was a person who could be respected and admired, rather than loved. She was proud of her achievement at university and in teaching, but, in a sense, marriage was a step down for her. She may have felt a lowering of self-esteem which made her fiercer in standing up for her superiority in the world. She accepted the role of being her husband's companion and supporting him as the bread winner. Like many women, she suppressed other interests she had, for this purpose. She suppressed her writing; it might have been in conflict with how everything was in her life.

She was used to having servants, and treated children as subordinates. She was probably disappointed not to have a son. The family had too many women in it (or just too many children), and maybe she was glad not to have them around her, throwing things off balance. She liked to have one child with her at a time whom she could control. It was a kind of 'divide and rule' policy. She would tend to co-opt my older sister to be on the side of the parents, against the other two children.

She may have done fruit-bottling, but she was no 'doormat'. She was active in, and critical of, things political. But she didn't venture into political life at a serious level. She often wrote highly opinionated letters to the local newspaper. She was critical of everything, especially of anything to do with language. She somewhat lacked a sense of humour, and stood on her dignity or took things the wrong way, and took umbrage too easily.

She respected her husband for his social background and the good conduct of his life. She was, to an extent, chauvinistic in a way that he was not. She called England home. This was connected to attitudes about class and race, but not obviously. She tried to get her husband to read women writers, which he said he didn't like, by tricking him into reading books by women with men's names, such as George Eliot, and Henry Handel Richardson.

My cousin wrote that the Wilkinson men were gentle, and kindly or gracious, not particularly ambitious or materialistic, but not unsuccessful. That was generally true of the other men too, my father, and the Miles and Chidson men, even though they had fought in wars. My father was a mild-mannered, stiff-upper-lip, polite English gentleman. He was an optimist; though he said he had a bad temper he rarely displayed it beyond being 'peeved'. These men did not fit the Australian stereotype of the macho male. Nor did they have submissive wives; the women were strong-minded. My mother wanted her daughters to 'have some gumption', and not to be 'lily-livered', or a 'shrinking violet'.

I felt affection towards my mother for recognizing and expressing the kind of person I was as a child. She said I was highly strung; I was sensitive. My mother liked me, although we both tended to rub each other up the wrong way. She used to recite to me the nursery rhymes 'Mary, Mary, quite contrary', and 'There was a little girl, who had a little curl', in this regard. She called me 'The cat that walked by himself', from the story by Rudyard Kipling. I used to think of myself, because of the circumstances, as being like Mary in *The Secret Garden*. My older sister regards me as being very independent, and my younger sister sees me as rebellious. I am also not very gregarious. I was meant to be independent, but I was held back by emotional problems stemming from my childhood. I lacked self-confidence.

My cousins in Sydney feel attached to the land they still own, in Wahroonga. It is their tribal stamping-ground. I can understand it, but I feel no attachment to pieces of land. I was influenced by Buddhism. I live in a state of non-attachment, and I have become a recluse. I love birds and plants. I love my children. As for being too young for my age, as was alleged by my school, I may be a bit of a Peter Pan, and I like my childlike spirit which was not defeated. My sympathies are with alternative society movements, for women, peace, the environment, against the great conservative forces. I support pluralism as a matter of principle, because it is important for some people to do so.

I wonder about the pets and other things my parents bought for me: I had two horses, at different times, a dog, a violin, and a weaving loom. My sisters did not have anything comparable, and it seems to have been unfair. To an extent, then, I was spoilt, and it was unnecessary, or not to the point. Maybe it was done to patch things up in some way. Maybe the gifts were bribes.

I thought that Amah had gone to China in 1942, and had sent me the 'Goodluck' brooch from there. Only years later I found out from my father's letters that she was living in Singapore all the time. He had seen her after the war; she had a name, Ah Lok, and she had a daughter. Yet no one suggested taking me to thank her for the brooch, or just to see her again. To my parents Amah was a servant, I was a child, and it didn't matter.

My parents kept for me the letters I wrote to them from boarding school, and my school reports. After looking through them quickly I threw them away, because I felt they didn't represent my true life.

Ponderings and Poems

Are there truths about life? Are they passed on in the 'collective unconscious' (Jung), or the structure of the mind? Jesus said (but I have taken it out of context): 'To those that have shall be given, and from those that have not shall be taken away even that which they have' (Matthew 13:10-13). This is sad but true both of the psyche and of the economic life of the person. People are hurt and suppressed by hierarchism, which is an expression of pecking order, whether it is the real pecking order, or not, as in sexism and other 'isms'. (This begs the question, 'What is the "real" pecking-order?')

In the streets of Beijing a translator told me this maxim: 'It is better to walk a thousand miles than to read a thousand books'. (Exercise can cure depression, for one thing.) An old Chinese villager asked me, through someone who translated, 'Are you bad, or am I?'. I answered, 'We are both good'. On the train, the water lady boiled a limited amount of water between stations; she always shared it. If the people in one compartment had none left, she would bring them some from another compartment.

I imagine myself walking alone along the edge of a cliff at night; on one side there are occasionally the lights of houses in a village, on the other side there is only the blackness of the abyss. I must be careful not to trip. A Turkish person once told me: 'Life is better than nothing'.

I didn't read my mother's poems before her death, nor she mine. Now her poems and mine speak to one another. I like a sonnet Joan wrote when she was in her late teens:

LAUNCESTON

There where two greeting rivers come
Together, softly joining hands,
And wind on through the level lands,
Their age-long day of parting done,
Within a hollow, that the sun
Fills to the brim, the drowsy city stands
A-nodding, while the golden sands
Course slowly, as the rivers run.

Like a rolled collar, brown and green,
Behind her head the steep hill-slopes rise,
As if to shield her from surprise,
And let her slumber on unseen.
Careless, the muddy fringes of her dress
She trails. She knows not her own loveliness.

The following poems I wrote when I was eighteen and nineteen. I would have liked to have studied writing at university, but there didn't seem to be a place for poets.

THE LOVERS

On a salt-soaked beach
These breakers clapping,
Swords of lightning stricken by a thunder
Shuddering from under,
And slapping
The sand-rough cheek with an angry god's hand.

Like an old Norse myth
These lovers craving,
Sting of gauntlet by a hero insulted
Ebbing not the wanting,
She braving
His storm-fierce love with salt-teared cheek of sand.

The second poem is untitled:

When I was a child I was a god,
Was Apollo in my paddock, and it was not incongruous,
Had Midas' touch on a weed, nor was deceived,

Like the dandelion clock I held time in my hand.

Then dreams were reality. I put my pennies
In the rainbow for a money-box, and knew they were safe.
I held my standard as high as hope in the battle,
Was king, was conqueror, measured to a mountain,
Till truth routed my dreams, and the standard broke.

When I was a child I was a god,
But the mountain, the battle, the rainbow, were deceiving;
Youth flies in a puff of dandelion seeds, leaving us
Sorrowed by a bare stalk. If truth is
Reality, what will I believe in?

My daughter, Julia Passioura, wrote these poems at the School Without Walls in Canberra when she was sixteen:

VEIL OF EVIL
Why were the Jews killed
And beaten by the Nazis?
Why are black people hated
By the Ku Klux Klan?
Why are the poor so often
Snubbed by the rich?
Why are the lonely
Avoided all the time?
Why the veil of evil?
Why the hurt and pain?
Why oppress your children
When your parents did the same?

How do you draw the line
Between the stable and insane?
Why is it taking so long to learn
From mistakes mankind has made?
Why can't you see that,
For a happy life,
Love is the only way?

The second poem could be about a parent or child of either gender:

She lived in a world of rules,
She did just what she was told,
She gave birth to a son,
Her work it seemed was never done,
But as her child up he grew
She taught him all the rules she knew.

He moved out of his home,
To find that he lived on his own;
Though youth and beauty were at hand,
His will was not in his command,
His love it was a piece of thread,
He made a world inside his head,
But though his world helped him survive,
His tortured soul, it cried, it cried.

Appendix to Part Four

John Wilkinson Who Went to Boarding School for Fifteen Years

My ancestor John Wilkinson went to boarding school for fifteen years from the age of five after his father drowned in the Thames, as he relates in the following letter about his life (which I have slightly abridged). John Wilkinson even had to pay, as an adult, some of his school fees. The 'persecution' he speaks of might have arisen because his wife-to-be was pregnant at the time of their marriage (a common occurrence at any time in human history). He was writing, as an old man, to his late patron's brother, to ask for more financial support:

Alne near Easingwold, Nov. 1831.

Dear Sir Bethell!

By your kind condescension and affability to me when at Alne and York, I am induced to pray and beg you will excuse the cursory, curtailed and detailed account of my life from five years of age, which I here write down for your perusal. I was born in the parish of St James, Clerkenwell, London; my father was a respectable coal merchant. When I was five years old my father was accidently drowned in the river Thames, and my mother's uncle, who was a bachelor, and independent, took me under his care. Before I was six years old he sent me to a boarding school in the north of Yorkshire.

When I was fourteen years old, my uncle died suddenly intestate. Then I was left destitute of all relations and friends, under the buffetings of master, mistress, and a hundred boarders. I remained at school till I was turned twenty years old, and gave my master a promissory note for what he demanded. I was guided by conscience, though cruelly treated, and, it being a cheap school, it was under a hundred pounds.

I ventured into the wide world to provide for myself by teaching school in a country village, where I became very serious and studious. Before I was twenty-three years old I paid twenty pounds in part for board and education. Then I took a wife, not considering how we were to live. But God was our succourer and comforter; we were content and happy. I was solicited to teach school in a village, where I got into favour with the late Duke of Northumberland, then Lord Percy, and Major Pulleine, by privately teaching a nephew of the former, and two sons and two daughters of the latter. I received from them as much money as paid off my promissory note, to my great comfort.

At this time I had prepared myself for holy orders, and I met with severe persecution by malicious and false tongues, which was but of short duration. I got into orders with a stipend of twenty-five pounds. In a year or two, the curacy of Kirby Wiske fell vacant, and I was recommended by Lord Percy to the curacy, salary forty pounds a year. While I was there the rector died, and I wrote in a humble manner to the Duke of Northumberland (being the patron of the living) begging His Grace would prevail with the next incumbent to continue me in the curacy, and to add a little more to my salary in consequence of my small family.

The new rector, the Reverend Matthew Raine, came soon after to take up possession of the living. He asked me what my salary was, and I informed him, 'forty pounds a year'. He immediately said he should allow me forty guineas a year, and I remained there nine years and a half. The living was worth 500 pounds a year. I then was recommended to be curate to the Reverend Edward Dowdeswell, vicar of Alne, now Dr Dowdeswell. I received only fifty pounds a year till he got preferment. Then your late brother, being patron of the vicarage of Alne, presented the Honourable and Reverend T. Monson, Rector of Bedale, to the vicarage of Alne, to hold it under resignation till Mrs Bethell's youngest brother came of age. Mr Monson allowed me eighty pounds a year, with surplice fees. Shortly after Mr H. Chaloner was presented to the living I was discharged, which may be about nine years ago. Ever since I have been happy assisting the neighbouring clergymen occasionally for a guinea a Sunday, for the assistance and support of my family.

Had it not been for your late brother selecting me in the year 1804 or 05, without solicitation on my part, to be his steward, when his rest was disturbed with the thoughts of having so many people employed about him, and also by patronising me with the perpetual curacy of Ellerton in the year 1814, I might at this time be worse than nothing. The living at Ellerton brings me in seventy pounds a year. Your late brother allowed me fifty pounds a year for my services as steward. I would be happy to serve you on any occasion with truth, honesty, and fidelity, and without bribery.

My wife bore me six children, one boy and five daughters, all alive and healthy. My third daughter is married to an attorney of Wetherby, and she has two boys and one girl, all well. My son is married to an attorney's daughter of York, and she has borne him twelve children, six boys and six girls, all alive. My son is the vicar of Bubwith near Ellerton. My son-in-law, the attorney at Wetherby, doing well, was employed by your late brother in drawing up covenants between landlord and tenants upward of twenty years ago. I have yet four daughters unmarried and unprovided for, save probably they may each have a hundred pounds in expectation.

Now I am in suspense what will happen to me and my family.

I am in my seventy-fifth year and my wife in her seventy-first year. What I am in possession of now will die with me except furniture, stock and crop, which are not great.

Dear Sir Bethell,
Your obedient and faithful servant,
John Wilkinson.

John Wilkinson said nothing about his mother, but when he was fourteen he felt keenly the loss of his great uncle. However, he was lucky to have all the education he had, as his upbringing could have been worse. He was an ordained minister, and had studied some courses. But he could not rise in his chosen profession without a university degree and, I believe, better social connections. He probably obtained the financial help he sought, because he was the curate at St Mary's Church, Alne, in 1840, not long before his death. He was able to leave fifty pounds to each of his four unmarried daughters.

John Wilkinson's patron, Sir Christopher Bethell-Codrington, was using a title illegitimately. His uncle Sir William Codrington, the second baronet of Dodington, had disinherited his own son in favour of his nephews, Christopher and two brothers, who were orphans, but he did not pass on the title to them. Christopher had spent a fortune by the time he died, which was soon after John Wilkinson's death.

The Wilkinson Descent

John Wilkinson married in 1779 Esther, daughter of John and Jane Elsdon of Dalton, North Yorkshire. She was possibly grand-daughter of Sir Christopher Elsdon of Northumberland, who was beheaded for his part in a Pretender uprising, and whose estates were confiscated except for a small dower house at Kirby Hill, near Richmond, North Yorkshire. The name Elsdon is not common in those parts. His daughters were Jane, Anne, Louisa (Mrs Maude, who had children), Eliza, and Harriet (Mrs John Hartley of Leeds).

His son, John, BA of All Souls College, Oxford (where the Codrington library is), was vicar of Bubwith and Gate Helmsley, near York. He married in 1808 Ann Joanna, daughter of Christopher Newstead, an attorney of York, and had twelve children but few descendants. (Some black silhouette miniatures of this family survive.)

His son William, BA of Trinity College, Dublin, was vicar of Ellerton Priory and Bubwith, East Yorkshire, for over forty years. He married in 1843 Dorothy, daughter of John William and Alethea Wright of Eyam, Derbyshire, and had five sons and a daughter. Only their youngest child, Christopher, had children; he was born when his mother was forty-six. (Some of the Wright's family silver was passed on in our family, and when my aunt met some Wrights living near her in Wahroonga, she was able to show them the silver as proof of her descent from their family, of Eyam Hall.)

The son Christopher was MA of Cambridge in Mathematics, Philosophy, Political Economy, and Logic. He always remembered being in the Cambridge Union when Charles Darwin made a famous speech about the origin of the species. He was recruited by Bishop Montgomery. He is written about in Alexander, A 1996, *Blue, Black and White, the History of the Launceston Church Grammar School*. He married Florence Shann, who was well-educated and spoke French. (The Shanns, who may have been from old Shann Hall near Methley, West Yorkshire, were cloth merchants at 2 Meadow Lane, Leeds, from about 1700.)

Florence's mother was a beautiful girl, born Elizabeth Berry. She died of tuberculosis in her early twenties. Before her short life ended, she married Frank Shann and had Frances, who died, and Florence. When Florence was three years old, her father went to seek his fortune in Australia, and he left her behind in Yorkshire. Florence was brought up in Ripon by her aunt and legal guardian, Hannah More Shann, a charming and cultivated single woman; she was named after the philanthropist and teacher, Hannah More. (Hannah and Frank were from a family of fifteen children, some of whom died young.) Frank Shann married again in Australia, and had another family.

Christopher and Florence Wilkinson had six children:

Dorothy (1883-1947) MA, Dip Ed, was headmistress of SCEGGS. She is written about in the *Australian Dictionary of Biography*, and in Cameron, M. 1994, *S.C.E.G.G.S. a Centenary History of Sydney Church of England Girls' Grammar School*.

John (1884-1977) was educated at the Launceston Church Grammar School. He joined the British Army, and served in Singapore, India, with the King's African Rifles, and in Ireland and England. On a visit to Tasmania he became engaged to Gwen Bailey, but they didn't marry for nine years because of the intervention of the First World War. Perhaps that was why they didn't have children. His cousin, Robert Leighton, left him a property at Goodmanham, East Yorkshire. He was brought back from retirement in the Second World War to work at Aldershot, and retired as an honorary brigadier. His wife and he were in Australia 1946-9. Their trip was extended because Gwen had a serious illness. They lived with her sister 'Owey' Stevenson, and her family, in Wahroonga. John married secondly Katherine Wanklyn, and lived in New Zealand.

Cuthbert (1886-1958) was educated in England, and was an engineer at Vickers, Sheffield, and Malaya and Siam. He married Gertrude Clark. They did not have children. Later, they lived in Sydney, at Dover Heights near the cliff, and Gertrude taught at SCEGGS.

Marjorie (1891-1975) married Ingle Parramore, of Beaufront, Tasmania, and had Thomas; she married secondly Thomas Miles, a tin mine manager and author who served in two world wars, and had Christopher, Richard, Joy, Elizabeth, and Patricia. Thomas Miles's father, Captain Edward Miles, a master mariner of Hobart, started the first tin-mining in the world in a harbour, by dredging, in 1906 at Phuket, Thailand, where there is a memorial to him. His family carried on the business for sixty years; see the *Australian Dictionary of Biography*, and Miles, T.A. *Tin International*, January-March, 1967.

Joyce (1894-1993), a VAD in WW1, married Hume Chidson, a barrister in England and Malaya, who was brought up in Oregon, USA and fought in the Machine Gun Corps in WW1. They had Mary, Jane and John.

Joan (1901-1991) BA Hons., a teacher, married William Webber, an English rubber planter in Malaya, and later a stock broker in Tasmania, and had Dorothy, Sylvia and Margaret.

(Between 1942 and 1945 William Webber was a prisoner of war on the Thai-Burma Railway for about a year, and was put into the hospital with a leg ulcer. He was then given the job of treasurer for the canteen at Chungkai until the end of the war, and this circumstance, he said, saved his life. His bookkeeping did not reflect the full amount of food and medicine that was entering the camp.)

Fuller details of names, dates, etc, are available in a family tree.

Some Verse

The Reverend William Wilkinson and his son Christopher annotated Charles Mackay's *Lost Beauties of the English Language*, 1879, with Yorkshire and Lancashire dialect. William left in the book, as a bookmark, a poem about a Mr Hotham who was beating his wife. I believe he was genuinely concerned, but felt constrained to write about it humorously, and in dialect:

> *For James Kirby of Bubwith, East Yorks:*
> *A ran-a-dan-dan,*
> *I ride the stan,*
> *It's naa-ther for ma sake nor hour sakes,*
> *'At I ride the stan,*
> *Bud it's for owd Roachy 'Otham,*
> *Who's been bee-atin' his wife,*
> *He bee-at 'er within an inch of her life,*
> *He naa-ther took stock, stick nor peg,*
> *Bud he up wi's fee-at and punched her ower't leg,*
> *'Ip-'ip-'urraa-ah! 'ip-'ip-'urraa-ah!*
> *'E banged her, 'e banged 'er, 'e banged 'er, indeed*
> *He bee-at 'er, 'e bee-at her! a foor sha stood need.*

Joan, my mother, liked the nursery rhyme about the old woman and her dog, which she sang with a refrain between each line. She recited whimsical ditties from *Alice's Adventures in Wonderland*, and witty or wicked limericks. I regret I lost the limerick about the Bishop of Durham that was passed on by the Wilkinson vicars. My mother sang songs like 'Your baby has gone down the plug hole' or 'There was I, waiting at the church'. Some of them had a slightly racist character, like the following one:

> *The last of all our lamas*
> *Has gone beyond the door,*
> *He'll never wear pyjamas*
> *Any more, any more.*
> *At the summit of a chasm*
> *He tried to pass a yak,*
> *It took a sneezing spasm,*
> *And blew him off the track.*
> (Repeat the first verse, starting with 'Oh'.)

When I was a child, I thought the lama in the song was a llama.

My mother had a tongue-twister: 'Tiglath Pileser has gone to Mesopotamia'.

I wrote this tailpiece not long ago:

EVOLUTION

> *Why are men so fast to come,*
> *And women slow?*
> *There is an evolutionary reason*
> *You ought to know:*

The woman who was quick to come
Got up and walked away;
Only the woman slow to come
Allowed the man his sway.
She bore the child;
The other, none.

Bibliography

References 1:
Unpublished material, mainly primary sources. The reference is held privately in Australia, and may be in a public institution as well.

Barstow, Elizabeth. Memoirs of Elizabeth Barstow of Garrow Hill, York, 1898; 'My Grandmother', 'Little Ann'. Copy in Yorkshire Archeological Society library, Leeds, West Yorkshire, and Dutch Royal Archives Library, The Netherlands.

Barwell, Graham, University of Wollongong. Some previously unknown John Donne manuscript material in Australia, paper presented at the Bibliographical Society of Australia and New Zealand annual conference, Oct. 1997.

Beal, Peter. Notes about the Donne manuscript of the Rudstons, and the Egerton-Cutler wedding verses, Sotheby's catalogues, 2002, 2004.

Beament, Roger. An introduction to the Barstows of the Vale of York.

Chidson, John. Notes about the Chidsons.

Codrington, William. Notes about the Codringtons, 2000.

Commonwealth of Australia. Report of passengers on board the *S.S. Dominion Monarch* on 26 May 1942 at Fremantle from Colombo. National Archives of Australia, k269.

Duggan, Penny. Notes about the Kellys and Webbers in Ireland.

Glinski, Miroslaw, Gdansk Historical Museum. Notes about the Barstows, the Almondes, and their house in Danzig; map of the Langgarten of 1867.

Gloucestershire archives. Document D1610/E168. Letter of John Wilkinson.

Janet Clarke Hall, University of Melbourne. Records of Dorothy and Joan Wilkinson.

Kelly, Caroline and Charles E. Webber. Some recollections which Caroline Theodosia Kelly ('Aunt Can') considers not worth recording, privately printed, 1902. Copy in genealogical office, National Library of Ireland.

Kelly family letters, National Archives of Ireland 2003/73/1 and 2003/73/3. Transcript genealogical office, National Library of Ireland.

Maclean, Lachlan. A letter about the Macleans of Duart Castle.

Miles, Richard. Notes about the Miles family.

Miles, Thomas A. Reminiscences and Coincidences, 1970.

Passioura, Julia. Poems.

Rudston family papers in the East Riding of Yorkshire Archives at Beverley, East Yorkshire. (Individual items are listed at the end of Part One.)

Rudston, Margaret. Transcripts of William Webber's letters.

Thomas, Bertram. Joan Webber, nee Wilkinson, 1991.

Tighe, Antony L. Letters I gave him: Mary Tighe (2) undated, Sarah Ponsonby (1) 1790, Lady Eleanor Butler (1) undated, Sarah Tighe (1) 1794, Caroline Hamilton (1) 1826 and poem

1859, and Lord Patrick Crichton Stuart (1) 1837. Transcript in genealogical office, National Library of Ireland.

Tillotson, John. Papers of the Rudston family of Hayton Hall ..., Australian National University, 1997.

Webber, Charles E. See Kelly, Caroline.

Webber, Evelyn. Notes and letters.

Webber family letters, National Archives of Ireland, 2003/73/1 and 2003/73/3. Transcript in genealogical office, National Library of Ireland.

Webber family tree, made by Lady Alice Coote (nee Webber), Everilda Gibbs (nee Webber), Tom Coote and George Gibbs.

Webber, Joan. Letters, poems and writings.

Webber, Oswald. An account of the Webber family in Ireland. Copy in the genealogical office, National Library of Ireland.

Webber, Oswald. Letters 1895-1901. National Army Museum, London.

Webber, Sylvia. Poems and writings.

Webber, Sylvia. Papers I hold: One letter of Caroline Kelly (undated), one letter of Daniel Webb Webber 1832, one letter of Oswald Webber 1880, one letter of Robert Jones 1881, one postcard of Montague Barstow and Baroness Orczy (undated), and various old notes about the Kellys, Barstows, Macleans, Irwins and Webbers. Transcript in genealogical office, National Library of Ireland.

Webber, Thomas W. Notes and letters. Transcript in genealogical office, National Library of Ireland.

Webber, Thomas W. Some horses and dogs that I have known, National Archives of Ireland, 2003/73/2.

Webber, Thomas W. Photo album in India 1860-1870, in British Library, Photo 1228.

Webber, William R. Letters 1923-1950.

Weigall, Dorothy. Letters, notes, and photos.

Wilkinson family papers of the Revd John Wilkinson, Revd William Wilkinson, Revd Christopher G. Wilkinson, Florence Wilkinson, Dorothy Wilkinson.

Wilkinson, John S. Memoirs.

Wingfield, Elizabeth (nee Kelly). Memoir in the form of twelve letters to her daughter 'Bena', written before Elizabeth's death in March, 1856. The memoir is titled 'Isabella Frances Wingfield. 24th Decr., 1860' for the date that a copy was given to Elizabeth's daughter Isabella (later typed). Copy in the genealogical office, National Library of Ireland.

References 2:

Published and internet sources. These references provided both primary and secondary source material.

Alexander, Alison. *Blue, black and white, the history of the Launceston church grammar school*. Launceston, Tas. 1996.

Alumni cantabrigienses ... J. Venn. Cambridge, CUP, 1922-1954.

Alumni dublinenses... G. Burtchaell and T. Sadleir eds. Dublin, A. Thom and Co., 1935.

Alumni oxonienses... University of Oxford, Nendeln, Lichtenstein, Kraus reprint, 1968.

Australian dictionary of biography. Melbourne, MUP, 1966-2007.

Baedeker, Karl. *Northern Germany - as far as the Bavarian and Austrian frontiers; handbook for travellers*. Leipzig, 1904.

Bailey, Anne and Robin. *An Early Tasmanian Story...* Blenallen Press, 2004.

Baines, E. *Baines' directory of the county of York*, 1829.

The Barnsley Chronicle, Barnsley, South Yorkshire, 19 and 26 February, 5 March, 1881.

Beal, Peter. An authorial collection of poems by Thomas Carew: the Gower manuscript, *English Manuscript Studies* 10, 2001.

Bell, G. (ed.) *The Hamwood papers of the ladies of Llangollen and Caroline Hamilton*. London, Macmillan, 1930.

Bence-Jones, Mark. *Burke's and Savill's guide to country houses*. London, Burke's Peerage, 1978-1981.

Bence-Jones, Mark. *Life in an Irish country house*. London, Constable, 1996.

Bible, authorised King James version with Apocrypha. Oxford, OUP, 1998.

Bogue, David. *The history of the Dissenters from the revolution to the year 1808*. London, 1833, vol.1.

books.google.com

Bowlby, John. *Child care and the growth of love*. London, Penguin, 1953.

Bowlby, John. *Attachment and loss*. London, Hogarth, 1982.

Bulmer, T. *Bulmer's history, topography and directory of East Yorkshire* (with Hull) ... Preston, T. Bulmer, 1892.

Burke, B. *A genealogical and heraldic history of the landed gentry of Great Britain and Ireland*. London, Harrison, 1882.

Burke, B. *A genealogical and heraldic history of the landed gentry of Great Britain*, London, Harrison 1914.

Burke, B. *A genealogical and heraldic history of the landed gentry of Ireland*, London, Harrison, 1904, 1912.

Burke, B. *A genealogical history of the dormant, abeyant, forfeited and extinct peerages of the British Empire.* London, reprinted by Harrison and Sons, 1962, (facsimile of 1883).

Burke, J. *A genealogical and heraldic dictionary of the landed gentry of Great Britain and Ireland.* London, Henry Colburn, 1846.

Burke, J. *A genealogical and heraldic history of the extinct and dormant baronetcies of England, Ireland and Scotland.* London, J.R. Smith, 1844.

Burke's Irish family records. H. Montgomery-Massingberd ed. London, Burke's Peerage, 1976.

Burke's peerage and baronetage. C. Mosley ed. London, Burke's Peerage, 1999, 2003.

Cameron, Marcia. *S.C.E.G.G.S. A centenary history of Sydney Church of England Girls' Grammar School.* Sydney, Allen and Unwin, 1994.

Castor, Helen. *Blood and roses: the Paston family in the fifteenth century.* London, Faber and Faber, 2004.

Clarendon, E. *The history of the Great Rebellion.* London, OUP for the Folio Society, 1967.

Concise Oxford dictionary. H. and F. Fowler eds. Oxford, Clarendon Press, 1912.

Crockford, J. *Crockford's clerical directory.* Oxford, OUP, 1860-.

Crookshank, A. and the Knight of Glin. *The painters of Ireland, c.1660-1920*. London, Barrie and Jenkins, 1978.

Crush, Margaret. *A first look at costume*. Franklin Watts, London, 1974.

Dictionary of national biography. L. Stephen and S. Lee, eds. London, Smith Elder, 1885-1900.

Dunlop, E. *The war diaries of Weary Dunlop*. Ringwood, Vic. Australia, Penguin Books Australia, 1990.

East Yorkshire Family History Society. *Hayton, Nunburnholme and Burnby monumental inscriptions*, 1999.

English, Barbara. *The great landowners of East Yorkshire 1530-1910*. New York, Harvester Wheatsheaf, 1990.

en.wikipedia.org

Evangelical magazine, and missionary chronicle. new ser. 34 (1856) London, F. Westley and A. Davis.

Foster, Joseph. *Pedigrees of the county families of Yorkshire* - vol.2, North and East Riding. London, W. Wilfred Head, 1874.

Geographers' A-Z Map Co. Ltd. *Handy road atlas Great Britain AZ*. Sevenoaks, Kent, 1997.

Gillett, E. and MacMahon, K. *A history of Hull*. Oxford, OUP, 1980.

Hall, John. *The memory of the just: a tribute to the memory of the late Rev. Thomas Kelly*, by Rev. John Hall, Athy. Dublin, John Robertson, 1855.

Hill, Christopher. *The century of revolution 1603-1714*. London, Routledge, 1980.

Hill, Christopher, and E. Dell eds. *The good old cause: the English revolution of 1640-60...* London, Lawrence and Wishart, 1949.

Hoskins, W.G. *The Age of Plunder,* Longman, 1976.

Hutchinson, Lucy. *Memoirs of the life of Colonel Hutchinson, governor of Nottingham.* London, J.M. Dent, 1913.

International genealogical index of the Church of the Latter-day Saints, at www.familysearch.org

Jackson, George. *The diaries and letters of Sir George Jackson KCH from the Peace of Amiens to the Battle of Talavera.* London, Richard Bentley and Son, 1872.

James, Lawrence. *Raj: the making and unmaking of British India.* London, Abacus, 1998.

James, Lawrence. *The rise and fall of the British Empire.* London, Abacus, 1996.

James, Lawrence. *The savage wars: British campaigns in Africa 1870-1920.* London, Hale, 1985.

Julian, John ed. *A dictionary of hymnology ...* London, 1892.

Lane-Poole, S. *Coins and medals: their place in history and art.* Chicago, Argonaut, 1968.

Langenscheidt's encyclopaedic dictionary of the English and German languages. O. Springer ed. London, Methuen, 1962-1975.

Lewis, S. *Topographical dictionary of Ireland.* London, 1837.

Linkin, Harriet K. ed. *The collected poems and journals of Mary Tighe.* Kentucky USA, The University of Kentucky Press, 2005.

Macquarie dictionary. A. Delbridge ed. Dee Why, N.S.W., Macquarie Library, 1985.

Marcinek, Roman. *Poland, a guide book*. Krakow, Kluszczynski, undated.

Maxwell, W.G. *The civil defence of Malaya*. London, Hutchinson, 1946.

Miles, T.A. Diamond jubilee of tin dredging. The story of the creation, building and commissioning of the first tin dredge. *TIN International* Jan. to March, 1967. London, Tin Publications.

Miller, K.A. *Emigrants and exiles: Ireland and the Irish exodus to North America*. New York, OUP, 1985.

Moffatt, Jonathan. *1941 directory of Malaya*, at www.malayanvolunteersgroup.org.uk

Neave, David and E. Waterson. *Lost houses of East Yorkshire*. Georgian Society for East Yorkshire, 1988.

Neill, A.S. *Summerhill*. Harmondsworth, Penguin Books, 1968.

open-encyclopedia.com

O'Donovan, John. *The tribes and customs of Hy-many*, ... Dublin, DUP, 1843.

O'Sullivan, D. *Carolan; the life, times, and music of an Irish harper*. London, Routledge and Kegan Paul, 1958.

Oxford companion to English literature. M. Drabble ed. Oxford, OUP, 1985.

Oxford dictionary of national biography. H. Matthew and B. Harrison, eds. Oxford, OUP, 2004.

Oxford English dictionary. J. Simpson and E. Weiner eds. Oxford, Clarendon Press, 1989.

Pevsner, N. *Yorkshire, the West Riding*. Harmondsworth, Penguin Books, 1959.

Pevsner, N. *Yorkshire, York and the East Riding.* Harmondsworth, Penguin, 1972.

Reader's Digest great world atlas. F. Debenham ed. London, Reader's Digest Association, 1969.

Reid, Carline. *Malayan climax.* Melbourne, Robertson and Mullens, 1944.

Roget, J. and S. Roget. *Roget's thesaurus of English words and* phrases. Harmondsworth, Penguin Books, 1957.

Rose, Andrew. *The Rudstons of Hayton and Allerthorpe,* website by Daniel Sefton, 2015.

Rosenkranz, Edwin. *The free city of Gdansk during the Napoleonic period.* Gdansk, 1980.

SBS world guide. Melbourne, Reed Reference Australia, 1995.

Shann, S. *School portrait.* Fitzroy, Vic. McPhee Gribble/Penguin Books, 1987.

Sheahan, J.J. *History of the town and port of Kingston upon Hull.* Beverley, J. Green, 1866.

Shennan, Margaret. *Out in the midday sun: the British in Malaya, 1880-1960.* London, John Murray, 2000.

Strickland, W.G. *A dictionary of Irish artists.* Dublin, Irish Academic, 1989 (facsimile of 1913).

Style manual for authors, editors and printers. Canberra, Australian Government Publishing Service, 1990.

Sydney Morning Herald newspaper, May-June 1942.

Thomson, David. *Europe since Napoleon.* Harmondsworth, Penguin Books, 1966.

Tickell, J. *The history of town and county of Kingston upon Hull* ... Hull, Thomas Lee and Co., 1796.

Victoria history of the county of York. W. Page ed. Folkestone, Dawsons of Pall Mall, 1974.

Victoria history of the county of York. East Riding. K. Allison and G. Kent eds. London, OUP, 1969.

Victoria history of the county of York: the city of York. P. Tillott ed. London, OUP, 1961.

Ward, H. and W. Roberts. *Romney: a biographical and critical essay with a catalogue raisonné of his works.* 2 vols. London, Thos. Agnew, 1904.

Webber, Thomas W. *The forests of upper India and their inhabitants.* London, Arnold, 1902.

Whitaker, Joseph. *Whitaker's almanack.* London, J. Whitaker, 1888.

White, W. *White's directory of Yorkshire*, 1840, 1846.

Whyte, Thomas. *The story of Woodstock in Inistioge.* Dublin, Cappagh Press, 2007.

Winstedt, Richard. *An unabridged Malay-English dictionary.* Singapore, Marican and sons, 1960.

www.awm.gov.au. Japanese midget submarine attack on Sydney harbour 30-31 May 1942, taken from G. Gill, *Royal Australian Navy 1942-1945.* Canberra, Australian War Memorial, 1968.

www.british-civil-wars.co.uk

www.french-linguistics.co.uk/dictionary/

www.historyonthenet.com

www.oceanlinermuseum.co.uk

www.rzygacz.webd.pl/index.php?id=12,73,0,0,1,0   (Dlugie Ogrody, Gdansk)

www.schliefkowitz.de

www.stirnet.com
www.textuality.de/maclean.html
www.thefreedictionary.com
www.upstreamvistula.org
Yeldham, Charlotte. A regency artist in Ireland: Maria Spilsbury Taylor (1776-1820). *Irish Architectural and Decorative Studies*, Dublin, Irish Georgian Society, vol.8, 2005.

Cover Illustrations

Front Cover

Top left: Fanny Webber (nee Kelly), miniature by Maria Comerford (private collection).

Top right: Caroline Kelly, oil painting by Maria Spilsbury Taylor, 1819 (private collection).

Lower right: 'Garrow Hill', the home of the Barstows, from a water colour painting by Thomas W. Webber (private collection). The house was purchased in 1835. It is now part of the Friends' Retreat mental hospital.

Back Cover

Top: Fanny, Elizabeth and Sally Kelly, pencil and wash by Sally Kelly, 1827 (private collection).

Middle: The Kelly children playing in the drawing room at Rossana. Detail from an oil painting by Maria Spilsbury Taylor, 1815. Left to right: Edmund, Fanny, William, Sally, Elizabeth, Tom (private collection).

Lists of Art Works Held by Members of My Family, Not Shown Here:

Oil paintings by Maria Spilsbury Taylor: Revd Thomas Kelly 1815; William Kelly as a child 1815; unknown youth probably Tom Kelly; Harriet St George (nee Kelly).

Oil painting of Revd Thomas Kelly, probably by the Irish artist Creggan.

Water colour paintings: Tom Kelly (2) 1806; Young girl with a little dog probably Caroline Kelly; Revd Thomas Kelly with three grandsons William, Thomas and Charles Webber by Caroline Kelly; Daniel Webb Webber with three grandsons by Fanny Kelly.

Miniatures including: Elizabeth Kelly nee Tighe, and Thomas and Charles Webber as children, by Maria Comerford; Mrs Sarah Tighe 1814, John Blachford, Robert Tighe, William Tighe of Woodstock, and Daniel Webb Webber, by John Comerford; Judge Kelly 1760 and his wife Fanny Hickey; William Kelly; William Downes Webber; Lord Downes.

Drawings: Revd Thomas Kelly by Fanny Kelly 1831; Daniel Webb Webber and three grandsons by Elizabeth Kelly; other drawings by the Kelly sisters; Revd Thomas Webber.